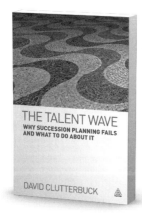

The Talent Wave

Why succession planning fails and what to do about it

David Clutterbuck

KoganPage

LONDON PHILADELPHIA NEW DELHI

First published in Great Britain and the United States in 2012 by Kogan Page Limited

120 Pentonville Road	1518 Walnut Street, Suite 1100	4737/23 Ansari Road
London N1 9JN	Philadelphia PA 19102	Daryaganj
United Kingdom	USA	New Delhi 110002
www.koganpage.com		India

© David Clutterbuck, 2012

The right of David Clutterbuck to be identified as the author of this work has been asserted by him in accordance with the Copyright, Designs and Patents Act 1988.

ISBN   978 0 7494 5697 9
E-ISBN   978 0 7494 6078 5

British Library Cataloguing-in-Publication Data

A CIP record for this book is available from the British Library.

Library of Congress Cataloging-in-Publication Data

Clutterbuck, David.
   The talent wave : why succession planning fails and what to do about it / David Clutterbuck.
      p. cm.
   Includes bibliographical references and index.
   ISBN 978-0-7494-5697-9 – ISBN 978-0-7494-6078-5 (ebook)   1. Executive succession–Planning. 2. Business planning.   3. Chief executive officers–Selection and appointment.   4. Organizational effectiveness.   I. Title.
   HD38.2.C57 2012
   658.4'07112–dc23
                                                                                                    2012007759

Typeset by Graphicraft Limited, Hong Kong
Printed and bound in India by Replika Press Pvt Ltd

The Talent Wave

CONTENTS

FOREWORD

With *The Talent Wave*, David Clutterbuck tackles the very real, very common challenge that every organization faces: leadership succession. Some organizations handle it well; some do not. Reading *The Talent Wave* will help those organizations who don't handle it well bring their performance up a notch – if not more!

David starts by addressing the dilemmas of organizations, including that talented leaders are in short supply and that succession planning processes are too rigid. This is a very real and challenging dilemma. Having worked with more than 120 major CEOs and their management teams, I've seen this first-hand in many organizations.

Part of the problem is that the leaders who are not prepared for succession are just that – not prepared. They often disregard it as something that will 'happen later,' that is until it is in fact happening, at which point it is too late! However, succession is a process that every leader faces eventually. Rather than be shocked when the time actually does come; how can organizations prepare their leaders for transition? What is the human side of succession? How can outgoing leaders leave their positions with class and dignity, passing the baton of leadership to incoming leaders who will have to be up to speed to manage a successful handoff?

The other part of the problem is that all of this has to take place while stakeholders, analysts, customers, and competitors are watching to make sure that value is being delivered, returns on investments are being made, commitments are being kept, and there are no signs of exhaustion or failure where the competition might strike. It is definitely challenging!

In *The Talent Wave*, David explores these critical challenges of succession and proposes the critical conversations that must take place if succession planning processes are to be successful. And, most importantly, he offers a practical solution to navigating the complexity and change of succession in today's rapidly changing business environment, which is simply to support and assist those rising to leadership positions rather than command and control the process. As organizations have become less hierarchical, so it seems must the succession planning process become less rigid and controlled.

My suggestion for you, the reader, is to take what you read here and apply it in the context of your own organization. Be courageous, learn from David's research and experience, and make your organization's succession planning process successful!

Life is good.

Marshall Goldsmith

Marshall Goldsmith was recently recognized as the world's most influential leadership thinker in the biannual *Thinkers50* study – sponsored by the *Harvard Business Review*. His 31 books include the *New York Times* bestsellers, *MOJO* and *What Got You Here Won't Get You There*.

ACKNOWLEDGEMENTS

This book would not have been possible without the hundreds of learning conversations with HR professionals, line managers, coaches and mentors, who have both helped me to shape and critiqued the concepts and approaches as they emerged. Most will be unconscious of their status as co-authors in the more than five years it has taken to pull all these ideas together – but I'd still like to thank them, both individually and collectively!

Introduction

If succession planning works, how do the wrong people so often get to the top?

> A combination of factors including a wave of pending retirements, global
> expansion and an increase in merger activity have raised the visibility of the
> succession planning process to that of 'mission-critical' within most firms.
>
> (Dr John Sullivan[1])

It doesn't seem to matter whether we are in or out of recession, or somewhere
in-between. Succession issues are increasingly occupying the attention of
both top management and senior Human resources (HR) professionals. One
of the reasons is the recognition that talented leaders, who fit the needs of
an organization or a function within it, are in relatively short supply and
becoming scarcer – in spite of overall population growth globally, there are
not enough seasoned, competent leaders to go round.

The statistics for population demographics are well rehearsed and similar
in most developed countries. According to the Center for Strategic and
International Studies Global Aging Initiative website:[2]

> For most of human history, until about a century ago, the elderly (people aged
> 65 and over) never amounted to more than 2 or 3 percent of the population.
> Today, in the developed world, they amount to 15 percent. By the year 2030,
> they will be around 25 percent. As recently as 1980, the median age of the
> oldest society on earth (Sweden) was 36. By the year 2030, the median age of
> the entire developed world is projected to be 45. In Japan and much of southern
> and eastern Europe, it will be over 50. As a whole, the developing world will
> remain much younger for the foreseeable future. Yet it too is aging – hence the
> term 'global aging.' Several major countries in East Asia and Latin America,
> including China, South Korea, and Mexico are projected to reach developed-
> world levels of old-age dependency by the middle of the century.

The ratio of new appointments resulting from need to replace a former
incumbent versus new roles created is heavily tipped in favour of the former,
with the balance tipping increasingly in that direction as baby boomers
quit the employment market.

Bringing leaders in from other organizations is costly and relatively risky, and becomes more so the higher up the organization you go. The likelihood that an executive recruited from outside into a key role will achieve the successes hoped for is less than 50 per cent, according to private conversations with headhunters. Organizations have very effective immune systems that reject change-bringers.

It's not surprising then that the majority of members of the Conference Board in New York worry about how they will identify and develop the leaders they need, at all levels, in an increasingly complex environment.[3]

So employers have to focus more and more on developing their own leaders and on maintaining a sufficient reserve of talent to both replace key losses and fuel business growth. But this isn't simple either – indeed, it is arguably the most intractable problem top teams face. The problems are multiple:

- The most talented people are under siege from other organizations, who seek to hire them away. In a volatile market, your least talented leaders are often the ones most likely to stay.

- Many people, who have the intellect and the behavioural skills to become part of the senior level talent pool, choose not to – for example, some law firms are now struggling to find enough people of the right calibre, who are willing to make the lifestyle trade-off involved in becoming partners.

- In spite of the investment in assessment centres and fast-track, business school-based education, many organizations simply don't know who their really talented people are. Judgements about individuals are often arbitrary, inconsistent and based on hearsay.[4] Even where companies use 360-degree feedback, they tend to place higher value on the assessments of potential by more senior managers, than on the experience of current direct reports – even though the latter data are far better predictors of future performance.

- Even where organizations have leadership competency frameworks that emphasize emotional intelligence and the ability to grow other people, they still tend to place the most weight in promotion decisions upon ability to hit or exceed targets. But this ability doesn't necessarily translate to higher levels of management. Moreover, psychopathic managers, who achieve results through fear, can often manipulate apparent performance and appear to tick all the right boxes.

- Charts and tables don't reflect the complexity of the interface between the organization and its employees and this is particularly true in the case of succession planning. Moreover, these processes are frequently and rapidly out of date because of change both inside and external to the organization.

- Employees and organizations are generally not very honest in their discussions about succession planning issues. In how many companies could you say, 'I'm planning on doing another two years here, to gain specific experience, then I expect to take that experience into another sector', without being dropped from the talent pool? And how many companies would say to employees: 'The risk of taking this job is that we'll withdraw our investment, if we don't hit targets within two years'?

It's no surprise, therefore, that many observers deduce that there is a crisis in succession planning, even if it is not universally acknowledged. Long one of the bastions of HR credibility, succession planning has a key role in maintaining HR's strategic credentials. The problem is that evidence for efficacy of the elaborate processes devised to predict which talent to invest in and who should be targeted for promotion is thin at best. Indeed, the little evidence we do have suggests that, if the 'right' people do get to the top, it is more in spite of succession planning systems than because of them. The recent dramatic failures of leadership in major financial service corporations suggest strongly that something is seriously awry. For example, at some point, the strategic planning system at the Royal Bank of Scotland must have concluded that 'Fred the Shred' was the best leader available. Of course, all leaders make some poor decisions, and succession planning is not about finding leaders, who never make mistakes. But the succession planning process at so many financial services companies was designed to promote a style of leadership which made eventual catastrophe inevitable.

Current approaches to succession planning leave much to be desired. They are routinely based on assumptions which are largely unevidenced and rooted in the mechanistic HR practices of a command and control culture. As a result, HR professionals are increasingly finding that the tools they have to manage the talent pipeline are insufficiently flexible to meet the demands of adaptive organizations and careers.

Estimates of the proportion of senior management appointments that work out are depressing – one survey in 2005 found that the world's largest companies 'mis-hired people 80 per cent of the time and mis-promoted people 75 per cent of the time'.[5] If any other business system so consistently produced poor results, it would have been thrown out long ago. Yet organizations cling on to existing methods of talent management and succession planning, mistaking mechanistic routines for systematic approaches. The result is a plethora of charts and plans that give a veneer of being in control, yet are obsolete before they are completed, and based on false premises both about the nature of talent and succession planning, and about the individuals within the process.

Here are just four of these common myths:

- Line managers are generally effective in recognizing and encouraging talent amongst their direct reports. (True only if the direct report is like themselves.)

- Clear job descriptions are important. (Success is much more associated with hiring the right person and allowing them to redefine the job to capitalize on their strengths – 'how would you do this role radically differently?' is a critical question in leadership transitions.)

- High performance in one role is a clear indicator of high potential in another. (In reality, high performance may be related more to the team context and to a specific match of a role and current competences. Talent in one organization may be very different from talent in another.)

- It's important to know precisely who is ready to step into each key role. (Only if you want to produce clones; far better to have a relatively large pool of people, to allow for changes that are likely to occur in the job role.)

Recognizing and acknowledging these myths frees up HR to propose and develop approaches that meet more accurately the realities of the modern employment environment and its rapidly evolving psychological contract. But having created the myth of being in control of succession planning, HR often struggles to convince line managers and business leaders – who want proof that HR knows what it is doing – that radical changes in approach are needed.

In essence, succession planning processes are often characterized by rigid systems that provide a veneer of being in control, but only just conceal the chaos beneath. There is an increasingly urgent need for more dynamic, flexible approaches to succession planning, rooted in the realities of a connected society, where mutability and informality are the norm.

A key part of the problem is that most of the assumptions about succession and talent derive from a simple, linear systems perspective. Yet we are dealing here with complex, adaptive systems, which are essentially uncontrollable, but which can be influenced. What's needed is a radical shift of mindset towards enabling talent to make its own way, instead of trying to predict the unpredictable.

Alternative approaches to succession planning and talent management

So what's the solution? How can we create dynamic approaches to succession planning that accommodate the complexity and shifting sands of the employee–company relationship?

One part of the solution is to question all our assumptions about what talent is and how we assist it in rising to leadership positions. Notice the subtle shift in language here. The role of HR, our researches suggest, is not to *control* the succession planning process, but to *enable* it. Instead of charts and competency frameworks, we need to create opportunities and initiate conversations that sustain and enhance the alignment between the constantly fluctuating demands of environment, the company and the individual employee. These changes happen so rapidly that believing you can control them is no more than self-deception. The key question for HR is: 'How can we support the processes and conversations that will happen anyway, in ways that will benefit both the company and its employees?'

In this book, I explore in more detail where traditional approaches to succession planning have gone so badly wrong. I challenge received wisdom about common approaches to succession planning. I also provide some answers to the question on page 1: 'How do the wrong people so often get to the top?'

But being an iconoclast brings with it the responsibility to offer an alternative. So I also attempt to extract what is sufficiently fit for purpose from common practice in succession planning, to be worth retaining in or adapting to a more honest, flexible and individualized approach. And I try to draw lessons from failure, with the aim of helping HR protect organizations from leaders who bring short-term results and medium-term disaster.

The second part of this book offers a practical solution to many of the succession planning conundrums. It attempts to define four types of conversation which underpin a healthy relationship between an organization and its employees, in respect of talent management and succession planning. The first of these relates to the conversations that employees have in their own heads and with trusted confidantes about their ambitions and career aspirations. The second relates to their current working environment – the conversations they have with bosses, peers and HR about themselves and their work. The third consists of the broader, context-making conversations between an organization and its employees more generally. In essence, it is about the psychological contract between employees and employer with regard to development and career planning. The fourth kind of conversation brings in the external world and, in particular, the social networks employees and employers use. The boundary between the organization and the outside world has always been an artificial one. Indeed, many millions of employees have traditionally regarded their primary loyalty as being to their profession – for example, doctor or lawyer – rather than to a particular employer. Now employers are learning that they can no longer think of people in one dimension (as employees), but must think of them as multifaceted personalities who are influenced by a wide range of social contacts and environments. To truly engage with employees, especially from Generations Y & Z,[6] they must engage with their networks as well.

This, then, is a book of two halves and, I hope, two kinds of 'Aha!' moment. The first half looks at what is wrong with our assumptions and practices in succession. The 'Aha!' is the insight that comes with the realization that the world is not as we thought. The second half is an alternative perspective on succession planning that offers different and, I propose, more realistic and more effective approaches. The 'Aha!' here comes from recognition of new possibilities. I hope that you experience a good many 'Ahas!' as you read!

Notes

1 http://drjohnsullivan.com/articles-mainmenu-27/articles/workforce-planning-mainmenu-41/226–succession-planning-why-recruiting-needs-to-focus-on-internal-movement

2 http://csis.org/program/global-aging-initiative

3 Barraett, A & Beeson, J (2002) Developing Business Leaders for 2010, The Conference Board, New York

4 Sorcher, M & Brant, J (2002) Are you picking the right leaders? Harvard Business Review, Feb pp 122–29

5 Topgrading: How Leading Companies Win by Hiring, Coaching, and Keeping the Best People, *Portfolio*, 2005

6 Generation Y refers to people entering the workforce in the late 90s and early 2000s – hence they are sometimes called millenials. Gen Z is the digital generation following on their heels. Both have very different expectations of the workplace than previous waves, called Generation X (entering the workplace in the 1980s and early 1990s) and Babyboomers (who started work in the 1960s and 1970s and are now entering retirement).

What's wrong with succession planning?

Recently I met with the heads of human resources of Global 100 companies, and in a confidential survey they stated that their companies mis-hired people 80 per cent of the time and mis-promoted people 75 per cent of the time. That's right, HR's chosen methods of selecting talent produce high performers only 20–25 per cent of the time.

(US consultant Brad Smart)

As a formal practice, succession planning has a relatively recent history. True, kings, emperors and prophets have all sought to ensure their succession, by overseeing the development of favourite sons or followers (with, at best, mixed results!) But the sense of succession planning as a structured process encompassing leadership at multiple layers in organizations probably began with the British Army and Civil Service in the 19th century. It has been given momentum by two 20th-century forces: the increasing complexity of modern corporations and the need by the new discipline of Human Resources (HR) to justify its existence. Faced with large numbers of employees, who they can never hope to get to know intimately, HR's instinctive and natural response has been to impose policy and process. Policy and process can be applied mechanically, with the inevitable result that they will, as Peter Drucker often observed, have an innate tendency to deliver the opposite of the intended result; or they can be applied systemically, recognizing the complexity of human systems and accommodating special circumstances on the grounds that all talent is special.

And here lies at least part of the problem. The qualities that make people talented are often also those that make them unique, difficult to classify (for which, read 'stereotype') and unpredictable. The more HR tries to make talented people fit standardized talent management and succession planning processes, the more likely it is to fail.

Consider the following quote from coaching guru Peter Hawkins: 'Too much talent development is just the fastest escalator up yesterday's mountain' (private communication). What he means is that by the time an organization has defined what it means by talent, developed the inevitable competency frameworks to box people into this definition and begun to shift the focus on career moves accordingly, the world has moved on and it is all obsolete. The critical question, he asserts, is: 'How do you use future talent to speed the creation of tomorrow and future proof the world?' While there are no doubt some basic competencies of a leader, such as listening to and developing others, the more specific a competency framework becomes, the less likely it is to be relevant in a few years' time. And even if it remains relevant, the emphasis on different competencies will probably have shifted.

Conventional wisdom on succession planning says that managers can recognize and nurture talent in the people below them; and that organizations should continuously classify employees according to their potential to take on greater responsibility. As we shall explore in this and later chapters, this is at best wishful thinking; at worst, a dangerous distraction from the real business of engaging business leaders and employees in continuous, dynamic and evolving dialogue about the relationships between them.

HR professionals are in a dilemma. They know that the standard forms of succession planning are 'clunky' and possibly even directly inimical to the development and promotion of talented people. They realize that what enables people to succeed is rarely as obvious as managers would like it to be. In his book *Outliers*, Malcolm Gladwell (2008) examines the careers of a range of high achievers from sport and business. He provides evidence, for example, that the most successful US sportsmen get to the top because they are born early in the school year, when they have up to 12 months' advantage in terms of strength and maturity over their age peers in the selection process; and that the information technology (IT) billionaires just happened to be born within a short opportunity window, when they had few competitors and were able to access computing time which had never previously been available. The suspicion that similar fortunate coincidences underlie the progress of designated talent inside organizations is hard to dispel; but the fear of what might be uncovered in seeking these patterns of hidden privilege tends to deter serious investigation.

It's perhaps no surprise then, that HR has not convinced top management of the value of succession planning. According to the Human Capital Institute, 70 per cent of succession plans fail within two years, because they lose management support. There is, however, a silver lining in this lack of confidence in HR's ability to deliver effective succession planning. When organizations turn from succession planning as something they do *to* people and treat it instead as something they do *with* them – when HR sees its role as enabling, rather than controlling – a much wider range of possibilities opens up.

But before we enter this controversial debate, let's at least try to define what succession planning is, or is meant to be.

What is succession planning?

According to the *Encyclopaedia of Industrial and Organizational Psychology*, succession planning is the process by which an organization makes sure that it will have the right leaders in the right place at the right time. The encyclopaedia places the origins of formal succession planning processes in the post-World War II need for 'replacement planning' – finding people to step into key roles that had been vacated due to the promotion or death of the previous incumbents. Inherent in this approach is the notion of shortage of candidates for these roles.

Succession planning, therefore, initially referred to a relatively simplistic process of:

- identifying who would or could step into the shoes of the most senior leaders;
- grooming them over a period of years as 'crown prince'; and
- supporting their transition into their new leadership role.

Potential chief executives, for example, might be identified by the incumbent five or ten years before the expected transition, coached over a period in which they are given increased responsibilities and exposure to formative experiences, including deputizing for the incumbent, and finally mentored by the previous chief executive officer (CEO) (in their own new role as chairman) in the first year or so in the job.

Replacement planning gave way in the 1970s and 1980s to the concept of succession management: creating a pool of potential successors from which the fittest could be selected when the need arose. Assessment centres and competency frameworks have their roots at least in part in this somewhat Darwinian perspective. The best would rise to the top through a rigorous planned process of education, evaluation and opportunities to develop their track record. Unfortunately, much of this effort proved irrelevant, because the processes weren't robust or responsive enough to respond to challenges such as poaching of talent, change in technology or the inbuilt tendency of executives faced with a choice about who to appoint to a vacancy to ignore all the graphs and spreadsheets and simply go for the candidate they liked most (or who reminded them most of themselves). While evidence either way is thin, it is probable that succession planning, as practised by HR, had a negligible impact on the quality of leadership appointments, beyond that which might have occurred by chance.

The scope of succession planning has widened a great deal since then, in a number of ways. Firstly, the succession planning process reaches much further down into the organization, with brave and often futile attempts to allocate successors for the majority of managerial and senior professional roles.

Secondly, the time horizons have shortened – five to ten years to develop a new CEO isn't realistic, when CEOs themselves have a much shorter lifespan in their roles. Even in much more junior roles, the pace of change has made it much more difficult to groom an individual for a specific role. In HR, for example, in a random sample of 20 multinational companies, all but one had experienced radical shifts in role for most of their HR professionals. The most common structural changes were towards HR business partnerships and from regional to global roles. While this was by no means an empirical study, the experience of these organizations raises the question: 'How do we identify successors for jobs that don't exist yet or are likely to be radically different in the near future?'

In the past decade or so, succession planning has become integrated into strategic talent management, a broader process that recognizes that leaders do not constitute the only talent pool in an organization. In essence, this attempts to create a stronger and more strategic link between the development of the business and the development of the people within it. Paraphernalia of HR processes, including competence frameworks and assessment centres, have grown up to support this integration. This link with talent management suggests a wider definition of succession planning, which can be expressed in the following questions:

- Who are proven *performers* who deliver the right results in the right way?
- Which of these has the *potential* to grow into positions at a higher level?
- What do they need to get *ready for promotion*, and how fast will they be ready?
- Which candidate is the best all-around *fit* for a particular role or opening?

These questions seem pretty all-encompassing and straightforward. In practice, however, they have proven to be extremely difficult to answer in a way that stands up to scrutiny. Performance, potential, promotability and job fit turn out to be far more tenuous concepts than they might appear at first sight, and many of the problems with modern succession planning come from naive and sometimes arbitrary attempts to pin down these concepts. A wider definition would also include:

- making sure that there are enough suitable people to step into any significant role as it becomes vacant or is created;
- motivating and developing them to adapt to the new role as fast as possible, with minimum damage;
- ensuring that every role is a learning resource, in which the incumbent can develop not only skills relevant to that job, but also the capability to embrace different and/or larger jobs;
- recognizing that roles and their incumbents are constantly evolving.

Some definitions of succession planning:

A process by which one or more successors are identified for key posts (or groups of similar key posts), and career moves and/or development activities are planned for these successors... Succession planning sits inside a much wider set of resourcing and development processes that we might call succession management. This encompasses the management resourcing strategy, aggregate analysis of demand/supply (HR planning and auditing), skills analysis, the job filling process, and management development (including graduates and high fliers).

(Hirsh, 2000: 1)

Succession planning refers to an effort by organizations to select and develop future leaders who are prepared to replace current leaders.

(Encyclopaedia of Career Development)

Succession planning is the means by which an organization prepares for and replaces managers, executives and other key employees who leave their positions, and is critically important to the organization's continued and future success.

(Wilkinson, :1)

[Succession planning and management] is the process that helps ensure the stability of tenure of personnel. It is perhaps best understood as any effort designed to ensure the continued effective performance of an organization, division, department, or work group by making provision for the development, replacement, and strategic application of key people over time.

(Rothwell, 2000: 5–6)

Succession planning is a structured process involving the identification and preparation of a potential successor to assume a new role.

(Garman and Glawe, 2004)

My own definition of succession planning is:

A dynamic process of aligning employee aspirations and talents with the constantly evolving needs of the organization and of providing employees with the resources and support they need to grow into new roles. The key points here are:

- *Dynamic*: the process evolves constantly with changes in the internal and external environment of the organization, and the aspirations and circumstances of the employees.

- *Resources and support*: this is an enabling process, not one that seeks to exert control.

Models of succession planning

The *Encyclopaedia of Industrial and Organizational Psychology* offers five critical elements of the succession planning process, against which I offer some critical questions:

- *Business review*: What is the business strategy and what does that mean generally for leadership qualities and talent pools?
- *Talent needs forecast*: How many people will we need in critical roles, with what experience and capabilities and what will our selection criteria be?
- *Talent inventory*: Who have we got? At what stage of development are they in terms of slotting into key leadership roles? What potential do they have to grow into bigger roles? What kind of roles would give them growth opportunities and in what kind of roles could they contribute most to the organization?
- *Talent review*: What plans do we have to develop individuals and talent pools, in line with the evolving business need? (Note the word 'evolving'. Even six months may be too long to wait to review.)
- *Follow-up and progress review*: Are the succession and development plans being implemented and are they delivering results? (And what are our criteria for measuring whether it's working?)

Key themes in succession planning

An open or closed process?

Succession planning can either (as was traditionally the case) be a secret process or an open one, or somewhere in-between. Secret succession plans result in managers giving strong hints to favoured candidates, so the secret is at best partial. Downsides listed by HR professionals include unintentionally encouraging talented people to leave, because they can't get a straight answer about where their careers are headed. Another problem with secret processes is that they tend to become divorced from reality. In one case, the HR function of a multinational company proudly and regularly informed the top team that there were on average four names pencilled against every critical role in the company. Then a director asked the simple question: 'How many of these people would take the job, if it were offered to them?' The ratio fell to less than one per position.

Worse still is the leaky secret process. When destiny is communicated in nods and winks, trust is an early casualty. Those left out of the inner circle intuit their position and resent the favoured few, especially if they feel that the selection process is arbitrary or unfair. Those who have been given the nod become impatient if promotion is not sufficiently rapid, and switch off from extracting more learning from the role they are in. Both tend to be psychologically attuned to the headhunter's call.

On the other hand, open succession plans can switch off talented people who have been left on the sidelines. For them, the question becomes: 'Do I work hard to demonstrate that I am much more talented than they have realized; or do I take the easier route and find an employer who will value what I have to offer?'

Yet there are many potential upsides to open succession planning. In particular, openness opens greater possibilities for flexibility. People and organizations constantly change. A static succession plan – for example, one that is revised every year or so – may bear little resemblance to the internal marketplace of talent need and availability. A core theme of this book is that having continuous, open conversations between employer and employees – conversations in which assumptions are constantly being challenged and tested – can be far more effective than any closed-door process. Perhaps most importantly, an open process provides the opportunity for people who feel they have been miscast or overlooked to challenge how the organization perceives them. Appraisal processes in many organizations are still deeply biased against people who do not fit the ideal profile (which can be based on an unconscious stereotype of 'people like us'). Assessments of potential tend to focus on perceived weaknesses, rather than strengths, and to undervalue the importance of having different mindsets, to challenge narrow thinking. A recurring theme in my studies (Goldsmith and Clutterbuck, 1997) of how excellent companies lose their way is that succession planning becomes selective inbreeding.

US academic William Rothwell (Rothwell, 2005) distinguishes between succession planning in open and closed cultures. He defines the difference as follows: 'An open corporate culture is one in which the organization's leaders trust workers and are willing to disclose important information. They do not keep secrets. A closed corporate culture, in contrast, is secretive.' In closed cultures, managers do not trust workers and assume that 'exemplary performers will stop exerting maximum efforts if they believe they have promotion assured'; whereas in open cultures 'the issue is not whether to tell people they are successors but how to tell them', given the uncertainty that surrounds any planning process.

Increasingly, however, even managers in closed corporate cultures may be forced to learn how to reveal information about succession. Telling people can be a retention strategy. And the loss of exemplary performers can be particularly hurtful.

Job modelling

Job modelling is based on the assumption that psychologists can analyse the requirements (called 'person capabilities') of a leadership role and identify how closely the candidates available might meet them. Tools include psychometric tests of leadership potential and current capability, readiness for greater responsibility, and so on. Reputable psychologists offering these services stress that the test results and interpretations are simply part of the judgement process, along with performance appraisals and observations of more senior managers. However, human nature tends towards selecting out those bits of an analysis that support preformed opinions and ignoring those that don't. Moreover, the qualities perceived to be required of a role can vary widely according to perspective. Roles are shaped by their incumbents. Incumbents, their peers and their bosses develop a set of assumptions about the role and the competences needed to fulfil it – based mainly on the status quo. The greater the consensus amongst this group, the narrower and less imaginative the person specification is likely to be.

Aimed at a narrow or broad audience?

Research by the Institute of Employment Studies (IES) (Hirsh, 2000) indicates that 'the most common model for centralised, corporate succession planning is one that covers only the most senior jobs in the organization (the top two or three tiers) plus short-term and longer-term successors for these posts. The latter group are often manifest as a corporate fast stream or high potential population who are being actively developed in mid-career through job moves across business streams, functions or geographical boundaries.' However, says the IES report: 'Many large organizations also adopt a devolved model where the same approach is applied to a much larger population (usually managerial and professional) but this process is managed by devolved business divisions, functions, sites or countries. It has to be said that few organizations successfully sustain the devolved model, usually because it is not really seen as a high priority and not adequately facilitated by HR.'

Tactical or strategic?

Put another way, is succession planning about replacement, or about making the most intelligent use possible of the talent within an organization? According to the Aberdeen Group report (Lombardi, 2010): 'Succession can no longer be simple disaster contingency in the event that a leadership role suddenly becomes open. If the competition changes, if the economy changes, if consumer expectations change, the skills that helped to lead the company before may no longer fit. It will be important to have a deep and diverse cadre of talented leaders in order for the organization to endure.'

Making room for succession

An interesting and logical inference from the *Encyclopaedia of Industrial and Organizational Psychology* definition (though not one on which it expands) is that succession planning should also encompass moving leaders on. It implies some form of continuous monitoring to ensure that, as the environment changes, leaders are evaluated on their ability to deliver under the changed circumstances and encouraged (or required) to vacate their roles to others better adapted to the new environment. So, should effective approaches to succession planning include knowing when it is time for leaders to move on, and helping them to do so without creating rancour and disruption? Of course, boards of directors do fire chief executives, but that is almost always for one of three reasons: conflict with the chairman, missing the numbers, or a major reputational failure (eg BP's CEO Tony Hayward in the wake of the Gulf of Orleans oil spill).

In the mid-1990s Walter Goldsmith and I reprised our business bestseller, *The Winning Streak* (Goldsmith and Clutterbuck, 1997), and identified a number of critical balances that companies which had been highly successful for a sustained period paid particular attention to. One of those balances related to how they replaced the person at the top, and key to this was the attitude of the CEO. As Sir Gerald Whent of Vodafone expressed it: 'One of the great things of being a good business leader is knowing when to go.'

I struggled hard in the research for this book to find role models of CEOs who had the perspicacity to recognize that succession planning included planning their own exit. One of the few exceptions was Andy Bond, former CEO of UK retailer Asda.

CASE STUDY Succession planning includes knowing when to go

Andy Bond was CEO of Asda, one of the largest supermarket chains in the UK, for five years. Then, when everything was going exceptionally well, he announced that he would quit. Wal-Mart, the parent company, persuaded him to become chair and delay his exit for a year, but Bond knew it was time to give up the substantial corporate salary and go. Here's how he explains his decision making:

'I have a set of principles that have guided my career. One of them is that there should always be a balance between what is right for me and what's right for the company. When I looked at how long I should stay, I also had several criteria. The key one was that every leader should recognise the need to stay long enough to write one chapter in the book of the company, but that they can't write two. I'd achieved a lot of success, but my energy and my ability to make things happen was diminishing. Tough decisions I took had consequences that needed a different resolution. It's harder for you, having made those decisions, than for someone else, who didn't.

'You get to the top by being motivated and driven. That doesn't change as CEO. But you have opportunities to do other things. At first you brick those off, because you don't want to be distracted from the main job. But the job gets easier as you go along. Then you start to think, 'I can do the job in four days and spend the other day on a government committee'.

But the company needs you full-time. The moment you start getting distracted in this way, it's time to go.'

The problem in most organizations, he explains, is that emotional and legal contracts make it difficult to have open conversations about leaving. Lawyers will normally advise saying nothing until the day you decide to go, which leaves very little opportunity for a planned, smooth transition. Quitting can be seen as an act of betrayal and may even lead to immediate, same-day departure in extreme cases. Bond took the risk of laying his cards on the table and offering to do all that he could to help the transition work. His Wal-Mart bosses responded maturely, after attempting to persuade him to stay, and they worked together on the succession process. 'As a leader, it's your responsibility to create a smooth transition,' he declares. 'After all, as a CEO, it's most likely the last job you'll do for that company.' Interestingly, he has found that family firms and private equity companies can often be the most mature and pragmatic in dealing with this kind of transition.

Leadership as an individual or collective responsibility

This is another theme that I shall return to later in the book. Succession planning processes – and organization charts in general – place far more emphasis on who has the title than on who actually does the work, takes the decisions, and so on. The 'cult of the hero' embeds much of leadership literature. True, there are examples of charismatic leaders, such as Bill Gates or Steve Jobs, whose personality and individual leadership style have been fundamental to the success of their businesses. But charismatic leaders either leave a leadership desert when they move on, or they build around them a team of highly effective leaders who happen to have different, complementary qualities. The recognition that the title and the responsibilities may not rest in the same person was partly behind the concept of 'parliamentary management' proposed in the 1970s by Einar Thorsrud, the pioneer of semi-autonomous workgroups. In his vision, there would always be a 'leadership team in opposition', ready to offer an alternative, should the occasion arise (Clutterbuck, 1975). While it might help to keep leadership teams more alert, there are, of course, practical objections to this idea, outside of cost. For a start, corporate governance is already excessively politicized, without making it more so; and the experience of political governance is not encouraging in terms of avoiding short-termism. In Thorsrud's own institute, the role of chief executive rotated between the most senior employees, according to who had the time and energy. A similar arrangement occurs in some professional services partnerships. How successful this distributed leadership is, may well be related to the size of the leadership group. Too small and it becomes an oligarchy; too large and too much energy dissipates into gaining consensus for decisions.

Most of our high-performing companies in *The Winning Streak* research had leadership groups, where it didn't matter a great deal who had the title

CEO – it was the cohesion and complementary competences the group exhibited which counted.

Lessons we drew and which have been reinforced over the years include:

- Succession planning processes concentrate too much on who should step into a role and when; and not enough on who should step out of a role and when. Both are important. One of the main reasons people leave organizations is because no one has recognized and responded to their need to move on from a role. When outward transitions do occur – whether for good reasons or bad – it is relatively rare for enough consideration to be given to managing that transition for the benefit of the incumbent's existing team. One of the few situations where this transition is frequently managed well is where the CEO becomes chairman and mentors his or her successor. But this has to be a true mentoring relationship, not an excuse for continued interference! One of the common themes in literature on succession at the top of organizations is Founder's Syndrome: reluctance by a founder to step down (or stepping down only in name, while continuing to interfere and try to run the company).

- Strong leaders who have a firm grip on power can often spell disaster for the company if they can't let go. Consider these comments, from Peter Jobs and Patrick Mannix, CEO and HR director respectively of Reuters at the time:
  - 'Nothing can grow in the shade of the banyan tree. I think everyone has their own formula for running a business, but part of that should be subordination of the ego. You can walk around any country graveyard to remind yourself that you will be underground eventually. It's sensible therefore to say, "How long do I want this company to go on after me?"'
  - 'If the company is very dependent on the chief executive, then you have a hell of a problem when it comes to succession.'

- Appointing 'crown princes' or heirs apparent is a guarantee for a talent drain, with the added risk that the role or the person identified to fill it – or both – will have changed by the time the transition is required. In our *Winning Streak* study, Bob Lawson, CEO of Electrocomponents, commented: 'The moment there is a guaranteed successor, why are you still around?' And Dominic Cadbury, of Cadbury's: 'If you've only got one successor, I think that's not a very healthy sign of good management.'

Ownership

In the early 1990s, companies such as British Airways recognized that as long as succession planning was seen as an HR process, it would lack credibility with line managers. Its solution, now more commonplace, was to establish a succession planning steering group, which was owned by the line (ie led and dominated in terms of numbers) and supported by HR. However, owning an issue does not necessarily mean driving it. Says one HR director: 'It's a constant battle to maintain top management's interest in succession planning. Quite frankly, they find the whole thing boring, especially when compared with making deals and other high adrenalin activities.' Engaging top management in coherent and informed discussion and evaluation of succession planning can be done – there are a number of good examples around the world – but it tends to involve falling back to a process-driven approach carried out at annual intervals, and with considerable energy required from the CEO to ensure that leaders take the responsibility seriously.

An annual or continuous process?

For many organizations, succession planning is an annual binge, rather than a continuous, dynamic process. The annual approach has the benefit that it is easier to ensure it happens across the business and to impose some level of standardization on how the process is carried out. However, research into wider issues of strategic planning (of which succession planning is just one subset) indicates that continuous strategizing is more strongly associated with corporate high performance than is an annual review process. Michael Mankins and Richard Steele (2006) found that, on average, companies with standard decision-making processes make only 2.5 major strategic decisions a year (ones with potential to increase or decrease profit by more than 10 per cent or more over the long term), while high-performing companies take more than double that. They conclude that all too often:

> strategic planning becomes merely a codification of judgements top management has already made, rather than a vehicle for identifying and debating the critical decisions the company needs to make to produce superior performance...
> Executives plan periodically (66 per cent of them) and by unit (66 per cent of them). Yet they decide continuously (100 per cent) and issue by issue (70 per cent). No surprise that only 11 per cent are highly satisfied that strategic planning is worth the effort...

All of this resonates with the standard approach to succession planning: a discontinuous process, largely performed by rote and confirming decisions which have already been made. This is, of course, not universally so. Some organizations do review talent much more frequently and they do introduce a high level of challenge to managers' views of their own direct reports. However, the talent review process may still be largely tactical and confirmatory, rather than genuinely strategic and questioning. Says one HR director:

> We have got to be quite good at challenging the suitability of individuals for promotion generally and for specific roles. But I'd hesitate to say we are genuinely strategic. It's not often that we ask questions, such as: How do we

want the roles we are aiming these talented people at to evolve? What is this role like in other organizations? Will the roles really be needed in five years' time? We keep moving pieces on the chessboard, when maybe we should be playing a completely different game.

The dangers of assuming that the world will stand still while the organization implements a strategy were illustrated by a McKinsey study (Anon, 2009). Once a strategy is agreed, directors often tend to be very reluctant to revisit it, even if circumstances have changed. There is a sense that 'we have put in all that effort – the last thing we want is to have to go through it all again'. But that's exactly what they should be doing, according to McKinsey. One of the short case studies in the article concerned a board which was facilitated in articulating the key premises for the company's strategic plan for the year. Then each director was interviewed by a consultant, to establish which of the premises were still valid in their view. Most turned out to be no longer tenable. Without this intervention, the board could have continued backing a flawed strategy for much longer, because everyone assumed that the others were still behind it.

If this is what happens at corporate strategy level, with all the attention and effort paid to 'getting it right', then how much more vulnerable is the succession planning strategy? In discussing this issue with HR directors, it seems that one of the main reasons for sticking with an annual strategic review of succession is that top management resists spending the time on a more frequent process; and that the term 'strategic review' applies only loosely, in that there is a reluctance to challenge the assumptions upon which the strategy is based. Such in-depth challenge happens most commonly when the function and role of HR as a whole is being reviewed. I have found that many HR professionals privately believe that succession planning strategy should be reviewed radically every six months, and in the light of specific environmental changes every two or three months.

Like any other strategic process, succession planning needs a vision and/ or mission to give it purpose or shape. It also needs to be linked firmly to the business values, and to be integrated into other strategic processes. Annual succession planning reviews tend inevitably to emphasize replacement and continuity as core purposes. With continuous review, however, there is more likely to be a values-based mindset. For example, for some organizations the purpose of succession planning becomes to ensure their flexibility and ability to respond rapidly and effectively to external and internal change. An analogy that works for me in describing these two approaches is between the chessboard (fixed locations for all the pieces, only certain types of predetermined move allowed) and swarm behaviour. In the latter, seen in schools of fish or flocks of birds in flight, shifts in direction occur instantaneously, with every member of the school or flight responding in unison. How animals in the wild achieve these remarkable acrobatics is still not fully understood, but it is clearly related to powerful and instinctive communication. Clearly, the swarm effect resonates more closely with a complex, adaptive system and epitomizes the agile organization.

Aligning aspirations and values

Another perspective on succession planning strategy is that it should aim to integrate, as far as possible, the collective aspirations of employees (or at least the talent pool) with the business aspirations (vision and values). Of course, the workforce and the talent pool are made up of lots of individuals, with different aspirations. If strategy is an intelligent and adaptive response to the corporate environment, then it's important to be able to react to and accommodate both internal and external change. Understanding how employee aspirations evolve, and exploring how employees perceive the business values (do they incorporate them into their own view of the world in general or see them as simply something relevant to the workplace?) are essential prerequisites for swarm-like agility of response.

What constitutes evidence?

Here's an optimistic statement from a recent LinkedIn exchange: 'By grounding your [succession planning] decision in data, you're able to remove bias and focus on making a decision that will be the best for the business, which is ultimately important for the organization and its people.' If only it were that simple!

Clearly, organizations aspire to base succession planning decisions on data that is both credible and valid. However, credible and valid are not necessarily the same thing. Managers and academics tend to have different perspectives on what constitutes credibility, for example.

Part of the problem is that managers often aren't very good at working out what is valid evidence and what is not. The literature on managerial decision-making reveals a dozen or more common errors that distort managers' thinking when they make decisions of this kind (Hammond and Keeney, 2006). Most of these apply to succession planning. Among them are the following:

- The anchoring trap – when considering a decision, the mind gives disproportionate weight to the first information it receives. First impressions don't just count, they linger. In the same way that parents often still treat their offspring as children when they are adults and have children of their own, managers tend to stick with their initial view of other people's talents, motivations and 'fit'. Disturbingly, when a global logistics company measured the perceived impact of executive coaching on managers' performance (it measured the same behaviours both before and after the coaching intervention), the coachees perceived that they had made significant changes, and their direct reports largely confirmed this. Peers noticed some improvements, but direct bosses hardly any. They weren't able to get past their initial perceptions.

- Status quo trap – decision-makers prefer to opt for solutions that preserve the status quo. (Breaking the status quo means taking action and that involves risk and responsibility, which open us to regret and criticism – so our ego pushes us toward the status quo solution.) In succession planning, this prevents us from looking too closely at our decisions regarding who has or hasn't got leadership potential. Once someone is on the list (or has been rejected), it can require a dramatic event to cause us to re-evaluate.

- Sunk-cost trap – when old investments are no longer recoverable, people are subconsciously unwilling to admit it was a mistake. It's even worse when the organizational penalties for bad decisions are severe. This trap is particularly pernicious in succession planning and talent management terms. Having decided that an employee is talented and having invested time, money and reputation (being able to spot talent) in them, managers are naturally reluctant to admit they were wrong. So they tend to place more weight on the employee's successes and less on their failures.

- Confirming evidence trap – letting your instincts be confirmed by listening only to people or data that support them. It affects where we go to collect evidence and how we interpret information we receive. We tend to decide what we want to do before we work out why we want to do it; and to be more engaged by things (or people) we like than things (or people) we don't. One of the most damaging cycles I have seen in the workplace (too many times) starts with an implicit assumption by a manager about, say, a direct report's 'lack of motivation'. The initial assumption may be based on an unconscious association in the manager's mind with a previous employee, who has some characteristic in common with this person – say, they are tall and like to take time to consider answers to questions. From that point on, the manager's mind is likely to be more attentive to situations where the employee appears to be unenthusiastic, than those where they demonstrate strong task engagement. If the person is also an introvert, then it becomes even easier to miss their enthusiasms. Add to this situation an element of cultural and/or racial diversity and the stage is set for massive misvaluing of the individual and their talents. This damaging cycle can equally start with overly positive implicit associations.

- Framing trap – people are risk averse when an issue is framed in terms of seeking gains; but risk seeking when the same problem is posed in terms of avoiding losses. So when a promotion is into a role where things are functioning reasonably well, there is a tendency to appoint a safe candidate (often as close as possible to the previous incumbent). Only when things are going badly do we seriously consider less conventional candidates. According to the Canadian Institute for Advanced Research (Anon, 2008): 'When women break through the glass ceiling, becoming presidents, CEOs or taking on other leadership roles, these tend to be in organizations that are experiencing severe difficulty. As a result, ground beneath them is more likely to crumble, sending them plummeting – over the Glass Cliff. This has led to a widespread and dangerous misperception that women leaders cause poor performance, when in fact, our research suggests it is the other way around.'

And the answer to poor strategic decision making? According to Professor Ram Charan (2006), it lies in the quality of conversation about strategic issues: 'To transform a culture of indecision, leaders must... see to it that the organization's social operating mechanisms – that is, the meetings, budget and strategy reviews and other situations through which the people of a corporation do business – have honest dialogue at their centre.' Decisive dialogue, he maintains:

- encourages incisiveness and creativity;
- brings coherence to fragmented and unrelated ideas;
- allows tensions to surface and be dealt with;
- promotes emotional commitment.

Integrating succession planning and development

It seems pretty obvious that if you want someone to progress into larger roles with greater responsibility, you should invest in their development. But that doesn't always translate into a seamless process, for a number of reasons. Among them:

- Budgetary restraints or demands of the individual's current role make developmental activity a relatively low priority activity.

- Development to whose agenda and for what? If the organization has a specific role in mind and an accurate picture of the individual's development needs, then it might be relatively easy to design a development plan to fit the circumstances. However, this assumes that the individual shares the same view of both where they want their career to go and the learning they need to acquire to get there. (It also tends to lock both parties into a path which, with changes in circumstances, may not be right for either the organization or the employee.) If the objective is to produce an employee who is more generally promotable, the potential clash between organizational and individual agendas may be greater or lesser according to the quality of the conversations that happen between them.

- The incentives for developing. For example, an issue for companies working in some oil states is how to persuade local employees to invest in their own development, rather than sit back and expect promotion to happen to them, simply because of their nationality and political pressure to increase the pace of indigenization. More close to home, a financial services company's unspoken cultural assumptions were that people got promoted for delivering results and being seen to work hard (for which read 'long hours'). Members of the designated talent pool and their managers effectively conspired to avoid developmental events provided by human resources, on the basis that client needs took priority. The result was that openings at higher levels were filled with people who lacked appropriate leadership skills, and who replicated the contra-development behaviours by their own managers.

- Where HR and line management place the emphasis between identifying talent and developing it. Says the head of talent management in a multinational professional services company: 'We spend 80 per cent of our effort identifying talent; and 20 per cent developing them. Then we wonder why so many of them leave or get dropped from the talent pool. We are quite good at sending them off on courses, though their bosses sometimes complain. What's missing is the *continuous attention* to their development. What they get is short bursts when someone remembers, rather than frequent conversations about what they need to learn to move into the next role and where they can get the intellectual stretch they need.'

Diversity issues

If succession planning processes really worked, the people that reach the top would mirror the talent that enters at the bottom. From just a gender perspective, that clearly isn't so. Research by McKinsey shows little difference between men and women in terms of their ambition to progress in organizations, both at entry and middle management levels. Say the authors of a 2011 report (Barsh and Yee, 2011). 'For evidence of the problem, look no further than the blocked, leaky corporate-talent pipeline: women account for roughly 53 per cent of entry-level professional employees in the largest US industrial corporations, our research shows. But according to Catalyst, a leading advocacy group for women, they hold only 37 per cent of middle-management positions, 28 per cent of vice-president and senior-managerial roles, and 14 per cent of seats on executive committees. McKinsey research shows similar numbers for women on executive committees outside the United States – from a high of 17 per cent in Sweden to just 2 per cent in Germany and India. Our analysis further reveals that at every step along the US pipeline, the odds of advancement for men are about twice those for women. And nearly four times as many men as women at large companies make the jump from the executive committee to CEO. Part of the reason is that almost twice as many executive-level women as men (60 per cent versus 35 per cent) occupy staff roles that are less likely to lead to the top job.'

It is still relatively rare to see succession planning and diversity management closely integrated. Yet succession planning processes can undermine diversity objectives if they do not take account of critical influences of race and gender on career trajectories. Women who take time out to have children, or who have caring responsibilities (indeed, people of either gender who are carers) can easily be marginalized by succession planning processes that, for example, equate talent with judgement-laden qualities such as 'commitment'.

David Thomas, an academic at Harvard, has compared career progression amongst black and white professionals and managers (Thomas, 2001). He finds that promising white professionals tend to enter fast tracks early in their careers, whereas high-potential minorities typically take off after they have reached middle management. He found that both white and black managers benefited from having a mentor at key points in their careers, but that there were significant differences in the kind of mentoring they received.

An interesting sideline on this issue comes from recent research from two US academics, who have investigated how people gain appointments to the board. (Most boards in the US are predominantly non-executive.) James Westphal and Ithai Stern (2007) examined the most commonly successful strategy of 'ingratiation' (which in academic speak encompasses a range of behaviours, intended to build a good impression) in the context of competing for a board role. These behaviours may be sycophantic at one extreme, or simply effective reputation management at the other.

Their analysis of responses from 760 directors finds that ingratiatory behaviours towards the CEO and other existing directors do indeed increase the chances of appointment to the board. However, the effect is much stronger for white males. Indeed, the same behaviours in women and people from ethnic minorities may even be seen as a negative attribute by those with the power to appoint.

If fitting in doesn't work, what other strategies might ethnic minorities apply to gain board appointments? Other studies (Cannella and Harris, 2002) suggest that developing specialist expertise relevant to the board (for example, in company law) is a pragmatic route into director roles – becoming 'super-qualified' eventually opens up doors.

There are serious implications here for both individuals and organizations. Women and minorities aiming for the board may need consciously to establish and work to different strategies than their white male counterparts. Coaches and mentors working with these individuals need to be aware of the need for different strategies and to help the coachee understand the issue from both their own perspective and that of the existing majority directors. And boards need to institute procedures that confront and overcome the institutionalized discrimination that occurs from evaluating behaviour differently in people of different gender or racial backgrounds in the context of appointments and succession planning. Indeed, it is recommended that all appointment committees regularly assess their procedures through a diversity audit.

If line managers are responsible for recommending who should join the talent pool, another raft of issues emerges, relating to implicit bias. When supervisors perceive someone else as significantly different from themselves, they are more likely to see their performance as poor, more likely to have a relationship that involves conflict and, in some circumstances, is abusive (Bennett *et al*, 2011). If the succession planning system is to be fair, it must contain mechanisms for recognizing and counteracting such bias.

Burnout

An increasingly common concern for many organizations' succession planning processes is that while fast-tracking gives talented people opportunities much earlier in their careers, it can also give rise to burnout. In part, this is because these individuals do not have sufficient time to experience failure and develop the resilience they need in higher roles.

The burnout phenomenon can be ascribed in large part to a failure of organizations and high flyers to have honest conversations about work and its impact. Tim Casserley and David Megginson (2009) refer to the collusive process that occurs between the organization and the employee. When progress depends on perceived performance and performance is defined by how hard (and long) someone works, the foundation is laid for a destructive spiral. They explain (page xv):

> more often than not, those who burn out collude with dysfunctional working environments. They choose to make work and career central to their lives... High flyers' addiction to action and adrenalized work styles often hide an identity that is strongly externally referenced – on work and career – rather than anything from within. There is also an element of paranoia. A belief that pushing back, asking for more time or resources or confronting unreasonable demands will adversely affect career prospects.

Given that competency frameworks for senior leaders now increasingly emphasize qualities such as authenticity, awareness of their environment and courage, such collusions could be seen as shaping exactly the kind of leaders organizations would not want to get to the top – assuming they avoid burnout before they get there!

Only for a small proportion of executives, who burn out, is the experience a beneficial one. For these fortunate few, burnout provides the transformative experience that accelerates maturity and systemic growth. 'By virtue of being a personal trauma, burnout caused [these] high flyers to confront their own fallibilities, helped them gain a sense of perspective, humility and humanity, and be clearer about their own identity' (p xv). This baptism of fire is a pretty wasteful way of developing talent, however. A more intelligent strategy would be to:

- Recognize the symptoms of potential burnout early and intervene (through coaching, counselling or, in serious cases, through therapy) to enable the maturing process to occur in less traumatic ways.

- Break the association between working long hours and performance, which leads people who do more to be higher up the list of potential promotional talent than people who think more. The more senior leaders become, the more important it is for them to be able to work smart, rather than long. A simple motivational shift can be to reward people on the contribution they make to the goals that really matter for the department or team, rather than on some vague definition of performance.

- Create an environment of psychological safety where people can challenge excessive work demands without fear of wrecking their careers. Critical to this is enabling people to have open dialogue about stress-inductors, ask for help and support for colleagues, and renegotiate priorities. In my experience, wherever a team has made this shift, the actual workload diminishes, partly because some tasks simply aren't as important or urgent as people thought they were, and partly because spending more time on preparation and planning reduces error, rework and crisis tasks.

- Rethink what we mean by 'commitment' and identify the role that commitment plays in decisions about talent and succession. Again, breaking the automatic link between commitment and long hours is a healthy intervention.

Who owns the talent?

The model still used in many companies is the military chain of command, or 'dead men's shoes'. The person with potential may not be waiting for one specific opening, but because the opportunity pool is limited, so is the talent pool. Depth of experience is valued highly. This is most common in organizations that operate through functional silos. An alternative model assumes that talent is owned by the organization, not by individual businesses; it moves designated high flyers around frequently, to ensure they gain breadth of experience. Much less common than either of these is the organization that offers people a choice, at different periods in their careers, of whether to enter a closed or open talent pool (one aimed at a specific range of potential roles, versus one that provides a platform for a much wider range of roles), and builds bridges between these – yet for many people, this is a much closer reflection of the career progression they would like.

Implicit in many organizations' view of the talent pool is the philosophy of 'up or out'. Yet there are many reasons why people may wish to broaden their capabilities by horizontal career moves – for example, to allow for a period of high demand from their non-work lives. Going up may enable an individual to expand their leadership competence; but moving sideways can result in building cross-disciplinary operational skills, which are an ideal platform for more rapid subsequent progression and which may be highly valuable to the organization. Moreover, the 'up or out' philosophy is potentially discriminatory against people from minority or disadvantaged groups, who have different career trajectories than people from the dominant group, with longer intervals between promotions at early stages of their careers.

Mentoring has proven particularly valuable in helping both individuals and organizations recognize the value of horizontal progression. Mentors often act as intermediaries, enabling the individual to make both the personal and the business case for a non-vertical career path, while still retaining a position in the talent pool.

How organizations go about succession planning

Organizations vary widely in how they approach succession planning, from the highly informal to the highly formal. The assumption of good practice, however, is that more formality (for which read 'process management') is better than less. And more formality leads inevitably to automated or semi-automated systems. Yet a general rule of IT is that automating an ineffective paper system simply makes things worse, and this applies equally to succession planning.

The most commonly used tool or system in succession planning is the nine-box grid. We shall examine this in more detail in Chapter 4, but the basic assumption is that you can assign a position for every employee within a matrix where the two dimensions are performance and potential. How each employee is assessed varies, but common practice is to assemble a panel of line managers and HR professionals to achieve a consensus. Ideally, each of these assessors has had sufficient recent contact with the employee to have formed an opinion, based on some level of personal observation or interaction with the employee. Because this process has great potential to lack objectivity, other evidence may be included, such as appraisal, 360-degree feedback, or data from assessment/development centres, training courses and so on.

So how objective is this process? Two big questions arise here:

1 How effective is decision making generally in the organization, and in this situation specifically?

2 How robust are our definitions and assessments of performance and potential?

It has been my experience that selection panels working through the talent pool have little or no recognition that the psychological traps described above even exist, let alone have processes to manage them. There appear to be no solid ways of measuring the quality of decision making in succession planning, other than whether individuals rated highly performed well in their next promotion. Here we have two problems. How do we know that other candidates, who were rated less favourably on the grid, might not have done a better job? And, of course, the sunk cost trap leads managers to convince themselves that the new appointee is doing fine, and to be more forgiving of mistakes. There is often also an unconscious extension of greater support towards top-rated talent than towards colleagues rated less generously in the nine-box grid – hence their actual or potential failures are smoothed out by the system rather than by any action of their own. We will explore some of these questions in Chapter 4.

Effective succession planning

US academic William Rothwell (2005) describes succession planning in terms of seven steps, each containing questions intended to stimulate thinking and dialogue. These questions are:

Step 1 What results are desired from a succession planning and management program, and what management commitment exists to support those results?

Step 2 What results are people expected to get in their work now, and what competencies are essential to help them achieve those results? This is about what distinguishes high and low performers in the same role or similar roles.

Step 3 How does the organization evaluate individual performance? The organization may have a performance management system, but how robust is it? And do people in the organization regard it as a valuable support for doing their role or as another nuisance activity?

Step 4 How does the organization plan for future competencies?

Step 5 How can individual future potential be assessed? This requires the organization to reflect deeply on what future competencies will be needed.

Step 6 How can the developmental gap between present individual performance and the present competency model be narrowed, and how can the developmental gap between future potential and the future competency model be narrowed? Key to this element are the issues of Personal Development Plans and personal learning competencies. Given that the quality of development planning often decreases with increased hierarchical level, this can be quite a difficult question to answer honestly (Clutterbuck *et al*, 2010).

Step 7 How can the relative success of the succession planning and management program be evaluated?

Rothwell maintains that companies which have addressed all these questions have succession planning processes that are much more effective than the average. Clearly, it is important and beneficial for HR and top management to engage in constructive dialogue around these issues. Yet, as we shall explore in Chapters 9 to 12, even more value may be gained from engaging the talent pool, or even the workforce as a whole in dialogue around these issues. Whether the same answers would come out of this dialogue is an intriguing question!

A handful of studies has attempted to gather data around what an effective succession planning process looks like. The Aberdeen Group has for several years been studying how companies manage succession planning. In its 2010 report (Lombardi, 2010), it found that the proportion of companies with some form of formal succession planning in place increased from 53 per cent in 2008 to 75 per cent in 2010. The report evaluates the effectiveness of succession planning primarily against three criteria:

- The percentage of newly promoted leaders in key positions rated as 'exceeds expectations' in their most recent performance reviews.
- The percentage of positions with at least one ready and willing successor identified.
- Year-on-year reduction in time to fill key positions (in the worst-performing companies, this time was increasing year on year).

The research found radical differences between the best and worst in class. Among characteristics of best-in-class companies are that:

- Leaders are held directly responsible for developing talent.
- The performance of the succession strategy is evaluated each year.
- Best-in-class companies 'are less likely to use behavioural or cognitive ability assessments. Instead they rely on multi-rater or 360-degree assessments to gain a more comprehensive view of the individual. At the same time, they are more likely to look outside of the business to gain insight, incorporating customer or client feedback into the mix.'

So that's what companies do, at various levels of competence and effectiveness. On the surface, the criteria these researchers have used seem reasonable and valid. Or are they?

Evaluating the effectiveness of succession planning

Tom Peters is credited with the aphorism 'What gets measured gets done'. Certainly, experts in the field of succession planning have invested a great deal of effort into creating effectiveness measures. While many organizations still don't measure this at all, those that do tend to put their faith in a bundle of indicators mostly based on ratios. Some of the most common are the following.

The proportion of key roles for which succession planning is in place

On the face of it, this is a practical measure, but it assesses part of the process rather than an outcome. Moreover, it doesn't indicate whether the 'right' candidates are waiting in the wings, only that there is at least one person with the capability to step into the role. Important additional considerations here include:

- What transition would be needed for each candidate to fill this role? If the candidate is key to another project, for example, it may take six months to extract them. Or, if they have little experience in the job area, it may take an equal time before they know enough about the role to manage it without making costly mistakes. The cost of transition is difficult to calculate (so few companies attempt it) but can be considerable! One of the most dangerous situations occurs when a newly appointed manager is under pressure to deliver results and 'hit the ground running'. If they make major decisions before they truly understand the role, then it can seriously damage both the team and their own career track record.
- How does it fit with the candidate's own perspective on their next career moves? (The 'wrong' promotion is a significant cause for people to seek to leave the company.)
- How developmental would this role be for each candidate?

Retention of high potentials

This is an outcome measure, but again can be misleading if the company has defined talent too narrowly. A public sector organization with which I worked had focused most of its efforts on retaining and promoting people who fitted its definition of talent. Implicit in this definition was that talented people sought wider roles with greater responsibility for managing others. Through the review process of a mentoring programme, it emerged that some of the employees who would be most difficult to replace were deeply unhappy about their career prospects. These were mostly technical experts, whose interests lay in progressing in terms of technical responsibility rather than people responsibilities. Because they were off the talent radar, the discontent among these employees (amongst whom there was, when HR investigated, a steadily rising turnover rate) had gone unnoticed. The organization responded intelligently by re-examining how it defined talent and by creating a dual career stream structure.

Ratio of internal versus external hires

What's a good ratio of internal to external hires? A straw poll of recruitment professionals yielded me a wide variation, but the basic rule seems to be that there is no basic rule. The appropriate ratio for a particular organization at a particular time depends on a number of factors, including:

- Whether the organization is in a stable or phase shift stage of growth or decline. For example, small entrepreneurial businesses go through stages of evolution where they outgrow the competencies of the existing employees. Similarly, organizations going through a major culture shift may need to import people who have both the desired mindset and the ability to infect others with it. A big issue in this context is where these people are imported into the organization. As a recent graduate, I joined a public sector organization which was under strong pressure to change its culture, having a public reputation of being both institutionally and overtly racist. Our selection process included a test of our attitudes towards people from other cultures and races. Top management thought it could change the organization by seeding the lowest levels with people who held more enlightened attitudes. Not surprisingly, within 18 months most of these new recruits had quit. Changing organizations from the bottom, or even with an alliance of top and bottom, is extremely difficult. You have to involve all levels to achieve an impact. While many organizations measure the ratio of internal to external hires, it is rare to see them analyse how the ratio varies across the organization, or between different categories of employee. It's also rare to see these data used in a strategic way.

- How the organization recruits and grows people. There seems to be a significant difference between those that recruit on values fit and those that recruit for skills and experience. Several decades ago, a brewery chain in the UK experimented in how it hired new publicans. Half of its intake in the experiment were people who already knew the trade; the other half were people who had little or no experience in the role, but who demonstrated that they had appropriate values (gregariousness, customer focus, commercial acumen and so on). Not surprisingly, those hired on their values outperformed the control group substantially in their first year of trading. Companies such as Dyson or Ben & Jerry's which place high emphasis on hiring for values fit are better able to sustain internal promotion. They also have a greater need to do so, to maintain the integrity of their culture, as was demonstrated in a Swedish study of high-growth companies (Ahrens, 2005).

The utility of data on internal and external hiring lies partly in being able to put a monetary value on the succession planning process. Every internal hire, in theory, is a significant cost saving. Internal hires incur only marginal recruitment costs, they typically accept a lower salary hike than external candidates, and because they are already acculturalized, are less likely to leave within the first 12 months. In theory, benchmarking against other companies can be a useful indicator – but only if they are in a similar situation.

The reality is that organizations need an appropriate mix of internal and external appointments. Going all out for external hires tends to lead to a breakdown in cultural cohesion. Yet insufficient external recruitment tends to stultify an organization. A government agency put a long-lasting freeze on external appointments. In the short term, this resulted in improvements in performance, as although talented people were hired away, more openings occurred for internal talent. However, the shallowness of the talent pool meant that it ran dry after about a year. A lifting of the ban on external recruitment came too late – there were now simply too many 'blockers' in middle and senior management positions to respond effectively to change in the organization's environment. Within 18 months, it was disbanded and its roles reassigned to other agencies.

Success in the new role

On the positive side, this is at least an outcome-based measure, intended to tell you how well the succession planning process actually works. However, what do we mean by success? And over what period?

A starting point might be: what is the purpose of appointing this person to this role? Purposes might be to improve sales or customer satisfaction, or to deliver a project on time. But they might equally, in the case of a member of the talent pool, be to give exposure to new experiences and challenges. Indeed, an important element in the development of future leaders is for them to experience *failure*. In which case, success might be the quality of the learning they take away from the experience.

A simplistic response – all too often used – is to look for SMART goals: Specific, Measurable, Attainable, Relevant and Timebound. But SMART goals only appear to work on a very narrow range of task-based, relatively obvious outcomes. The more senior or more knowledge based the role an employee occupies, the more they are expected to work with fuzzy goals, creating shape as they go. Focusing on simplistic goals, say the authors of *Goals Gone Wild* (Ordonez *et al*, 2009), has a number of negative outcomes:

- Because goals focus attention, they reduce people's attentiveness to other factors that may help them achieve or contribute more. The lack of context (staring at the ground rather than seeing the trees) makes it easier to focus on the *wrong* goals. (I would add that it also makes people less able to recognize when a goal has become inappropriate.)

- Narrow, short-term goals tend to promote 'myopic, short-term behaviour that harms the organization in the long run'.
- People motivated by specific, challenging goals tend to adopt riskier strategies than do those with less challenging or vague goals.
- Over-focused goal setting can induce unethical behaviour, especially where people just miss challenging goals.
- 'SMART goals inhibit learning' – 'An individual who is narrowly focused on a performance goal will be less likely to try alternative methods that could help her learn how to perform a task'.
- SMART goals may increase extrinsic motivation, but they may also harm intrinsic motivation, because shifting an employee's focus from internal to external rewards is likely to have negative effects on, for example, job engagement (Deci *et al*, 1999).

In the context of measuring the success of an appointment, it is the relatively simplistic goals – and the easiest to achieve – that tend to be achievable in the first 6–12 months. But at senior level, the most significant impacts an executive makes in a new role may require a much longer period to become clear. So organizations end up measuring what is measurable, not what is meaningful.

Another problem with measuring success is, who makes the judgement? Is it just the person's boss, or a portfolio of stakeholders, including customers and direct reports? The more narrowly you define success, the easier it is for people to manipulate results to put themselves in a good light, and the more narrowly managers are likely to perceive their role. So the numbers may be delivered, but the capability of the team may not grow, or may even be diminished. High-potential employees so often are rewarded for winning the battle, while losing the war – but by the time this becomes obvious, they have moved on. Using 360 degree feedback helps to provide a wider perspective of success, but as we shall see in later chapters, this too is open to manipulation and requires care in interpreting results. In short, the wider the definition of success and the more people able to contribute to defining it and assessing it, the more accurate a view of talent and performance is likely to emerge.

Time to become fully operational in new role

This overcomes some of the problems associated with measuring success in the role, but of course requires a definition of what 'fully operational' means, and from whose perspective. Moreover, it is difficult to specify what a reasonable period should be, given that people come into a role with different levels of experience and resources available. Take some real examples:

- A young manager, used to getting things done through command and control, is given a learning role where they can only deliver by influencing peers and superiors.

- A manager taking over a problem department, with limited flexibility in replacing team members and therefore unable to create their ideal team.
- A senior executive appointed to a role where there is ongoing conflict amongst their peers, whose support they need.

Such situations are very common in the workplace. Yet 'as functional as might be expected in the circumstances' isn't likely to pass muster as a measure. It's difficult to create meaningful measures that recognize the complexities of the interrelationship between the individual and their context!

Bench strength

This is defined as management headcount ready for promotion divided by management headcount; ie the percentage of high-potential employees who have been identified as ready for promotion. Typically, a bench strength index would classify managers as ready for a critical role now, in 12 months or 24 months. Comparing the index year on year is intended to provide a perspective on the health of the succession pipeline.

But again, what does 'ready for promotion' mean? Is it into a specific role, or more generally, into any relevant leadership role that comes up? The two situations may require very different characteristics. And will people actually want the roles that open up?

Other measures

A variety of other measures have been suggested for assessing the effectiveness of succession planning by US academic Dr John Sullivan. Extrapolating from these and adding some of my own, there are both process measures and outcome measures.

Process measures:

- Do line managers know about and use the succession planning process and plan?
- In what proportion of actual promotions or appointments was the succession planning process used?
- Does every person identified in the plan have a written progression plan, which they can self-manage? Are these supported by the organization? Are they actually carried out?
- Are line managers rewarded for supporting the development of people on the plan and for releasing talent from their own teams?
- Is there a plan to retain and support people, who haven't moved for several years?

- What proportion of internal moves are natural progressions (or 'dead man's shoes')? Sullivan suggests that a healthy succession planning process will include a solid proportion of moves that involve someone from another department, a more junior level or a break in the seniority chain. It's important to ensure, he maintains, that the succession planning process does more than throw up 'obvious' candidates. Does the plan include some external candidates, who have been identified and sounded out?

- What proportion of moves place people in the right place within a business cycle? Different phases of development require different types of leadership, so start-up may require someone with strong skills of innovation and team building, while a function in its mature phase may need a manager skilled at extracting efficiencies.

- How timely is readiness for the next promotion? Sullivan recommends six months ahead as the ideal, on the grounds that people who are ready well before that, or well after, are likely to go off the boil. Essentially, this is a measure of how well aligned development processes are with processes to predict job openings.

- What proportion of people on the succession plan are subsequently removed from it, although they are still employed? Some movement is to be expected, as life circumstances change.

- What level of organizational commitment do people on the plan have? This can be compared with the organization's employees in general, or with a broad industry benchmark, or year on year.

- How well does the mix of people on the plan reflect the diversity of people employed by the organization?

Outcome measures:

- What proportion of people who are promoted receive a further promotion within three years?

- What proportion stay in the new role for at least a year? (The period here will depend on the pace of change in the organization, but a good appointment would normally need at least a year to make a lasting impact and be able to move without costly disruption to the role.)

- What is the retention level of people on the plan? Of people who were considered or interviewed for the plan and not included?

- How quickly are vacancies filled? Sullivan recommends 30 days as the baseline for jobs remaining unfilled.

- How has the succession planning process contributed to the diversity of actual appointments?

And perhaps most important of all, but rarely asked: 'How effective do *employees* think the succession planning process is?'

The bottom line on evaluation of succession planning seems to be that it is nowhere near as simple as it might seem at first sight. Simplistic measures may give a false sense that all is well. Once again, the more extensive and the more inclusive the dialogue around the succession planning process, the more likely that an accurate picture can be gained as to how well it is working!

A special problem of succession planning in smaller companies

One of the observations from small business coaching and mentoring is that the competences needed to lead change as the organization becomes bigger. So effective mentoring in this sector tends to concentrate on helping the entrepreneur grow in alignment with the development of the business – no easy task! But the entrepreneur is only one individual, and most people in the company at an early stage of its evolution will have only a limited capability to be effective leaders of a larger entity. So at each phase of growth there is a need to import managerial and leadership talent, most of whom will not have what it takes to lead in the subsequent phase of growth. Of course, if the company doesn't experience rapid growth, there is less of a problem. But where it does grow rapidly, there are significant emotional stresses – especially for the founders – as valued employees gradually become left behind.

Managing succession in such an environment requires a very different approach to the norm. Companies such as Dyson (once but no longer a small company) have resolved many of the problems by viewing all new hires not as recruits for a specific role, but as potential leaders. As long as growth continues, they are able to meet from within both the demand for talent and the aspirations of bright employees.

So how do the wrong people get to the top?

Given that this is a chapter largely about definitions, it helps to define what we mean by a right person or a wrong person. Inevitably, the answer is complex. The 'right' person might be defined as 'someone with the personal resources, skills and abilities to provide leadership appropriate to the time and circumstances'. Resources here might include integrity, resilience and personal credibility. What is appropriate will vary according to the size and kind of organization, the challenges it faces, the composition of the rest of the team, the scope of responsibilities and so on. Inherent in this definition is a sense that as time and circumstances change, what constitutes the 'right' leader will also change. Some of the broader changes that are occurring in what is expected of an effective leader are explored in more detail in Chapter 3.

The 'wrong' leader can therefore be of at least three types. Type A consists of leaders whose fit with their role has become increasingly uncomfortable. For example, in the decade that I worked for a multinational publisher, I watched it acquire companies, complete with their entrepreneurial leaders. In many cases those leaders departed rapidly, because the demands of operating within a bureaucratic organization were very different from the free-wheeling style of leadership they had been used to.

Type B 'wrong' leaders have stumbled into a misfit job by accident. They may have been promoted beyond their competence level, having performed well in the previous job. Or they may have been persuaded to take on a role as a 'safe pair of hands'; or the requirements and constraints of the role may have been mis-sold to them. The misfit is a misfortune that has happened to them, rather than a result of overweening ambition.

Type C 'wrong' leaders are people whose hunger for power and self-gratification makes them unsuitable for leadership in almost any business context. As a workshop exercise, I have asked people to define where in an organization a psychopath might be employed in a way that they would bring sustainable benefit (apart from to themselves). It's hard to find such roles, because while psychopaths often appear to deliver short-term targets, the longer-term cost of doing so typically outweighs the benefits. The only roles consistently identified where the psychopath is a good fit are in the organizational structure of Hades!

This section could arguably have been better entitled, 'How psychopaths get to the top?' – for they do, and frequently. The words 'sociopathy' and 'psychopathy' often tend to be used interchangeably. Both exhibit similar behaviours, but sociopathy is typically regarded as being more influenced by environment than psychopathy, which is innate. So just how well embedded are these individuals in business organizations? Studies by Paul Babiak and his colleagues suggest that they rise to the top far more frequently than has previously been thought – that perhaps as many as one CEO in 25 has strong psychopathic tendencies. In one of their papers (Babiak *et al*, 2010), based on a study of 203 executives selected into leadership development programmes, they report that: 'Psychopathy was positively associated with in-house ratings of *charisma/presentation style* (creativity, good strategic thinking and communication skills) but negatively associated with ratings of *responsibility/performance* (being a team player, management skills, and overall accomplishments).' In other words, these individuals package themselves well, but perform poorly. Says Babiak in a *Horizon* documentary (7 September 2011): 'Part of the problem is that the very things we're look-ing for in our leaders, the psychopath can easily mimic. Their natural tendency is to be charming. Take that charm and couch it in the right busi-ness language and it sounds like charismatic leadership.' The move to new styles of leadership and new expectations of leaders ought, in theory, to make it more difficult for psychopaths to rise in organizations – after all, the new leadership is meant to be authentic, concerned with developing and motivating people. In practice, however, these are all qualities that a charismatic and devious person can fake with relative ease. If anything, we may have made it easier for the psychopath to rise.

Here's a story I have heard repeated frequently, in one form or another. There were several candidates for a senior job role. All had a good track record of achievement, but one person stood out. The others had all, at some point in their careers, taken the decision to delay a promotion while they supported their teams through a difficult project or transition. They all had very good relationships with previous teams they had led, and kept in touch with them. They had had relatively few employers – between three and four, on average. The exception on both counts was a manager whose career had been built over the bodies of direct reports who disagreed with him or who he saw as disloyal. This person had invested a great deal in his own reputation management, particularly with top management, as someone who 'made and saw through tough decisions'. He had had the largest number of employers and there was a pattern, in both his personal life and his work life, of initial intense relationships that didn't last. In an assessment centre it became clear to us that this person, engaging and charming as he could be when he wanted to, was sociopathic. In team exercises, when he thought he was not being observed, he cynically manipulated other participants.

We informed the leadership group that this person was a hidden liability to the business; that he would always seek to do things for his own advantage, rather than for the business. But they told us, 'He gets things done. We can control him and we know where we want to use him.' Of course, they were deluding themselves. They couldn't control him and by the time they realized he was manipulating *them*, he had caused the company to lose some real talent it couldn't replace. In the end, the operations he took charge of after his promotion had to be sold off at a fire sale price – to the company he'd joined when he was finally rumbled! They were lucky, however. If he'd stayed, he could have taken over a much larger chunk of the company and perhaps brought it all down.

What goes on in the minds of leaders who ignore the warning signs of a psychopath in the wings? No one knows for sure, but perhaps part of the answer lies in the mythology of Western leadership – the assumption that a leader has to be something of a ruthless bastard to succeed. It's true that studies of leadership often conclude that successful leaders exhibit more than a trace of obsessiveness and determination in pursuing grand visions. The distinction lies in where that obsessiveness is put into service. The psychopath pursues a dream rooted in his or her own aggrandisement – for example, creating the world's biggest bank, or consultancy, or whatever. The true leader is not interested in big, or even most profitable, but in a vision that emphasizes, for example, quality and values. True, a psychopathic leader may use the words 'values' and 'quality', as they would any other resource for manipulation, but they are tools towards a different end, rather than the end in itself. When did you last hear a psychopathic leader announce that their primary goal was to make their company the greatest place to work?

In a recent conversation with a group of psychologists, who are also coaches, a theme that caused some excitability was the ability of psychopathic managers to manipulate systems such as competency frameworks. Each of the people present was able to recall one or more managers who was able to tick all the boxes in terms of demonstrating the required behaviours, yet was deeply psychologically flawed as a leader.

Why succession planning doesn't work: a summary

Many, if not most succession planning programmes are limited in their effectiveness for a number of reasons. Among them:

1 They are overly reliant on line managers' perceptions of their direct reports' performance. Yet research shows this to be an unreliable predictor of future leadership capability (Alimo-Metcalfe, 1998). A more accurate predictor is the view of the person's own direct reports.

2 They are embedded in inflexible competency frameworks that do not take sufficient account of the changing demands of jobs.

3 They pin down jobs with detailed job descriptions and thereby limit the range of people who are considered, or who opt to apply. Yet the reality is that people shape jobs around themselves and their own preferences, strengths and weaknesses. A more productive perspective might be to define the outputs for a role and seek candidates who can potentially transform it.

4 They take inadequate account of role evolution. Roles evolve to fit the circumstances which influence them and which they are intended to influence. When I ask groups of managers, 'By how much would you estimate your role has changed in the past six months?' often the great majority say that it has done so substantially. In research I carried out a decade ago (Clutterbuck, 2000), funded by the European Union and what is now Exemplas, I explored how teams managed their learning. It soon emerged that there were many types of team and that two of the factors that influenced team type were the stability of the task and the stability of membership. While it is probably true that the majority of people work in stable teams (ones where the membership and tasks are consistent for a reasonable period), they are often also members of

other teams where the membership and/or task is constantly changing. And many employees work only in such 'unstable' teams.

5   They have inadequate definitions of talent, linking it too closely to rapid and continued upward progress and perceptions of an 'ideal' manager or leader. These definitions may be too vague, or too narrow, or paradoxically both at the same time! They fail to recognize that people can be talented in the role that they are in, and that expanding that role may be more beneficial all round than placing them in a new role. (The link between impact on the organization's goals and hierarchical level is assumed, but often questionable!)

6   They assume that high performers at one level will become high performers at the next. The Peter Principle (Peter and Hull, 1969) has been around for a long time, but it is easy to find examples where the lesson has not been learned.

7   They do not take enough account of gender differences. Ambition may be expressed in different ways in men and women. Men are more likely to expect to pick up skills once they achieve a new job role; women to expect to gather the skills beforehand. And as we have seen above, people from different racial backgrounds may have different career trajectories.

8   They ignore work–life balance as a factor in people's decisions to go for more senior jobs. So innovative solutions, such as job sharing, don't get considered. This limits the talent pool and has a disproportionate effect on the willingness of women to seek top roles. One large legal firm admitted to me a while ago that it had lowered the bar (so to speak) for becoming a partner, because so many of the smartest and most talented employees would not sacrifice their home life to adopt the life which they observed existing partners to lead.

9   They leave it too late to give people breadth of experience as well as depth within a silo. So when managers are promoted into roles where they need to adopt an integrative, cross-functional approach, they lack the appropriate experience and skills. While the stages of leader mental development outlined in books such as the *The Leadership Pipeline* (Charan *et al*, 2001) are helpful in defining generic ways of thinking at different levels of responsibility, the foundation for this different thinking needs to be laid down at a much earlier stage in a person's career. One of the most formative experiences for me was having a mentor at a much more senior level who shared with me how he thought about issues in the workplace.

10 They collude in the fiction that employees will remain for the long term, when all the evidence suggests that they will leave after a few years. This nostalgic hankering for the good old days when people

stayed with the same employer all their working life tends to blind us to the realities of the modern workplace. Having employees move on has many positives. It opens up opportunities for others; creates alumni networks which can be highly beneficial in terms of future trade (ask McKinsey or any of its competitors); and former employees are a potential recruitment pool of people who now have additional, valuable skills and knowledge. Yet time and again, we see companies treat people who resign as traitors – even in some cases insisting that they clear their desks immediately. As a result, much of the data on people in the talent pool is wildly inaccurate in terms of their intention to stay; the penalties of honesty mean that employees, too, must maintain the fiction that they will be around for the long term.

11 They have a one-size-fits-all talent development process. Yet every genuine high flyer I have interviewed, coached or mentored has gained greatest value from learning and development opportunities that they have created for themselves. They see well-meaning attempts by HR to provide a generic development route as largely incidental to their development. They do value informal interventions that help them work out what they want and why. Then they want either the freedom to get on with it on their own, or specific, personalized development opportunities. They may need continued support in making choices, but these tend to be from informal routes, such as mentoring.

12 They take inadequate account of how 'adult' people are. Managers show a wide range of levels in their socio-emotional perspective (how they perceive themselves and their values in relation to the world around them) and their cognitive ability (the level of complexity, which they are able to engage in their thinking – *not* the same thing as IQ). It could be argued that a high proportion of corporate failures and poor decision making is related to having executives whose level of socio-emotional and/or cognitive maturity is wrong for the role they hold. US-based psychologist Otto Laske (2009) makes a powerful case for HR to be proactive in assessing the maturity of executives and for intervening directly in helping managers make the transition from one level to the next. Unfortunately, seniority and maturity don't always go together in organizations!

13 They attribute too much of the success or failure of a team to the leader (Martinko and Gardner, 1987) and too little to the people around them and the context in which the leader is operating. (It's a lot easier to be a success in an expanding market than a shrinking one, for example!)

14 They place people in boxes. Even if the evaluation of the employee is accurate and they are in the correct box, this can create more

problems than it resolves. As soon as the employee is boxed, his or her horizons adjust accordingly and the performance level becomes a self-fulfilling prophecy.

15 They have inadequate processes to define what is a critical job role, where it is most important to have at least one potential successor. In a large European bank, for example, the HR team found that rigorous examinations of role criticality led to about a third of roles being dropped and replaced by others.

16 They do not take sufficient cognisance of the differences in attitudes towards careers and career self-management between generations. Succession management processes tend to be designed by baby-boomers, for implementation by Generation X and imposed upon Generation Y. Many of the failures of succession planning can be laid in part at least to lack of intergenerational communication about expectations.

17 They focus on competency sets that represent idealized versions of leadership, forgetting or ignoring that the most effective leaders are often people who have flaws and are aware of them, but compensate for them in the support networks they create around them. Is it not remarkable that the leaders of business who we remember positively tend to be the mavericks like Sir John Harvey-Jones, or Archie Norman, who do not fit the mould? As a result, the search for excellence tends to produce an environment that favours the rise of conforming mediocrity; or worse still, manipulative players who know how to play the game.

18 They concentrate almost exclusively on one side of the succession process – the inward direction – and very little on the equally important issue of when the incumbent is no longer the best person for the role. Roles either change or, as in our case study of Andy Bond, the leader reaches a natural point in their achievement cycle when it is time to hand over to someone with a fresh set of talents, strengths and perspectives.

19 They view succession planning as a linear system, when it is in reality a complex, adaptive system. Trying to control the uncontrollable frequently results in simplistic solutions, which in turn can only be justified by simplistic measures of efficacy.

20 Finally (although this list is far from exhaustive) current approaches to succession planning are typically staggeringly ineffective in creating deep engagement from stakeholders – line managers, top management, employees (whether tagged as talent or not) and, as often as not, HR itself.

These are all themes that I develop further in this book, along with suggestions of practical alternative solutions.

Summary

In this chapter, I have attempted to capture some of the reasons why executives and many HR professionals are so dissatisfied with succession planning – and, to a lesser extent, with talent management – as currently practised. In the next chapter, I explore the difficult task of deciding what (or who) is talent, and the practicalities of nurturing talent. If succession planning is about putting talented people in the right place at the right time, then talent management is about identifying talent and preparing them to fill roles which the company needs to fill in the future – even if it is not clear what those will look like, nor what they will demand of those who occupy them. So the processes of succession planning and talent management are mutually supportive and intertwined; or at least they should be. And this is the starting point for the next chapter, which takes a deeper look at the nature and purpose of talent management.

A systemic perspective on succession and talent

A complex system that works is invariably found to have evolved from a simple system that worked. A complex system designed from scratch never works and cannot be patched up to make it work. You have to start over, beginning with a working simple system.

(Gall, 1975)

... as a living entity, a company is always insecure, never stable, always subject to shifting relationships between the company and the outside world.

(Arie de Geus, 1997)

The assumptions that HR departments and managers make about succession planning derive from the mindset they apply to the issue. The mindset behind traditional succession planning and talent management is linear: it assumes that simple rules of input and output apply. In this mindset, people's ability to perform well in more senior roles is predictable. What makes for effective performance in a particular role is consistent and can be analysed, in the form of competencies. Inexperience or lack of specific competences in an employee can be addressed through a combination of appraisal and development, equipping them with what they need to be successful in their next role. Failure is the fault of the individual, who has not lived up to their potential. The goal for HR and senior management is to achieve predictability, consistency and hence control.

An alternative, more accurate mindset is that succession planning and talent management are complex adaptive systems, or even complex evolving systems.[1] Such systems can't be controlled, and attempts to do so tend to deliver worse results than if they were left alone. So, for example, damming rivers frequently results in much greater and longer-lasting environmental damage than the floods the dams were intended to control.

Research into complex systems has revealed a number of characteristics, which are relevant in the context of succession planning. Complex adaptive systems are:

- *Emergent.* Elements in the system appear to interact randomly, yet produce a functioning mechanism. As we saw in Chapter 1, no one tells a school of fish or a flock of birds to shift direction in unison – it just happens. In the new vision of succession planning, the aim is less to fit employees into a grand plan than to channel their energies and ambitions, encouraging the development of 'deep capabilities' and trusting that the creative ferment will deliver the right person at the right time, most of the time.

- *Co-evolutionary.* They adapt to change in their environment, but they also stimulate change in their environment. In succession planning terms, talented people adjust their ambitions and develop new skills in line with their observations of opportunities in the corporate and/or professional environment. In doing so, they create new opportunities, both for the business and for themselves.

- *Self-organization.* No one is in charge of the process. It just happens. The system constantly reorganizes in reaction to feedback from its parts. In succession planning terms, this is the difference between HR producing detailed succession plans which are immediately out of date, and viewing every vacancy that occurs as an opportunity to recreate the role in the light of what a wide variety of candidates could bring to it. Note, I am not suggesting here that there is no role for HR – far from it. What I am questioning is the need for and indeed the practicality of trying to take charge of and control the system.

- *Suboptimal efficiency.* Emergent systems emphasize effectiveness over efficiency. 'Good enough' will always win out over transitorily perfect. In succession planning terms, this translates to, for example, talent being less about how well people match a predetermined list of competencies than about how adaptable they are in using their strengths to meet the demands of a job role, while being 'good enough' in areas of lesser strength. Current succession planning processes tend to look for supermen and superwomen; as a result they are liable to produce evolutionary dead-ends, adapted to perform well until the environment changes and new strengths are required!

- *Requisite variety.* The strength of a complex adaptive system lies to a great extent in how varied its components are. A key lesson from the observation of large corporations as they lose their competitive edge is that this decline is often accompanied by a lengthy period of weeding out diversity. Mavericks – people who don't fit the mould – get frustrated because they can't do things which they believe need to be done, and because their promotion is often blocked in favour of colleagues who present the 'right' attitudes and competencies. It takes a rare and highly talented individual to bide their time until they can release their individuality, as did Sir John Harvey-Jones at ICI. Of course, all organizations have a sense of whether someone fits their culture, and they need to protect against people who are radically counter-culture. It is when that instinct leads to increasingly narrow definitions of talent that clones and closed thinking become a major threat to the organization. Rigid competency frameworks can therefore speed up and entrench the loss of diversity.

Diversity is, of course, closely correlated with both creativity and conflict (see, for example, Earley and Mosakowski, 2000). The clearest conclusion from the extensive research in this area is that highest performance in teams is related to a combination of diversity and the *quality of conversations* between members, which enable them to defuse conflict or use it positively and constructively.

- *Connectivity*. One of the most exciting new areas of neuroscience research is the connecteome. The human brain is probably the most complex of known adaptive systems, constantly reshaping itself to the external and internal environment. What makes the brain so powerful and so difficult to understand is not the billions of neurons within it, but how these connect to each other. The connecteome is the ever-changing map of these connections and as such it makes the more familiar genome and proteome (both themselves horrendously complicated) look relatively simple! In complex adaptive systems, the relationships between 'neurons' is much more important than the neurons themselves.

  Current theories of succession planning generally do not take into account how individual employees interact with each other and with peers outside the organization. The development and promotion process is not a simple reiteration between the employee, the organization and the employee's boss. It is a deeply complex web of interconnections, shifting constantly in terms of strength, influence and direction. And what underpins this connectivity? The nature, quality and frequency of conversations between these individual connections.

- *Simple rules*. Underneath the complexity of an adaptive system often lie a small number of simple rules. A common analogy is the kaleidoscope, which is able to produce a myriad of complex patterns from simple arrangements of components. So what simple rules would apply to succession planning? The simple answer is that we don't know. To date, no significant research has taken a systems view to the issue, to my knowledge. However, observations from research and practice suggest that the following simple rules may be relevant:

  – All other factors being equal (eg broad satisfaction with pay and benefits) *employees seek roles which provide an appropriate balance between stretch, exploit and coast.* Stretch is job content that is intellectually challenging and stimulates personal growth. Exploit is applying stretch knowledge in other situations – some learning still occurring but more incremental, less dramatic. Coast is routine work that has little learning attached to it. People seek different combinations of stretch, exploit and coast according to their circumstances, motivation and self-belief – and they may frequently adjust the combinations they seek.

– *Diversity of talent thrives in an atmosphere of psychological safety.* Teams and organizations where people are encouraged and feel free to speak their minds, make suggestions and be recognized for their contributions – where conversations are creative and open – are strongly associated with quality of learning (Edmondson, 1999) and emergence of leaders who do not match an organizational norm.

– *Employees tend to have to have been working substantially at the level above, before they are promoted to that level.* In a study I led some years ago (Clutterbuck and Dearlove, 1995) into the evolution of career paths, it became clear that shifts in job role were much more complex than simply stepping into a vacancy at the next level. The analogy was another complex (though not necessarily adaptive) system: a bubble in the lower of two layers of moving liquid. The bubble gains momentum by expanding (absorbing other bubbles) and drifting with currents – it does not go straight up. In order to break into the next layer, it has to deform the barrier between the layers, until so much of the bubble is within the higher level that it forces its way through. In the same way, a young manager develops capability and gains experience at one level, taking on some new responsibilities and losing others. Eventually, they take on some responsibilities that belong within the next level. Only when the proportion of higher-level responsibilities is greater than the lower level ones, does promotion follow.

One of my personal experiences as a young manager was being promoted from a manager to a manager of managers. When I asked how the decision had been made, I was told that I had demonstrated that I was 'thinking like a manager at the more senior level'. While thinking patterns and responsibilities are not entirely the same thing, it can be argued that they are closely connected. It seems that two factors have a particular influence on this process of gaining greater responsibility and higher level thinking patterns: the opportunity to deputize for more senior managers, and the frequency and quality of conversations with those more senior managers. For me, all those years ago, both those opportunities came from building a mentoring relationship with my boss's boss.

- *The strongest connections exert the strongest influence.* If someone's strongest connections are within an organization, they are likely to look first for promotion internally. If their strongest connections are external, the opposite will be the case. When new recruits leave within a year, it is likely that they have 'failed to put down roots'. Succession planning should include processes to encourage the growth of the 'organizational connecteome'.

  There are no doubt other simple rules to be discovered and this is an area I look forward to exploring in future.

● *Iteration.* Frequent feedback loops can greatly magnify the impact of small changes. This process is sometimes called the Butterfly Effect. The impact of a single perfunctory development review between a manager and a direct report may seem small. But if the direct report decides not to bother preparing for the next review and tells colleagues of his experience, they may decide it is not worth preparing for their own reviews. Moreover, all the direct reports may adopt a similar laissez-faire approach towards reviews for their own staff. Because all systems tend to follow the path of least resistance (and because managers often tend to regard tasks like developmental reviews as messy and an interruption to the more enjoyable problem-solving parts of their job), what started as a single feedback loop becomes a torrent of resistance.

● *Russian dolls.* Complex adaptive systems are often subsets of other systems or made up of subsystems. For example, the succession planning system is interconnected with HR systems for recruitment, reward, appraisal, performance management, employee surveys, training and development, employee engagement and so on. It is also influenced by systems relating to information technology (IT) and technology more generally, formal and informal systems within work teams, and how employees relate to their professions, their own and other cultures, and other key colleagues and superiors. While it may be possible to infer some general rules about the interactions between these systems, at the level of the individual employee or the individual job, role predictability becomes far too complex.

While not wanting to stretch the metaphor of the complex adaptive system too far, it does seem to me that it has a number of powerful and highly relevant characteristics. First, it gives permission for HR not to keep trying to do the impossible. Second, it pushes responsibility for succession and career planning back where it belongs, with talented individuals. They may need occasional help, but they don't need to have the process managed for them.

This is a theme we will come back to time and again in the rest of this book. Many of the problems identified in Chapter 1 are the result of thinking about succession and talent from a simple, linear perspective. As we shall see in Chapter 4, this is particularly so in the context of identifying and developing talent.

Generation F: ambassadors of the complex adapative system

Gary Hamel, at London Business School, points out (Hamel, 2009) that the Facebook generation, Generation F, is acquiring mindsets and behaviours from their constant interface with the world wide web. He identifies 12 aspects of this mindset – and all of them are reflections of a complex, adaptive system. Here I rephrase and comment on just some of his 12 aspects, in the context of talent and succession:

- 'On the web, all ideas compete on an equal footing.' Using power from above to squash an idea won't work. If innovation is a prized talent for an organization, leaders and HR should be monitoring where the ideas come from (and it won't mostly be from the top!).

- What you do counts for more than the badges you hold. Job titles and qualifications are less important than what you are seen to contribute.

- Hierarchies happen. Organizations tend to impose relatively static hierarchies; on the web people earn respect and attention, rather than expect it to come from position. In the talent and succession planning stakes, who is most respected by their peers?

- 'Leaders serve rather than preside.' On the web, people switch off when ordered about; in organizations, servant-leadership is proving a more viable option than command and control. Do our definitions of talent adequately recognize those who demonstrate servant-leader qualities at an early stage?

- 'Tasks are chosen, not assigned.' On the web, people work on what interests them. While we don't necessarily have that freedom at work, genuine talent will always look to move on when the job role begins to lose its challenge.

- 'Groups are self-defining and self-organizing.' People choose who they want to work with. Internal social networking within organizations is already allowing this to happen – it just isn't obvious to leaders who are not part of those networks. Succession planning has to take account of people's ability to bring together informal, ad hoc groups which make things happen (often without waiting for formal authority).

- 'Resources get attracted, not allocated.' People with leadership abilities fit for the modern organization will have to be able to find resources by persuading others to invest in their ideas and energy.

- 'Power comes from sharing information, not hoarding it.' Career success in tomorrow's organization will increasingly depend on the quality of a person's networks and their reputation for generosity in providing knowledge and ideas to other people.

The bottom line here is that all organizations have a tremendous and existing resource which they can tap into, to help address the changes that will be needed to adapt to the realities of talent development and succession as complex, adaptive systems. But are HR and leaders – most of whom come from generations with very different mindsets – ready to listen to people at the bottom of the pyramid?

Challenges for HR

What does a systemic perspective look like in practice? A starting point, at least, is that it recognizes complexity and seeks connections. And one of the best ways to achieve both of those characteristics is to question constantly both the context in which talent management and succession planning take place, and the assumptions we make in trying to understand that context. The good news is that HR professionals, when given permission to raise such questions, often do so with enthusiasm and perceptiveness. Here, for example, is a list of questions generated by just one small group of senior HR people at a Clutterbuck Associates' networking breakfast:

- Is talent management about developing competencies or developing leadership?
- Does greatest value come from focusing succession planning on short-term solutions (filling slots as they become vacant) or on quality conversations and building organizational capability?
- How can you free competence frameworks from culture bias?
- Do you home-grow or import talent? (At McDonald's for example, reportedly 80 per cent of the board started out by flipping burgers.)
- How useful is the concept of readiness for promotion when in practice, by the time people are ready, the organizational need has often passed?
- How committed to succession planning and talent management are the leaders? (KPMG's HR told top management to give real support, or they would not bother to implement the talent management programmes!)
- What do we do with talented people (assuming we can identify who they are)? Cocoon them? Integrate them? Or set them free to find their own paths?
- How does HR find out when talent is blocked? And what do they do about it?
- Is there any evidence that organizations which manage succession planning are better than those that don't?

It's questions such as these that give hope that HR can rise to the challenge of creating more dynamic, more flexible, systemic solutions to talent and succession.

Note

1 Complex adaptive systems continuously adapt in response to changes around them, but do not learn from the process. Complex evolving systems constantly learn from change. This enables them to consciously influence their environment, predict and prepare for likely future changes.

What do we mean by leadership?

'Leadership myth tells us that it is lonely at the top. Not so. The most effective leaders we know are involved and in touch with those they lead'

(James Kouzes and Barry Posner, 1987)

This chapter sets out to provide a context for thinking about succession planning and talent management, in respect of leadership. If the main purpose for investing in talent management and succession planning is to ensure an adequate supply of effective leaders as the organization needs them, then it would help if we had a clear idea about what leadership is. If only it were that simple!

There are hundreds of books and thousands of articles written about leadership, many of them highly insightful. A relative minority take a genuine evidence-based approach and try to establish the common characteristics and behaviours of leaders who are manifestly successful and to extrapolate from these data competencies which can be used to select future leaders. I have followed the same path, particularly in the research for *The Winning Streak* (Goldsmith and Clutterbuck, 1984) and its follow-up study, *Winning Streak II* a decade or so later (Goldsmith and Clutterbuck, 1997). But there are two basic problems with this approach. One is that 'manifestly successful' is itself a questionable concept. As Malcolm Gladwell points out in his book *Outliers* (2008), success in a wide variety of fields often depends upon factors which have little to do with innate qualities and a lot to do with luck and contextual factors, such as month of birth. Other writers building on the same theme take an even stronger line that talent is mostly hard work and application (Coyle, 2009) – although the evidence for this view is far from compelling. Only in recent years have we started to see studies, such as those by Ruth Wageman *et al* (2008), which take a more contextual view of leadership success. Their analysis of leadership teams in 120 large organizations internationally measured effectiveness in relation to a variety of stakeholders, rather than just on financial performance of the business. So manifest success is dependent on the perspective – or more accurately, the number of perspectives – from which you view a leader or a leadership team.

The second problem is the assumption that there is one 'good' style of leadership. It doesn't take a lot of observation to conclude that different contexts demand different leadership qualities. At the simplest level, there seem to be three critical modes for large organizations in terms of leadership requirement: survival, revival and thrival. A much-quoted example of a leader who was highly effective in survival mode, but unsuitable for revival or thrival mode, was Sir Winston Churchill. Part of the problem for BP's former leader Tony Hayward was, it can be argued, that the context changed from one that needed a thrival (steady state) leader to one that needed a survival leader. Other studies suggest that different types of leadership are needed during their high-growth period and when market growth slows down.

The monolithic view of leadership – that a 'good' leader can be effective in any circumstance – underlies most succession planning processes. This rigidity, coupled with the reluctance of individual leaders to step down till they have to, severely inhibits the ability of an organization to respond rapidly to environmental change. The current leader has to be seen to be failing before action is taken, yet by then a great deal of damage may have been done. I recall several organizations, in which I have worked with top teams, where the environment has changed but the leadership team has not (except, in a couple of cases, for the resignation of frustrated individuals who pointed out the need for change and were ignored). In each case, those responsible for appointing the leaders hesitated to take action, because they wanted to be fair and 'give them a chance to prove they can adapt'. In every case, the ultimate result was the appointment of a new CEO from outside the organization and removal of most of the executive leadership, when the situation became too serious to be ignored.

The problem is that leaders and leadership teams frequently:

- Fail to recognize or acknowledge changes in the world around them which do not fit their current perspective and preferred approach to leadership.
- Are resistant to (and perhaps incapable of) honest self-appraisal with regard to their own ability to cope with unfamiliar contexts.
- Overestimate their ability to change leadership style.
- Tend to view radical change as something they can *do to* the organization, rather than something that has to occur within themselves. (Change is always uncomfortable, but less so if you can transfer the pain to someone else!)

A more flexible approach would be to recognize and value a much wider range of leadership qualities and to engage in continuous debate about the evolving nature of leadership required in the current and near future. At the same time, people at all levels would be encouraged to step in and out of leadership roles as circumstances change. Rather than being seen as a stigma or sign of failure, stepping aside into a different role would be valued and rewarded. Pie in the sky? Well, it's not hard to find examples in smaller organizations. For example, an entrepreneur has grown his business to about 50 people, inspiring employees with his ideas and enthusiasm. Does he now continue to lead the business – a role which is taking him further and further from the hands-on activities he enjoys – or bring in professional managers, who can internationalize the company, and step down into the role of leading product development?

Post-recessionary leadership

One of the positive outcomes of recession is that it stimulates organizations to re-examine the qualities they expect of leaders. The leadership style of some of the worst-affected companies, particularly in financial services, has shown how disastrous 'disconnected' leaders can be. By disconnected, I mean leaders whose charisma and drive to achieve takes the business efficiently in directions which threaten its survival. The very strengths that made these people seem attractive as leaders are also their most signal weaknesses.

Connected leaders, by contrast:

- Engage themselves with the organization, at all levels, in particular through two-way learning activities such as coaching and mentoring.
- Encourage and facilitate constructive dissent, while crafting an inclusive vision that combines corporate and individual values and ambitions.
- Explore the balance of their strengths and weaknesses and ensure that their teams provide appropriate counterbalances.
- Act as role models for the values the organization espouses (and are willing to be challenged when their decisions or actions do not appear to align with those values).
- Demonstrate humility.
- Are role models for learning.
- Maintain links with the outside world that provide different perspectives and avoid groupthink.
- See their role as asking the right questions and helping others find the right answers.
- Have a deep sense of ethicality.

The failed leadership teams of the recent recession demonstrated few of these qualities. So how do we build leadership teams who will behave in a more connected way? Part of the answer is to look for people who are truly 'rounded and grounded' – whose experience, skills and personalities exhibit balance and personal insight. For example, all leaders need to have a streak of ruthlessness, to make tough decisions when needed; but post-recessionary leaders need to balance this with an equal tendency for compassion.

Another part of the answer is to ensure the leadership team spends sufficient time reflecting on what it is doing and why, and to equip them with the skills to do this effectively. Often this needs external help, both to bring alternative perspectives but also to develop the habit of collective self-coaching. Such reflection is not an occasional 'away-day' activity – it needs to be an integral part of day-to-day operation and to take up a significant proportion of the team's time. What happens instead, in so many leadership teams, is that most of the time is spent on dealing with current and past crises, or urgent immediate tasks such as yet another acquisition, before previous acquisitions have been properly absorbed.

In short, therefore, post-recessionary leadership is less about personalities than collective capability; less about pace of business growth than quality of growth; less about winning than succeeding; less about what leaders do than what they enable others to do. We've heard much of it before, in different guises, but now perhaps there is a genuine desire to change the nature of business leadership for the better.

Just to be clear, all of these observations I have offered above are based on hundreds of dialogues with HR professionals and leaders. They are not the result of detailed statistical analysis of questionnaires or a similar reductionist academic approach, for a very specific reason: it's difficult to impossible to measure what you can't define, and it's hard to define something that is so heavily dependent on context. We'll look in Chapter 4 at how competencies try (and largely fail) to bridge that gap, but for now let's look at some of the attempts to describe what effective leaders do.

Tim Casserley and Bill Critchley (2010) similarly compare what they describe as the old and the new paradigm of leadership:

- Concern with performance versus concern with human sustainability as prerequisite for performance.
- Identify skills or competences versus foster and integrate core individual processes of reflection on action, psychological intelligence and physiological well-being.
- Modify leaders' behaviour based on those competencies versus negotiate agreement between core processes and culture of organization.
- Leadership is drilled into people via off-job training versus leadership emerges from reflection on action in dealing with real-life adversity.
- Focus on development of one-size-fits-all competencies, with no attempt to adapt these to leader's specific context and challenges, versus focus on the quality of the relationship between the individual leader's core processes and the culture of the organization.

Some critical leadership roles

Another way of looking at leadership is to identify leadership roles – spaces that leaders inhabit to some extent irrespective of their nominal responsibilities. To illustrate the point, let's look briefly at two of them: intrapreneur and developer of people.

Intrapreneur

Intrapreneurs are internal entrepreneurs. Large corporate bureaucracies are generally suspicious of and antipathetic towards internal entrepreneurs, so when they survive and thrive it is because they learn how to work within the system without being tied down by it. They have the habit of asking for forgiveness rather than permission, and as long as they deliver the goods, they can progress rapidly. However, because they don't conform to the rules, they are more likely to be punished hard and lose their jobs if they fail.

Intrapreneurs have many of the same characteristics as entrepreneurs. Entrepreneurs are proactive individuals who make their own opportunities by questioning, experimenting and acting on their dissatisfaction with the status quo. They have the courage to stick their head over the parapet. They have high achievement orientation – they are decisive and determined. Additionally, they show commitment to others, and build strong teams around them (people who can compensate for their own weaknesses or areas of low interest). Intrapreneurs are very similar, but they also have to have the skills to manage organizational politics, especially when they scavenge for resources, and to build coalitions. They combine their entrepreneurial enthusiasm with a strong dose of commercial awareness and understanding of how large organizations function. They come to work every day knowing that they could be fired, and are comfortable that should that happen, they can take their skills and vision into the outside world.

How do you identify and develop potential intrapreneurs? Among the practical ways HR professionals have shared in our conversations are: giving them strong role models; letting them loose on projects of minor importance to build confidence and experience; protecting them with sponsorship (especially from others who have a vested interest in ensuring that an innovation does not work); and creating ways in which people can access resources to pursue ideas without having to fight through multiple layers of bureaucracy.

Developer of others

Sir John Harvey-Jones, former chairman of ICI, was vociferous in his praise for managers who nurtured talent even though they recognized that the younger people they mentored would most likely outstrip them and bypass them in the organizational hierarchy. The relative humility and lack of fierce ambition of these influential managers is typically seen as a fatal flaw, but Harvey-Jones perceived these managers as vital to the organization's survival and growth. HR systems and the myopic perception of macho management often tend to regard talent as thrusting and focused on achieving personal career goals, and to devalue more community-oriented behaviours, such as developing others. (An expectation that inevitably favours the psychopath.) So managers who are nurturing, focused on collective achievement and assisting the achievements of others, may be excluded from the talent pool.

Some practical ways to support and grow people developers include:

- Recognize their value by engaging them in the creation of people strategy and by giving public recognition for their achievements in growing others.

- Identify the added value they bring. Take the example of Einar, a middle-level executive in the marketing function of a multinational company. Placed consistently in assessments just above the middle of the performance–potential grid, he nonetheless had a talent for spotting and growing talent. Of eight internal appointments to roles equivalent to his own level over a two-year period, five had been either his direct reports or his mentees. When the company compared retention of people who had worked under Einar and transferred laterally within the company, it found that on average they stayed significantly longer than people who had worked for Einar's peers, and that they were generally regarded as high performers within their new roles. Putting a monetary value on Einar's hidden contribution wasn't easy, but the net result of the calculations was that he was shown to be a close second amongst his peers in terms of financial impact on the business. His potential rating in appraisal also rose substantially, but it was unclear how much of this was the result of revaluation of his performance and how much was related to his increased self-confidence.

- Break the link between the talent pool and expectation of upward progression. Find space for people who want to grow their roles laterally and who are content to accelerate the upward progress of others.

- Help them find sponsors who understand and will champion the people developer role. From time to time I encounter within organizations powerful networks of people developers, inspired and led from the top by CEOs who willingly and visibly take on themselves the role of 'people developer in chief'.

One of the pithiest endorsements of the leader as developer of others comes from William Cohen (1998), who says: 'My research debunks the myth that many people seem to have... that you become a leader by fighting your way to the top. Rather, you become a leader by helping others to the top. Helping your employees is as important, and many times more so, than trying to get the most work out of them.'

Leaders versus leadership

So far in this chapter and book, I have followed the normal pattern and referred to leaders and leadership as pretty much synonymous. There is, however, a big difference between the leader (an individual who takes a leading role in directing and motivating others) and leadership (a collective activity, in which the role is distributed). This differentiation is in part behind the concept of servant leadership (Greenleaf, 1977), which also places great store in the leader as developer role. Servant leadership encourages collaboration, trust, foresight, listening, and the ethical use of power and empowerment.

Kouzes and Posner (2011) once again express the core concept well:

> Leaders we admire do not place themselves at the center; they place others there. They do not seek the attention of people; they give it to others. They do not focus on satisfying their own aims and desires; they look for ways to respond to the needs and interests of their constituents. They are not self-centered; they concentrate on the constituent... Leaders serve a purpose and the people who have made it possible for them to lead... In serving a purpose, leaders strengthen credibility by demonstrating that they are not in it for themselves; instead, they have the interests of the institution, department, or team and its constituents at heart. Being a servant may not be what many leaders had in mind when they choose to take responsibility for the vision and direction of their organization or team, but serving others is the most glorious and rewarding of all leadership tasks.

Ah, you might say, but don't leaders also get things done? Surely the acid test of leadership is the performance of others? And of course that is true. Focusing excessively on the 'soft' side of leadership runs the risk of not being able to take the tough decisions that are sometimes needed.

If I were forced to make my own definition of leadership it would simply be:

> Having the right conversations, with the right people, at the right time to make things happen.

Sometimes those conversations can be nurturing and deeply empathetic – the core of servant leadership. Sometimes they can be tough and challenging, not necessarily in the sense of being aggressive, but in the way they force people to face up to reality and to make difficult (and better) decisions. Sometimes the toughest conversations of all are those the leader has with himself or herself. Or to restate the definition above:

> Leadership is dialogue that moves mountains

Flawed leadership

Alongside the plethora of literature on what makes an effective leader, there is a growing interest among academics in flawed leadership: what causes apparently successful leaders to crash and burn (Casserley and Megginson, 2009).

Jack Zenger and Joseph Folkman (2009) maintain, based on their leadership skills studies, that a future leader must have the minimal acceptable amount of each of the following characteristics: an ability to learn from mistakes and develop new skills; interpersonal competency; being open to new ideas; taking personal responsibility for results; and an ability to take the initiative. To not have an adequate amount of even one of these, they maintain, is to have a 'fatal flaw'.

From my dialogues with HR professionals, fatal flaws appear to come in two types: those that may derail individual careers and those that have the potential to do much wider damage. One particularly damaging example of the latter is the inability to take a sufficiently wide perspective of the organization and its role in society. Macho, profit-is-all cultures are created by and encourage the advancement of people who take a myopic, materialistic view of success. People with a wider, more grounded perspective either leave or play a dual life, with different values at work and at home. When this fatal flaw is endemic in the leadership and in the leadership pipeline, unethical and inhumane practices are almost inevitable. At France Telecom, for example, it took 35 suicides by employees, over a two-year period, before action was taken to reform the leadership.

Vanderbroeck (2010) sees fatal flaws less as personality traits than as failures of attention. He maintains that managers frequently lose sight of fundamental values because they are seduced by lesser values. For example, they may – often without realizing it consciously – place higher value on creating wealth than on quality of family life. He explains: 'The only thing that can help leaders escape these traps is a strong set of moral values and the belief that they are contributing to a higher purpose. Leaders face many dilemmas and conflicting situations. By basing their decisions on these values rather than only what seems to serve the ephemeral interests of their employer, they can create true lasting value.'

If we look at flawed leaders who have brought disaster on their companies, a recurrent feature appears to be that they do not demonstrate a passion for higher values. True, the organizations may have values statements, but how authentically do they embody those values?

Nonetheless, if we put the concept of flaws into context, *all* leaders are flawed. Many times, a fatal flaw is simply a strength overused or allowed to run rampant. Says one of my e-mail correspondents: 'Maybe it is the people around the flawed leader, who need to change their thinking'. If leaders collectively are responsible for supporting each others' strengths and counterbalancing each others' weaknesses, perhaps that comes very close to a generic definition of effective leadership.

Summary

The aim of this chapter was not to present a comprehensive overview of research into leadership. That would be rather a daunting task! Rather, I have tried to signpost some of the major themes about leadership that might influence our thinking about managing talent and succession, and to demonstrate that there is very little consensus about what makes good leadership. Leadership frameworks, discussed in the next chapter, therefore inevitably involve a greater or lesser degree of arbitrary judgement about what qualities a leader in a specific organization (or a specific role in a specific organization) should possess and exhibit.

CASE STUDY Leader development as a complex, dynamic process

International security firm G4S has more than 600,000 employees. When it decided to design a new development programme for its most senior talent, it recognized that it would achieve far more by allowing the participants to take greater control over their own development. The 24 members of the Senior Leadership Network (SLN) are involved in project groups similar to action learning sets, each working on a significant business issue. They can decide for themselves who does what and can even delegate the work if they wish; what matters is getting the projects done and what they can learn from it. Jo Dunne, director of talent and resourcing, explains that they can opt to work on aspects that employ their own areas of expertise, or take on tasks that take them out of their comfort zone, or, if they wish, play a minor role and let other project team members carry them.

The CEO meets with the teams regularly to share his thinking about the businesses priorities and challenges – what's keeping him awake at night – and this helps the SLN members select what projects they want to sign up to and what roles they want to take, to build their own capability and credibility. Some SLN members have external coaches to help with this. The top team remains sufficiently involved to gain a reasonable clear perception of collective and individual capability. The roles which individuals gravitate to provide an indication of their core talents and the full-time roles they might thrive in. By constantly moving the SLN members from one project to another and letting them take control of the process, G4S is turning what started out as a simple, linear approach into a dynamic adaptive one. One of the results already has been the acceleration of a five-year organization change plan to less than two years.

The critical challenges: what is talent?

Chief financial officer (CFO) to Chief executive officer (CEO): 'What happens if we invest in developing our people and then they leave the company?' CEO answers, 'What happens if we don't, and they stay?'

(internet exchange, May 2011)

This chapter attempts to get to grips with two questions which are critical precursors to any conversation about succession planning in an organization:

1 What do we mean when we talk about talent? Does the way we perceive talent limit or enhance people's perception of what they could achieve?

2 How do we identify people who have existing or potential talent? (Or more precisely, people who have or could develop high strength in the right kind of talents for our evolving needs?) Does our current approach reveal all or most of the talent in the organization; and how do we know?

What do we mean by talent?

Like so many terms used in management and HR, talent can mean very different things to different people. When we speak of having *a talent*, we generally mean a particular skill or aptitude – for example, a talent for languages. The *Oxford English Dictionary* defines talent as: 'A special natural ability or aptitude, usually for something expressed or implied; a natural capacity for success in some department of mental or physical ability.' Someone who is talented is 'Endowed with talent or talents... gifted, clever, accomplished'.

When we talk about the talent in an organization, however, the concept becomes a lot messier. People have a wide range of different talents, some of which are specific to a particular role or task, some of which are more generally useful in helping the organization fulfil its objectives. It's quite possible for an individual to be highly talented, but in areas that are not particularly useful to the organization. Talent as a football player is not the same as talent as a manager.

That's obvious, you might say. Yes, it is, but managers and HR professionals still refer to 'talent' either without defining the yardstick against which being talented is measured, or assuming that all the talented people in the organization can be measured against a generic, one-size-fits-all set of competences. Often these competences are encapsulated into a leadership framework. However, both of these approaches are deeply inadequate in defining something as unique, variable and evolving as talent.

Many of the corporate definitions of talent revolve around a person performing well in their current role and having potential to grow into more senior roles. Yet, as we saw in Chapter 1, individual performance is often highly dependent on other people and on context. And the notion of upward progress is also suspect. If consultancy InfoHRM is correct in its prediction that 50–70 per cent of the workforce will never be promoted again and 80 per cent will have no more than one promotion, that raises the question: 'If we can't provide promotions, what exactly do we mean by a career?' The consultancy's advice is to build many more lateral careers and to measure the career path ratio (the number of promotions in your organization divided by number of transfers). In most organizations, people only move for promotion, but they recommend four transfers for every one promotion.

On these figures, standard assumptions about who is talented leave us with only the 20 per cent of the workforce seen as having potential to move more than one rung up the ladder. These become the 'leadership pipeline'. Note the metaphor: a contained, evenly flowing, one-way movement, with taps at strategic points to decant the amount of talent needed at a particular time. I've yet to meet an HR professional who actually believes that talent flows in this ordered manner! I explore the problems with the pipeline metaphor in more detail in Chapter 7.

If only those who are perceived likely to have more than one promotion are seen as talent, then the pool narrows at each level of the hierarchy. It's probably true that only one in five directors has what it takes to become a chief executive, for example. This principle, although not always enunciated, is behind the concept of high potentials or 'hypos'.

The problems here are, first, that as we saw in Chapter 1 and will explore again later in this chapter, defining potential is a somewhat hit and miss affair; second, that talent is related to higher-level jobs as they are, rather than to what they may evolve into; and third, that the mass of employees – along with their talents – are relegated to the realms of the untalented. Moreover, giving someone the label of 'hypo' can also have negative effects.

Managers, having made the emotional investment in deciding the person has high potential, are emotionally constrained from recognizing that the decision was wrong. Knowing that they are on a fast track can also diminish employees' effort. (This is a significant issue in some countries where there are strong pressures for indigenization and a relatively small pool of locals to choose from. Knowing that they are likely to be promoted because of their nationality, male employees in particular may demonstrate less investment in their personal development and less engagement with their employer.) Drawing on the world of education, we see that praising a student too often fails to help them for three reasons. First, they think they've succeeded, so they don't try as hard. Second, praising them puts them under more pressure to do well, with the result that they try too hard and fail. And third, they know that sometimes praise is used as a not so subtle way to bribe them to do what others want (Dweck 1986, 2000).

If the talent that is being recognized and rewarded is the talent to rise in the organization, is it surprising that promotions go to those who know how to project an image of promotability? And who better to manipulate the organizational systems to that end than our old friend, the organizational psychopath?

We don't have to define talent in this narrow way. For example, if we delete the requirement of 'upward' from the element of progression in talent, we open up the possibility that lateral movement can be just as important and valuable to the organization. Some of the most effective and talented HR professionals I have met in multinational companies have been people with little or no aspiration to achieve higher status. Rather, they are ambitious to become more well-rounded professionals. They constantly acquire new knowledge and skills and they move through jobs at the same level, gathering expertise and experience. As a result, their value and contribution to the business grows year on year. Are these people really untalented? If we accept that they also are talented, then a definition of talent might be: 'A superior performing employee who has potential to contribute significantly more by developing his or her skills, knowledge and experience and who is motivated to do so.'

But we can go a step further. Suppose we abandon the idea of progression entirely? There are many plateaued managers and professionals who are nonetheless catalytic in the advancement of upwards-oriented talent. As we saw in Chapter 3, Sir John Harvey-Jones, former chairman of ICI, used to refer fondly to these people as pivotal in his career and those of many of his peers. We can define such a person as: 'A superior performing employee, whose substantial experience would be difficult to replace, and who contributes significantly to the development of other talented individuals.'

How do definitions of talent affect people's ambitions?

From my conversations with HR and line managers around the world it appears that the more narrowly we define talent or leadership talent:

- The less flexibility there is to accommodate changes in leadership requirements.

- The higher the turnover amongst potential leaders. If people don't identify with the profile of the ideal leader (or with the role models seen to exemplify the ideal) their loyalty to the organization will be lower.

- The greater the wastage of talent overall. This appears to be an issue particularly at junior grades, where the gross refining process takes place and any pebbles that don't fit the shape of the holes in the sieve are filtered out. In the flurry to find the nuggets of gold, other precious metals get overlooked. People who fit the right profile get most opportunities to prove what they can do; other talent leaves or, if it stays, continues to receive fewer opportunities to develop leadership skills, thus creating a self-fulfilling prophecy. Again, part of the problem lies in linear thinking. Until recent years, common wisdom said that babies all developed along the same curve and that some were just slower than others. Now we know that babies develop different skills at different times and that taking longer to walk or talk is not normally an indication of lack of ability. Development is highly individual and much more complex than conventional wisdom allows. Leadership talent spotting is dogged by similar unevidenced assumptions. People develop different aspects of leadership competences at different speeds and in different situations, in response to internal and external change.

Misdiagnosing talent at early stages in a career is unfortunately very easy. Many people find themselves barred from the talent pool of large organizations, because they don't tick all the boxes. It's a salutary thought that one of the UK's most successful entrepreneurs would not have made the cut in many companies' leadership programmes, because of his dyslexia. Similarly, a top broadcaster has been profoundly deaf in one ear from her childhood, but managed to conceal her disability until her reputation was well established, knowing that as a partially deaf junior reporter she would not have been given the opportunities that shaped her career.

The impact of misdiagnosis of talent has other, broad organizational implications. Those who are passed over can either leave and find more fertile ground for their talents; or they can stay and either accept their lower potential, or resent it. The Pygmalion effect (people perform up to or down to the level of belief that those in authority have about their ability) comes into play here with a vengeance. The lack of belief the organization shows in them saps energy and reduces their ambition (both for themselves and the organization). It's a reasonable conclusion that this will also have an effect on performance.

It is my firm belief that the more people an organization has who are perceived and perceive themselves as talented, the greater the energy that can be directed towards achieving shared objectives; and the higher the attractiveness of the organization to talented people.

How do we identify talent?

Talent management systems are built upon the assumption that talent can be identified with relative ease and accuracy. This assumption is questionable for a number of reasons.

First, in practice, talent is often emergent. It sometimes takes time to become obvious to the talent holder and to observers. Someone may need to be placed in a stretching situation, which stimulates them to exercise a talent, before they recognize it as such. Here's how one observer describes it: 'Talent can be described as an innate characteristic, a kind of genetic heritage that is typical of someone gifted with exceptional potential in a particular field. This potential becomes universally evident only when it is fully expressed; it is difficult to identify in the early stages and is the result of a long, hard process of refining and developing on the part of the person who has it' (Sinatra, 2010: 289–90).

Second, talent involves aptitude and application. Malcolm Gladwell (2008) makes a strong case that people we regard as exceptionally talented have: (1) been in the right place at the right time; and (2) put in many thousands of hours of practice. People of equal potential who have not been given the opportunity to gain the practice hours tend to be seen as less talented.

Third, perception of talent is prone to enormous bias. Some of the most common sources of bias include:

- *Gender bias.* Leadership potential is more associated with male candidates than females. Experiments to determine gender bias in candidates for fictitious CEO jobs show a fairly consistent preference for male candidates – except where several male predecessors have failed and the organization is in crisis (Bruckmüller and Branscombe, 2010). Perceptions of leadership competences are based upon male behaviours and therefore often fail to value female leader behaviours. The problem is made worse because 'Women on their way up the corporate ladder get caught in two traps: the assumption that women and men have the same leadership qualities and the belief that they must imitate male leadership behaviour in order to succeed' (Vanderbroeck, 2010). Feedback based on competences derived from studies of successful male leaders compound the problem even further by putting pressure on women to conform to inappropriate stereotypes. When leaders look for potential, they are also likely to introduce a gender and racial bias which leads to them to downgrade women and people from different racial groups in terms of talent. Research by international consultancy Catalyst (Warren, 2009) concludes that many talent management programmes unconsciously reflect and promote traits shown by the organization's mainly male leadership team. Even without competency frameworks to guide them, employees mirrored those traits that were perceived as having made the existing leaders successful. Hardly surprising, then, that employees tended to be viewed as less talented if they demonstrated qualities, characteristics and skills considered atypical, or feminine.

- *Physical characteristic bias.* White men with brown eyes are perceived as more dominant than those with blue eyes (Kleisner *et al*, 2010), although the effect is mediated by other facial characteristics. Height is also closely associated with dominance and leadership. Simply looking competent can have an effect – even though there is no proven correlation between appearance and reality (Antonakis and Dalgas, 2009). Being tall provides a significant advantage for women in terms of promotion and salary, because they are perceived as more authoritative, according to research for retailer Long Tall Sally (Anon, 2010).

- *Success bias.* Psychologist Prof Adrian Furnham defines talent in terms of ability to learn from experience. People who have made mistakes and learned from them ought, in principle, to be valued for their insights. However, human instinct tends to make us shy away from failure, so we assign more credibility to someone who has never failed (and therefore probably never tried that hard!). Tim Casserley and David Megginson state: 'Many organizations have models of leadership that tend to lionize success and denigrate stumbling. Their picture of how leaders develop is sanitized. Any notion of learning from adversity has been excised. The money is put on those whose careers have enjoyed an ever-upward trajectory, who have never stumbled (to anyone's knowledge) and who have always complied with the organization's tight, atavistic definitions of what good leadership should be. Those who do not comply, including the stumblers, are quietly removed from succession plans. The outcome is that such organizations end up with leaders, who are hopelessly ill-prepared, who not only lack humanity, but do not see themselves as entirely human, who act as if they were intergalactic time lords who transcend the earthly realm of us mere mortals' (Casserley and Megginson, 2009: xvi).

A comment from a Toolbox online discussion forum in August 2011 makes the point equally vividly: 'Performance ratings at this organization are very sticky. If you knock it out of the park the first year you work there, or are well liked for reasons other than your performance, the high rating will stick to you forever. Those with consistent high ratings continue to receive them despite glaring mistakes (sending wrong comp letters to senior execs, system implementations gone completely wrong, getting caught sending their own work to others in a totally inappropriate manner). The "future leaders and professionals" [programme] is really just a popularity contest and is not results based.'

- *Flattery bias.* When leaders override objective evidence to ensure the progress of favourites, what is happening? According to US author and coaching guru Marshall Goldsmith, it's in large part plain old 'sucking up' (Goldsmith, 2003). He explains: 'If leaders say they discourage sucking up, why does it happen so often? Here's a straightforward answer: Without meaning to, we all tend to create an environment where people learn to reward others with accolades that aren't really warranted. We can see this very clearly in other people. We just can't see it in ourselves... Here's how leaders can stop encouraging this behavior. Begin by admitting that we all have a tendency to favor those who favor us, even if we don't mean to. We should then rank our direct reports in three areas. First, how much do they like me? (I know you aren't sure. What matters is how much they act as if they like you.) Second, what is their contribution to our company and our customers? Third, how much positive, personal recognition do I give them? In many cases, if we are honest with ourselves, how much recognition we give someone is more often highly correlated with how much they seem to like us than it is with how well they perform. If that is the case, we may be encouraging the kind of behavior that we despise in others. Without meaning to, we are basking in hollow praise, which makes us hollow leaders.'

- *Leadership qualities bias.* Melvin Sorcher and James Brant (2002) have focused their studies particularly on CEO succession. They find that good candidates often get overlooked, because they don't meet unevidenced assumptions about what a CEO should be like. One of these assumptions related to ambition. They explain (p 136): 'A perceived lack of ambition has scuttled many a promotion. "I'm not sure how hungry she is" or "He seems to lack that fire in the belly" are common criticisms. Unfortunately, executives forget that a person's ambition can be understated. Indeed, we have found that exceptional leaders are modest and display little ambition, even though on the inside they are fiercely competitive. In fact, a high degree of personal humility is far more evident among exceptional leaders than raw ambition.'

Leader myopia

Some years ago, I was asked by a somewhat paternalistic financial services company to help it get the message across to a group of graduate trainees that they had limited career prospects in the organization. Drawn from two years' intakes, they were seen as having very little leadership potential. The company recognized that it had not treated them particularly well so far – the person running the graduate placement scheme had recently been moved on and had clearly been seen to have failed in the role.

We agreed to run a two-day 'Manage your own career' workshop for the graduates. First, however, they would work in three teams to carry out interviews inside and outside the company to produce a report on how career opportunities would evolve in the company and in the sector.

On the first day of the workshop, we gave them a thick, sealed ring binder and told them: 'This contains the company's plans for your future. You are not to unseal it until instructed to.' The initial sessions of the workshop covered themes such as intrapreneurship, then finally they were asked to open their binders. The first few pages were blank. So were all the others. 'You have to write and manage your own career plan', we told them.

In the afternoon, they were tasked with preparing a presentation to top management about their research project. They all gathered, waiting for us to tell them what to do. 'Oh no,' we said. 'It's your presentation. You decide how to put it together. We're off to the bar.'

From time to time, we put our heads round the door to see if they needed any specific help. They didn't. Within 30 minutes, one of the group, a young man who had been identified by his manager as particularly lacking in leadership potential, was in the centre of the room, directing traffic. There was a flurry of purposeful activity.

At 5pm, the directors arrived to hear the presentation, which was concise, structured and innovative. The graduates all took a turn in presenting and were for the most part confident and clear. Afterwards, the directors took me aside. 'Are these really the people we'd written off?' they asked.

On subsequent investigation, it emerged that the graduates had never really been given an opportunity to develop or demonstrate their leadership potential. They had been dumped upon unwilling managers who didn't have real roles for them to slot into, and had therefore used them for tasks well below their capabilities. A negative cycle had been established, in which lack of opportunity for the graduates to prove their worth led to poor appraisals from their managers. Within three months of the workshop, almost all had been promoted into more responsible jobs in other departments, with one, who had no interest in leading others, finding a specialist technical role in which he could expand. They were finally on the leadership ladder!

I was reminded of this story by an article in *The Times* (2008), which recounted the remarkable story of Cecile Pearl Witherington, parachuted into France during World War II to help organize resistance fighters. Her official report reads: 'She is loyal and reliable but has not the personality to act as a leader'. Yet before long she was leading a 3,000-strong army of resistance fighters, having stepped into the shoes of her commanding officer when he was captured by the enemy. In this role, she rebuilt a demoralized, disorganized scattering of irregulars into a potent machine to pin down enemy troops. At the end of the war, she presided over the surrender of 18,000 German troops.

What both of these stories indicate is the folly of tasking managers with identifying leaders – a theme I will return to shortly. Of course, management and leadership are two sides of the same coin, but people who are mentally attuned to emphasize the management perspective will always struggle to recognize leadership in those below them; indeed, they may feel threatened by it. Yet our appraisal and succession planning processes are so often designed to place the recognition of leadership potential on the shoulders of the very people who may be suppressing it. Given that so many companies complain of a lack of leadership talent, should employers abandon manager appraisal as counterproductive, or find better ways to identify the leaders of tomorrow?

Studies of talent management and succession by Chicago Change Partners (CCP) (Bishop, 2009) point to several related problems. In particular:

- Inadequate distinction between moderately talented and really talented. It's hard for a manager to admit that they don't have many talented people reporting to them – it makes them look and feel inferior. So appraisal systems tend to provide an inaccurate picture, which can lead top management and HR into a dangerous complacency about the depth and quality of the talent pipeline. CCP advises training managers on how to recognize and assess talent, and in particular on how to recognize learning ability in others.

- Lacking a *collective* blueprint of the values and behavioural elements required for successful emerging leaders, so leaders tend to make talent decisions based upon differing views of what success looks like.

There may, however, be a silver lining to the way things happen now. It's clear that many people who have strong leadership qualities do succeed and rise through organizations. Is it possible that having to overcome and work round the myopia of managers who are blind to leadership potential is a baptism of fire that helps to bring out the steel in leaders? If leaders emerge in spite of the organization, rather than with its help, does this make them all the stronger for it? Like training for the SAS (Special Air Service – the elite troops of the British Army), do potential leaders need to be taken through immense hardship, near breaking point, before they pass the test?

Which managers accurately spot promotable talented employees early in their career?

While all the evidence so far suggests that it is sensible to be wary of line manager assessment of leadership potential, it's also clear that some managers do have a talent for talent spotting. I am not aware of any valid research that explores how they do so, but some possibilities from observation and our conversations with HR professionals are that they:

- create opportunities for employees to seize challenges that will demonstrate current and latent talents;
- take time to listen to people, simply because they are interested in them and their jobs;
- have a perspective of talent that emphasizes diversity and the unexpected, rather than fitting a particular mould; and
- see and value other people more in terms of their strengths than their weaknesses.

Could organizations make more effective use of their talent spotters, by recognizing this as a critical role and by supporting them in exercising their talent-spotting skills more widely? For example, such people tend also to make effective mentors and leadership sponsors for action learning sets – roles that open up significant opportunities to encounter and observe potential talent. Or perhaps use them as a counterweight to the assessment centres. If the intuitive observations of experienced and accurate talent spotters disagree with the outcomes of the assessment centre, that should raise strong questions!

Does HR provide a safer pair of hands for assessing talent than line managers? Are they any more likely to come up with the right answer? Again, there doesn't appear to be a simple answer. What is clear is that HR typically talks about its role in terms of management rather than leadership (one HR director actually told me that 'HR leadership' was a non-sequitur!); and of process control rather than visionary engagement. Certainly, HR often sees its role in talent development and succession planning as one of moderating arbitrary behaviour by line managers. But linear systems tend to impose an arbitrariness of their own. So just how credible are the approaches HR applies to establish who is and who is not worthy of being in the talent pool?

A simpler way of identifying talent

Here's a proposition, based on asking HR professionals to define the critical qualities they associate with talent. People belong in the talent pool if they demonstrate:

1 significant continued investment in their own development;
2 a track record of assisting the development of others – for example, through coaching or mentoring;
3 ambition to achieve greater responsibilities;
4 a high motivation and ability to learn.

Without these basic competences, an employee is unlikely to develop the competences needed for more senior roles. Instead of viewing role- or managerial-level competencies as *fixed and generic*, organizations might do better to seek to fill roles with people who have the ability to work out the competences that are *currently and specifically* needed and to adapt themselves accordingly.

Paradoxically, one of the best ways to attract talent is to have a reputation for losing them. In a brief study of multinational companies that I conducted nearly 40 years ago, I explored the concept of what is now called 'talent factories' (Ready and Conger, 2007): organizations that had a reputation for producing such a lot of talent in particular disciplines that their alumni accounted for a disproportionate percentage of people in top roles of those disciplines in other companies. These included Ford for finance directors, Mars for HR professionals, and Procter & Gamble for marketeers. In each case, the company took in and invested deeply in highly talented young people, knowing that many of them would be stolen by headhunters at some point. The trade-off was that having a reputation for developing talent in these disciplines, the companies attracted very bright, motivated people into those functions. While these people stayed, they brought a high level of commitment and energy to their job roles. When they moved on – with the companies' blessing – they created an updraft that sucked in new talent, with new ideas; and they developed a network of talent such that, in some cases, they became recruitment agents or talent spotters for their corporate alumnus. In a few cases, I even found that alumni in senior roles in other companies steered talent in their own organization towards the talent factory, to spend a few years there, learning on an unofficial secondment.

A modern-day example is soft drinks company Innocent. The three founders of the business built a talent factory for entrepreneurs and have been rewarded by seeing a stream of employees leave to set up their own businesses. Says co-founder Richard Reed: 'We've always set out to attract people, who are entrepreneurial. We ran a job advert, where the headline said we were looking for people who will want to leave us' (Woodward, 2011). Other modern exemplars of the talent factory approach include PayPal and computer company Acorn.

The key to keeping such talent for a sufficiently long period that both they and the organization benefit substantially appears to lie in maintaining their level of interest and challenge. Google gives people 20 days' 'innovation leave' to follow their own ideas. Forward Internet Group, which has a similar policy of letting people pursue ideas outside of their formal job role, also maintains regular conversations with employees to ensure they are working on things they are passionate about. Founder Neil Hutchinson says that this is one of the reasons behind the firm's strong rate of employee retention.

The linear systems approach: competencies and grids

The two basic tools used in standard talent identification systems are competency frameworks and the nine-box grid, promoted within the book *The Leadership Pipeline* (Charan *et al*, 2001). Both competencies and the grid have been enthusiastically absorbed by HR, because they appear to impose a level of control and predictability on talent identification, talent management and succession planning.

The theory behind leadership competency frameworks is that it is possible to define generic competencies of effective leaders, to assess employees against these competencies and hence to predict how effective people will be in leadership roles, depending on the number of boxes they tick in the assessment process. In theory, this simple linear approach should ensure that people who get to the top perform the functions of a leader competently, regardless of the context in which they are required to exercise leadership. The problem is that there is almost no credible evidence that this linear approach works – and there are a lot of examples of people who have passed the competency assessments with ease, but have been disastrous leaders. Beverly Alimo-Metcalfe and John Alban-Metcalfe (2009: 14) illustrate the point graphically in a report for the CIPD:

> Competency frameworks alone are not sufficient for assessing the full
> range of leadership behaviours that are required for effective leadership
> and organizational success. Indeed, we argue that believing that possessing
> the competencies is sufficient for leadership is rather like believing that by
> equipping someone with a 'painting-by-numbers' kit, they can produce
> a Monet... most competency frameworks are singularly characterized by a lack
> of empirical evidence of their concurrent or predictive validity.

This is not to say that leadership competency frameworks don't have value as one part of the information bank that informs our understanding of an individual as a current or potential leader. Where HR so often goes wrong is to use these frameworks as primary inputs in decision making about individuals, when the demands of leadership and the capabilities of individuals are far more varied and complex than any mechanistic framework can encompass.

The theory behind the nine-box grid is that you can establish with a reasonable degree of accuracy where an employee lies in terms of their current performance and their potential for promotion; and that clumping them together in neat boxes allows the organization (or more specifically, HR) to devise different strategies for dealing with each clump. The argument in *The Leadership Pipeline* (Charan *et al*, 2001) is that having nine boxes to put people into is better than just four. What the book doesn't question is why you would want to put people into boxes at all (unless of course they are dead!), nor whether these snapshots are actually predictive of leadership capability, other than from the negative perspective of convincing people who have been placed in the less desirable boxes to lower any aspirations they might have had.

Let's look at both of these in more detail.

How far can we trust competency frameworks?

Competencies are a dream consultancy product. They sound rational, they require vast amounts of man-hours to create and validate, they are often designed (intentionally or not) to reinforce the stereotypical assumptions of existing leaders about what good leadership looks like, and they require a lot more consultancy man-hours to administer. Not, of course, that any of these factors carries weight with the organizations that promote competencies so energetically!

What is a competence? Peter Hawkins makes a useful distinction between competence and capability, both of which he says are about know-how: 'Competencies can be learned in the classroom, but capabilities can only be learned live and on the job. The danger [of over-emphasizing competencies] is that one can acquire a very large toolkit of skills, without developing the capability of knowing when to use each skill and in what way' (Hawkins, 2011: 155).

The chorus of disquiet with leadership competencies, and particularly their use as predictive or decision-making tools, has become increasingly loud in the past decade. One of the most forceful articles on the topic (Hollenbeck *et al*, 2006) identifies four deeply flawed assumptions behind the competency addiction. First, competency frameworks focus on the qualities of the 'great man', the mythical heroic leader, and ignore the fact that leadership is typically exerted by several people acting in concert. Second, they assume that having a set of competencies is equivalent to knowing how to use them together. It's like saying that a pile of jigsaw pieces is a picture – not true unless the bits are assembled in the right way. What matters is not a person's score in a competency test, but the way they use their talents to achieve objectives. Third, competences tend to assume that, 'because senior management usually blesses competencies and sometimes even helps generate them, they are the most effective way to think about leader behaviour' – an obvious tautology. Fourth, they assume that 'when HR systems are based on competencies, these systems actually work effectively', when there is little or no credible evidence to support this assertion.

Other critics of competencies frameworks include Marcus Buckingham (2001), who proposes approaches that focus primarily on using the strengths an individual has rather than trying to change their innate weaknesses;

Bolden and Gosling (2006) and Gravells and Wallace (2011). Among the concerns that these authors raise about leadership competencies are:

- They focus on what can be described and measured, which is not the same as what has most impact. (How do you measure authenticity, for example?)
- They are essentially reductionist, breaking down competencies into components, so they miss the larger picture.
- They are insufficiently flexible to take into account widely differing requirements of leaders in different situations.
- People who demonstrate excellence in the same role don't necessarily demonstrate the same set of competencies.
- Trying to make people fit the competency framework by concentrating on improving the skills where they are weakest might seem an obvious step, but there is little evidence that it leads to more leaders or better leaders. (Although ignoring weaknesses doesn't seem a particularly smart strategy, either!)
- Competency frameworks are based on qualities which have been associated with success so far, but that means they are backward-looking, when talent management demands they should be forward-looking.

Another theme echoed in my interviews and conversations on competences has been the question of whose perception of importance and significance the desired competencies are based on. As one correspondent expressed it: 'Gen X or baby boomers decide what talent looks like and apply their assumptions to Gen Y, who have no say in the process.'

If a job competency is 'an underlying characteristic of an individual that is causally related to effective or superior performance in a job' (Boyatzis, 1982), then, say Alimo-Metcalfe and Alban-Metcalfe (2009), it's important to distinguish between the skills of leadership (which can by and large be learned given sufficient application and intelligence) and the qualities and values of effective leadership. The latter, of course, will always be situational. A fundamental mistake made in designing and applying competency frameworks to specific roles is that the role itself is fixed. But as context changes, so does what constitutes an effective mix of values and qualities. For example, the leadership qualities required in the rapid growth phase of a sector are not necessarily the same as those in an industry that is well into maturing (Ahrens, 1999).

It seems that the more we try to limit, systematize and codify what we mean by leadership competence, the more we limit our ability to respond to the challenges of diverse leadership roles. A more pragmatic approach, recommended by a number of seasoned HR directors, is to look at leader capability from multiple perspectives. For example, Peter Drucker defined leadership competencies very simply: as listening, communication, re-engineering mistakes and subordinating one's own ego to the task or cause (Drucker, 1990). Or, supposing we substitute for competences a framework of *traits*? Traits can be described as strong habits of mind which may involve a varied mixture of skills, knowledge and aptitudes. For example, here's how the author Justin Menkes (2011) described the result of his analysis of hundreds of CEOs and aspiring CEOs:

1 *Realistic optimism*. Leaders with this trait possess confidence without self-delusion or irrationality. They pursue audacious goals, which others would typically view as impossible pipedreams, while at the same time remaining aware of the magnitude of the challenges confronting them and the difficulties that lie ahead.

2 *Subservience to purpose*. Leaders with this ability see their professional goal as so profound in importance that their lives become measured in value by how much they contribute to furthering that goal. What is more, they must be pursuing a professional goal in order to feel a purpose for living. In essence, that goal is their master and their reason for being.

3 *Finding order in chaos*. Leaders with this trait find taking on multidimensional problems invigorating, and their ability to bring clarity to quandaries that baffle others makes their contributions invaluable. This is essentially the same concept as *simplexity* (Goldsmith and Clutterbuck, 1997).

How helpful is intelligence as a competence?

Leaders need both IQ (reasoning intelligence) and EQ (emotional intelligence) to be effective. Combined, they add up to being smart. Until recently, it has been assumed that intelligence is relatively fixed, but that view is increasingly being challenged. Professors Guy Claxton and Bill Lucas (2010) argue that we should be looking instead at the concept of expandable intelligence: the ability to cope with complexities by using a wider range of mental processes than mental reasoning. They maintain:

> Getting on in the real world requires many kinds of smart activity. Intelligence is not a separate faculty, divorced from motivation and personality; it is more like an orchestra of skills and attitudes. Self-discipline and resilience, for example, count for much more, in predicting school grades than measured IQ. Real-life intelligence requires imagination, perseverance, perceptiveness, and collaboration, just as much as it needs solo, abstract reasoning.

They also point to experiments that show, in children at least, how expandable intelligence is, especially when people believe they can get smarter. One of the boxes assessment processes put people into is how intelligent they are perceived to be. This perception becomes a self-limiting belief. Claxton and Lucas also argue that the role of intuition is of equal importance to that of reasoning in decision making.

Is competence enough?

The arguments for competency frameworks are that they promote clarity, consistency and professionalism. They also represent a middle path between the nature versus nurture perspectives of how leaders are created. Yet the words 'leadership' and 'competence' are to some extent incompatible. Tom Peters once pointed out at a conference in London that having leaders who are merely competent may not be enough to meet the challenges of complex organizations and complex environments. Competence implies at best steadiness and reliability; at worst, mediocrity. In the framework of Warren Bennis's (2010) distinction between leadership and management, competence sits better with management than it does with leadership, which – in spite of thousands of studies and books – still remains largely contextual, individual, intangible and, to a considerable extent, mysterious. As a result, leadership competency frameworks inevitably take a 'pick and choose' approach to the characteristics and qualities on which they focus. Meta-studies of leadership find great variety of characteristics and little universality.

Jonathan Gravells and Sue Wallace (2011) identify a number of serious problems with competency models and classify them into four categories:

- *Comprehensiveness.* The assumption that every aspect of leadership can be described and hence learned is beguiling but utterly unevidenced. If it is possible, why do organizations have such a poor record of developing leaders? If leadership quality were truly predictable, surely we would by now have achieved some level of consistency in creating leaders. The reality is that whether someone will become a good or great leader is almost entirely unpredictable. We can't even claim that 'it takes one to know one'. Predictive studies of leadership potential show a negative correlation between managers' views of direct reports' leadership potential and what actually happens; though direct reports' perceptions of their own manager do correlate positively with the manager's leadership potential (Alimo-Metcalfe, 1998).

  The problem with trying to be comprehensive is that leadership is a situational skill. What makes a good leader in one context will not be appropriate in another. Changed circumstances require changed styles of leadership, and few leaders appear to have the insight and humility to recognize and accept that their style of leadership is no longer suitable. This phenomenon is perhaps linked to the perception of leadership as being vested in an individual, rather than being distributed amongst a team. If leadership were a quality process, it would provide the right leader, in the right place, at the right time. Given that everyone is a combination of strengths and weaknesses – and that over-reliance on a particular strength can be one of the most significant sources of weakness – surely effective talent management should be less about trying to equip every leader with the same competences and more about engaging them with situations that play to their strengths, while supporting them as necessary with colleagues who can compensate for their weaknesses?

● *Cloning.* Say Gravells and Wallace (2011): 'If leadership can be so prescribed, why are successful leaders all so very different in personality and approach? Where does this leave personal style? Even the most superficial study of successful leaders, whether world-renowned or working away in our own organizations, will reveal a glorious variety of personalities, styles and idiosyncrasies. This is presumably not because the competency police have yet to finish the job of getting everyone in line, but rather because variety is what works. Indeed, what marks out the most successful leaders is an authenticity that stems from this fit between their natural preferences and the way they lead. In other words, they tend to lead from their own personality and style, rather than trying to be someone they are not. Of course, this is not a straightforward either/or choice. Having a style of our own does not preclude learning helpful behaviours from leadership development or role models, but what we see in the most successful leaders is an ability to integrate this into their own leadership persona.'

  The danger, then, is that an over-reliance on a competency-based approach can result in inauthentic leadership and a presumption of managerial control which, at the extremes, inclines us to 'one-size-fits-all' development approaches and a tendency always to fit the person to the job, rather than the other way around. It may lead us to ignore the impact of environment and circumstances on the sort of leader we are. Bennis writes of leaders being forged in the 'crucible' of circumstances, by a combination of their own personal qualities and the way in which they make meaning of their experiences (Bennis and Thomas, 2002).

● *Common sense.* I am minded here of research into the workings of the human brain. For a long time, neuroscience focused on identifying which bits of the brain managed each process of awareness, thinking and reaction. Gradually it has emerged that, while some areas play a larger role than others in, say, accessing memories, the function of memory requires the activity of multiple areas of the brain acting in concert. Reducing something down to its parts does not tell you much of value about how those parts act together, in different combinations, to produce different results. Having a basket of specific skills – irrespective of whether they are 'hard' technical skills or 'soft' behavioural skills – does not necessarily add up to a fully functioning leader.

  Another analogy here for me is NLP or neuro-linguistic programming, often presented as an entire philosophy for communicating effectively. In practice, many people using NLP, including some who have achieved high levels of competence in applying the individual techniques, remain poor communicators and can even be highly dangerous and unintentionally abusive to clients. The problem stems in large part, I suggest, from an inability to integrate their discrete skills into an authentic form of dialogue, both with themselves and with others.

- *Classical perfection.* Be it the perfect landscape painting or the perfect male or female body, the closer to perfection something becomes, the less desirable it is. If a painting looks just like a photograph, why not just have a photograph? Perfection lacks passion; and leadership needs passion. Say Gravells and Wallace (2011): 'In our desire for consistency and control, have we foisted upon managers so complete an ideal of the perfect leader that no one can ever hope to attain it?... If we build detailed and all-encompassing competency structures to delineate how we want leaders to perform, we are equally at risk of implying that leadership success comes only from the ability to "tick all the boxes".'

  One of the most scathing comments about Tony Hayward, former CEO of BP, was that he had had a 28-year career doing the right things to rise to the top of a major company, only to become an anti-leadership case. Whatever the truth of this, the question remains that while ticking the boxes might have been good for his career, was it good for the company? The stories of failed leaders that pepper this chapter often have in common a theme of hubris, of not seeking or accepting personal criticism or challenge, of not admitting to weaknesses. Yet surely admitting weaknesses is a sign of true strength? One of the first issues I address with any leader I work with is how they will share with those around them, including direct reports, their personal development objectives. It makes them more approachable and human, and less defensive when their ideas and pet enthusiasms are challenged.

When acquiring competencies becomes like collecting scout badges, it's time to question what we are trying to achieve with these frameworks. If we are aiming to produce an all-purpose leader for all circumstances, we are chasing rainbows. It's like creating Olympic athletes: most people are going to fail and even those who succeed will have only a short career at their peak. Moreover, all that effort exerted into trying to change the individual into something they may not have the capacity to be is diverting energy from using their talents most effectively. A case in point, brought to me in the course of coach supervision, is a senior manager in a front-line public service, told by HR that his career progress and perhaps his current job were at risk because he did not demonstrate sufficient competence (as measured in an assessment centre) in what could loosely be called emotional intelligence. No matter that he was deeply respected and valued as a leader by his colleagues and the staff in his unit – he must change his behaviours. Listening to the coach describe this person, it rapidly became clear that he was potentially on the autistic spectrum. Yet he had managed to find highly effective coping mechanisms to let people know that he cared, to communicate his intense ethicality and humanity. While he struggled to demonstrate empathy, he revealed his compassion in the decisions and actions that he took. He also compensated for his own discomfort in inconsequential talk and glad-handing by using one of his top team to deputize, while making his own sentiments clear in other ways. Here was a highly effective leader, aware of his weaknesses and able to adjust for them with the support of his team, whose career was about to be derailed by a misguided attempt to enforce uniformity.

The nine-box grid: a reliable assessment or an illusion of rigour?

One of the icons of succession planning and talent management is the nine-box grid, which ranks people on their performance and potential. Those high in both are perceived to be talent ready or close to ready for promotion; various other strategies are recommended for other positions on the grid, which is a fundamental underpinning of the leadership pipeline. It sounds a logical approach, but what is the evidence that this approach is effective?

The basis of the grid (Table 4.1) is that people can be assessed accurately on two defining attributes of talent: performance and potential. Performance is what you achieve from what you do; potential is what you might achieve, with further experience and opportunity to develop. An immediate problem here for the HR planner is that neither of these mesh very easily with the concept of competencies. Competencies may have relevance to both, but they are not *equivalent* to either.

A further question is: 'What's the purpose of the grid?' As a workforce planning tool, its purpose may be to help HR and top management gain an overview of the extent of the talent available and the health of the supply

TABLE 4.1 The nine-box grid

	Performance		
Potential	Possible misfit	Potential star	Consistent star
	Developing	Core contributor	Rising star
	Attention!	Solid performer	Strong performer

of people for more senior roles. As a talent management tool, it may be used to decide the future of individuals: how ready they are for promotion, and what investment the organization intends to make in their development. In this workforce planning context, there is clear value in a framework that causes managers to think objectively and strategically about the talent beneath them. As a broad talent management tool, there is also value in HR being able to identify broad areas of weakness across the organization, or an undersupply of talent. Using the grid to assess the diversity of talent can also be beneficial. Where the biggest questions arise with regard to the grid's utility – and where concerns arise that it may do more harm than good – is in the context of making judgements about individuals. At the heart of the matter is a key question: *How confident can we be that we can assess performance and potential accurately enough to be predictive of future leadership success?*

Is performance really measurable?

Let's start by considering what we mean by performance. We tend to use the terms 'performance' and 'potential' as if they had very specific and shared meanings. But do they?

Let us assume performance is about meeting specific and measurable goals or outcomes. Immediate issues that arise to confound evaluation here include:

- *Whether the goals are shared or individual.* If shared, it is often extremely difficult to determine the contribution each person has played.

- *Whether the goals capture the essence of the job role.* Most jobs, particularly at senior level, are multifaceted and multidimensional. Measuring whether the individual achieves, say, specific sales targets or cost reduction in their department is relatively simple, but it tells you very little about them as a manager or leader. There have been a spate of examples in recent years of high flyers in multinational companies whose reputation has been built upon delivering the numbers, but at a significant human cost. In some cases, that cost has been the deaths, through heart attacks and other stress-induced illnesses, of direct reports. Simplistic measurements separate what a person achieves from how they achieve it. Performance data needs to reflect the person holistically, not in narrow slices.

- *How predictive performance in one role is of performance in the next.* If the employee is being groomed for a specific role, if that role is relatively fixed and if there are sufficient numbers of such roles to compare with, it *may* be possible to establish a pattern which will inform succession decisions. Reliable data of such kind seem to be surprisingly rare!

- *Who judges performance and how.* Assessment of achievement of even SMART goals (Specific, Measurable, Attainable, Relevant, Time-bound) can sometimes be much less objective than it appears. For example, 'improve sales by 20 per cent next quarter' sounds unequivocal. But does this relate to sales delivered and paid for during the period, or to orders taken, but not yet delivered, or to growth in the sales pipeline? And does it relate to gross income or profitability? Or to customer quality (eg expectation of repeat business)? It happens sometimes that the highest performers – those who meet or exceed their targets most often – are the people who contribute least to the bottom line. The employee, their boss, the customer and other stakeholders may all have different perspectives on the employee's performance. When performance relates to goals that are less easily pinned down under SMART principles, evaluation can be influenced by a whole range of factors, including how well liked the person is and how they present the data upon which they are judged.

- *How accurately can you separate out individual from collective performance?* One of the criticisms of the competencies approach is that, while there are undoubtedly examples of strong leaders who shape destiny through their own visionary and charismatic leadership, they are not the norm. Expecting every major organization to have such a leader is unrealistic. Even if they existed in the numbers required, the last thing an organization needs is hordes of such people spread throughout the leadership levels. In most organizations, success is bound up with the leadership *team*, where individual contribution may be much harder to identify. Even with the corporate disasters of recent years, the myth of the individual leader dies hard. But it is increasingly coming under question. Consultant Clive Landa, a veteran observer of top teams, provides three key reasons why collegiate leadership is becoming more of a viable option:

  - Most problems (and processes) are now complex and beyond individual grasp or solution.

  - Most people look to their leaders for their example of what 'works around here', and if they are to behave as team players they have to see those behaviours demonstrated above them.

  - External people (clients, regulators, investors, etc) view organizations through the filter of their leaders and want to see 'ambassadors' not Genghis Khans.

The automatic association of leadership with individuals is also challenged by William Tate (2009), former head of HR strategy at British Airways. He writes: 'The belief that organizations are successful because their individual managers are successful holds a powerful attraction for companies. Their vast expenditure on individual-based leadership development programmes evidences their faith in the trickle-up theory. But the assumed cause-and-effect link was demolished by Enron's collapse in 2001; high talent in wasn't matched by what came out.'

Tate uses the analogy of an orchestra and soloist: individual competence is important, but what matters most is collective competence. Concentrating development on the individual doesn't take the organization very far. A systemic model of leadership is needed – beyond the individual, beyond collective groups and teams, to the organizational system. Managers have been trained to notice individuals, be suspicious of collectives and not notice the system. For many managers, the system is a blind spot in their education, vocabulary and way of seeing things. Performance management suffers for this reason. Among Tate's conclusions are that:

- Organizations should aim to distribute leadership rather than concentrate it: 'Those who are closest to the reality of how the organization works or fails, as a system, should have a role in improving it.'

- Performance management and appraisal discussions should focus more on the system than on the individual. He proposes that 'managers have a dual responsibility: a management role to deliver today (within the system as it is) and a second role to safeguard tomorrow (by improving the system, which calls for leadership).'

- The gaps or spaces between responsibilities are both the main causes of failure and the greatest opportunities. 'Spaces are where individuals and functions come together in cooperation. Whereas individuals may be creative, innovation takes place in spaces.'

As roles within organizations become increasingly interconnected, it becomes more and more difficult to separate out individual performance from the performance of the formal or informal teams in which people work. There is a growing body of evidence around this issue:

- In a Swedish doctoral study, Johan Bertlett (2010) examined working climate, using 200 employees at Arlanda Airport. He found that the manager's ability to influence working climate (and therefore team performance) was limited by the willingness of the team members to collaborate – and that is influenced heavily by factors such as general corporate climate and whether employees are rewarded for taking on additional responsibility. Even very good managers struggle to motivate teams when external factors are driving uncooperative behaviours. He advocates that companies should treat manager and team as a unit for training and as equal contributors to performance.

- In the context of creativity, the myth of the individual creative leader is coming under increasing scrutiny. Indeed, 'the image of the lone genius inventing from scratch is a romantic fiction' (Haragon, 2000:

275). Says Alexander Fliaster of Insead (Fliaster, 2011): 'a growing body of research indicates that this fundamentally individualistic view is too romantic and unrealistic. Even worse, the myth of creativity as a "one-man show" may even be harmful. Countless examples demonstrate that the generation of creative ideas is mainly a collaborative process rather than merely an intrapersonal one. For instance, according to Andrew Hargadon from the University of California, American inventor Thomas Edison was described in the words of one of his fellow employees as 'a collective noun and... the work of many men.'

- In more recent times, Steve Jobs was asked to describe the 'seed' of the distinctive innovation ability of Apple Inc. Despite having employed a large number of highly creative individuals, Jobs told *Business Week* (Anon, 2004): 'Innovation comes from people meeting up in the hallways or calling each other at 10.30pm with a new idea... It's ad hoc meetings of six people called by someone who thinks he has figured out the coolest new thing ever and wants to know what other people think of his idea.'

- *Star performance is heavily contextual.* It certainly isn't necessarily transportable from one organization to another. A Harvard study found that top analysts in investment banks typically saw significant falls in performance over the five years following their move to another employer. The study concludes that performance is more closely related to the support system around an individual than is generally recognized (Groysberg, 2010).

Some options for adapting the talent identification process to accommodate this 'new' reality include:

- Place much greater emphasis in appraisals on team contribution.
- Give suspected talent opportunities to work in multiple teams.
- Shift the emphasis of training and development towards team skills.

A systemic view sees performance as the outcome of both the individual's capabilities and the context in which they operate. Changing the environment may encourage talented people to apply themselves more and in original ways, which will be of far more value than dragooning them into a 'pipeline'. At the simplest level, a manager who had been dropped from the high-flyer pool because he was judged not to be a sufficiently strategic thinker negotiated one day a week at home to work without interruption. Six months later, his devastating analysis of the business's information technology (IT) strategy led to a total rethink of this aspect of the business. Two things had changed: he had gained the time to reflect; and he had been helped in using reflective space by occasional conversations with a mentor, who enabled him to tap into skills that were already there but had been suppressed by the working environment.

The role of coaches and mentors increasingly includes helping the individual create and negotiate with the organization a development plan that is both more imaginative and more sustainable. In reflective space it is possible to question both one's own and other people's perceptions, to envisage a range of parallel futures, and to work to personal growth strategies that are simultaneously focused and highly flexible. In this way, it is not necessary to wait until the next formal performance or development review to react to changing opportunities – either the individual or the organization can take the initiative.

A conversation about performance

Here's a typical conversation I have with organizations about performance.

How do you define performance?
Delivering results
Just that?
That's what counts most!
Delivering results on your own or through others?
It depends...
On what?
On the job description and responsibilities.
When you say delivering results, is that at any cost?
Of course not. It has to be ethical and in line with the company values.
So what proportion of performance is based on delivering results and what on how you deliver it?
That's a matter of judgement. It's moveable... but if we're honest, delivering results counts for more, unless there are obvious problems, like high employee turnover, or really poor employee engagement scores or breaches of regulations.
Do people ever get promoted even though there are severe worries about how they get results?
It shouldn't happen, but it does.
And how much emphasis is placed on short-term versus long-term results in assessing performance?
It depends, but again, if we are honest, it's mainly about short-term results.
What part does sustainability play in assessing performance (ie the long-term viability of the team or the organization)?
Not a lot...

In general, what organizations mean by performance ranges from the vague to the incomprehensible. To understand why, let's tease out some of the themes from the conversation above.

Delivering results through self or others. Why do some managers work much longer hours than their peers? One of the most common reasons is that they are failing to delegate sufficiently. It's always quicker and easier to do things yourself than coach someone else to do them – the first time around. But doing it yourself quickly becomes a habit. If working long hours becomes associated with commitment and drive, rather than with inability to delegate, then it's not surprising that micro-managers get promoted.

Results at what cost? You don't have to look far to find examples where the drive to achieve challenging targets has led to disaster. One powerful example relates to the death of Everest climbers, because their obsession achieving their goal blinded them to the dangers they were in (Kayes, 2006). In the research my colleague David Megginson and I have been carrying out into goal fixation in coaching and mentoring, we have drawn on a wide and growing literature that demonstrates the dangers of managers whose behaviour is driven by stretching goals. The authors of *Goals Gone Wild* (Ordonez *et al*, 2009) point to multiple examples where goal fixation has led to organizational disaster. They identify another worrying phenomenon: it seems that the instinctive reaction when managers find that they are going to miss a challenging goal by a relatively narrow margin is to *cheat!* Fudged figures, skipped safety tests, fictional data – these are just some of the tactics they may use to beat the system.

When they cheat in this way, managers rationalize their behaviour by telling themselves, for example, that 'It's only a small adjustment', or 'It's for the good of the team, or the organization', when really it is their own ego that cannot cope with the thought of admitting failure when they have come so close. Part of the problem lies in the black-and-white nature of many goals (you either hit your targets or you don't). Gradated goals can be just as effective, without the behavioural downsides, but they are still comparatively rare.

How goals are delivered. Even where companies use 360-degree and other forms of feedback to gain a more balanced picture of both results and behaviour, there is a remarkable potential for misinformation. Research into how employees respond to 360-degree surveys suggests that they are more honest and critical towards better people managers, because they feel greater psychological safety. By contrast, even though the survey is supposed to be anonymous, the worst managers tend to score well because direct reports know how badly they will respond to criticism. Hence the survey can be a smokescreen behind which a psychopath can hide! Bruce Grimley's (1998) MSc dissertation on upward appraisal found a disturbing fly in the ointment. It seems that managers who create a team dynamic where the team feels encouraged to be critical, with the intention of raising performance, scored lower but more accurately than managers who 'rule by fear', whose scores are higher and less consistent.

Another linear assumption is that giving people feedback will result in improved performance, but it isn't that simple. While feedback can improve performance, in roughly a third of cases it has the opposite effect (Kluger and DeNisi, 1996). Upward feedback only delivers improvement in 50 per cent of cases and meta-studies of upward appraisal show that it generally delivers only small improvements overall (Atwater *et al*, 2000). Even worse, a Watson-Wyatt study appears to show an association between 360-degree feedback and a 10.6 per cent decline in shareholder value (Pfau and Kay, 2002). And the correlation between how bosses rate themselves and how their direct reports rate them is typically poor: bosses typically think they are better than they are rated by others! (Harris and Schaubroeck, 1988). Some 30 years ago, when I brought the concept of 360 degree feedback to Western Europe (from St Petersberg, then Leningrad, where it was designed by the Communist trade union to keep line managers under control) and carried out initial experiments, I had no idea what double-edged sword I was unsheathing!

This is not to say that we shouldn't use 360 – merely that as an indicator of either performance or potential it is insufficiently reliable to base succession decisions on. It is very useful to inform developmental conversations, especially when it is:

- specific rather than generic (ie about behaviours and skills important to the appraisee's role);
- owned by the appraisee (ie they influence what is assessed and by whom);
- completed by people whose opinion the appraisee values and perceives to be relevant;
- aimed at improving the quality of dialogue not just in one-off developmental conversations, but between the appraisee and all their key stakeholders.

In the book *Senior Leadership Teams* (Wageman *et al*, 2008), the authors measure performance by looking at how the top team of organizations delivers on its promises to a basket of shareholders, rather than assessing performance on the financial results of the business (which can easily be out of sync with leader behaviours). This systemic view of the leadership is much closer to the real world and would seem to be relevant at any level of leadership – but the grid is much too simplistic to capture this contextual perspective.

A decade ago, I carried out a study funded by the European Union to explore the dynamics of learning in different types of teams. Along the way, a model of team effectiveness emerged, based on where teams and their leaders focused attention. It seems that there are three key foci: *Task* (what the team does, and the goals and priorities attached to that); *Behaviour* (how the team works together and supports each other); and *Learning* (how the team becomes collectively more competent and resourceful). If we truly wish to gain a balanced view of a manager's performance, these three foci can provide a pragmatic starting point. Focusing on the broader, sustainable effectiveness and improvement of the team in these three areas may give a very different picture than focusing on the performance of the manager. To put the point another way: a manager's performance is equivalent to how they enable the team as a whole to work and grow together in pursuit of common goals, minus the interference they create, or fail to protect the team from.

Promotion on results. According to the Human Capital Institute, current performance is a good predictor of future performance only if the context of performance (level, scope, challenges and competency requirements) is similar. It argues that versatility is therefore a key competence for leaders of modern organizations. While a rigorous analysis of individual capabilities and the requirements of job roles using industrial or occupational psychology can improve the odds of putting the right person into the right job at the right time, it's a costly process and therefore one that is rarely used. Instead, companies rely on a mixture of performance appraisals and perceptions by managers, which emphasize observation of how the person does their current role. But the factors that make someone effective in their current role can be many and varied. For example:

- the support they receive from key colleagues in compensation for their weaknesses;
- the kind of tasks that most and least excite them;
- their ability to delegate;
- specific knowledge or interests that may not easily be transferable to other roles.

When results in the previous role play a key part in the promotion decision, there is often a danger that other important questions are overlooked. In particular:

- Is the promotion for development, or are they expected to have all the skills for the new role already? If for development, performance in the current role may be less relevant, because they need to leave these specific skills behind.
- Is the person's mix of strengths and weaknesses such that they are likely to default to reliving their current job in their next one?
- Just how similar or different are the requirements of the two roles?

Promotion on results also assumes that the new job role is fixed in terms of the competencies required. The industrial or organizational psychology approach is based on determining the characteristics ideally needed for the job role. A more challenging approach would be to question how the role might evolve, or be transformed.

Short-term versus long-term results. One of the dilemmas I encounter frequently in assessing the impact of executive coaching is that the relatively short-term, clearly specified outcomes tend also to be the easiest and require much less coaching expertise than the longer-term, messier, harder-to-define ones. Yet the quality of coaching delivered is typically assessed by HR on the former – which is why it may take a long time to distinguish between average and masterful coaches!

This same dilemma plagues measuring the performance of managers, particularly at a senior level. The bits of the role that really differentiate people tend to be the hardest to measure!

Sustainability. When a manager moves on, what legacy have they left behind them? A few organizations work on the principle that to be considered for promotion themselves, managers have to demonstrate that they have developed at least one person, inside or outside their team, to the point that they are ready to step into a role at the same level as the manager is currently.

More broadly, sustainability is a measure of how fit the team is to meet future challenges. Critical questions include:

- Is the team acquiring new knowledge and skills at a pace commensurate with changes in its environment?
- How resilient is it? (How capable is it of coping with set-backs?)
- How self-motivating is the team?
- What would be the impact on team performance of losing a key member?

Measuring role legacy is a concept of increasing interest. The principle here is that accountability in a role should continue for a reasonable period beyond the time a person holds it. Legacy is measured in a variety of ways, which may include:

- ability of the team to maintain the quality and quantity of performance;
- problems unresolved and opportunities created;
- ability of direct reports to deputize or stand in for the new role holder as they 'bed in';
- medium-term reputation of the team as seen by other teams.

Role legacy is probably best measured about three months after the change-over; after that, the influence of the new incumbent will confuse the picture. The assessment, based on interviews with key stakeholders by an independent party (eg someone from HR or from an unconnected part of the business) can be used to inform the succession planning process and become part of the developmental conversation with the manager, aimed at helping them address the legacy they will leave in their new role. A pattern of negative legacy assessments may provide valuable warning signs in terms of future appointments!

Forced ranking

Central to the performance assessment axis of the grid, and deeply embedded in the models of *The Leadership Pipeline* and *The War for Talent* (Michaels *et al*, 2001), is the concept of forced ranking, the development of which is attributed to General Electric (GE). Forced ranking requires managers to assign all their reports a position on a bell curve of performance. The top 20 per cent (A players) get the biggest rewards; the middle 70 per cent (B Players) are targeted for development; and the bottom 10 per cent (C players) get counselling or fired. The success of GE and some of the other companies studied in the *War for Talent* is taken as evidence that cause and effect exist between forced ranking and corporate performance. However, this ignores many other cases of companies, such as Enron, which had similar systems and have been brought to disaster. Jeffrey Pfeffer and Robert Sutton (2006) attack the logic behind the assumptions that forced ranking is beneficial (indeed they make a strong case that forced ranking does more harm than good), pointing out that to demonstrate cause and effect, the cause must be measured before the effect – the opposite to the *War for Talent* methodology.

They cite a study of 200 HR professionals, half of whose companies used forced ranking. 'Respondents reported that this approach resulted in lower productivity, inequity, scepticism, decreased employee engagement, reduced collaboration, damage to morale and mistrust in leadership' (p 7). Focusing in particular upon the dispersed pay element of the forced ranking approach, they add: 'we can't find a careful study that supports its value in settings, where cooperation, collaboration and information sharing are crucial to performance' (p 7).

If forced ranking of performance were shown to be beneficial, is it practical? Pfeffer and Sutton claim that only 15 per cent of doctors' decisions are evidence-based, and that for managers, the statistics are much worse. 'Managers are actually more ignorant than doctors about which prescriptions are reliable – and they are less eager to find out. If doctors practised medicine like many companies practise management, there would be many more unnecessarily sick and dead patients' (p 2).

As we have already seen, the evidence that line managers are competent at recognizing talent is poor to non-existent. Much the same appears to be the case for assessing performance. In our current research into goal management, a recurrent theme is that line managers are so busy with their own priorities that they fail to notice performance improvements in direct reports, even those that are obvious to the direct reports themselves and people reporting to them.

Is potential really measurable?

Similarly, potential is not as easy to assess as might be assumed. A dictionary definition of potential is: 'capable of coming into being; latent' (*Oxford English Dictionary*). Potential derives from potency – or strength – so one way of defining it is: 'the ability to achieve or contribute more by building upon personal strengths or aptitudes, while managing relevant weaknesses'. In physics, potential is related to the mathematical understanding of energy. In complex adaptive systems, potential is a tendency to move towards certain types of attractor. In short, potential can mean different things according to the perspective you adopt.

A practical definition of potential from a succession planning and talent management perspective might be:

> the capability of an individual to build upon existing strengths, knowledge and experience to perform effectively at higher levels of responsibility, within an appropriate environment.

The last four words are particularly significant. Someone might have great potential as an Olympic swimmer, but it is unlikely to be realized if they live in a desert!

Issues that arise in evaluating potential from the perspective of succession planning include:

- *Context.* The ability to realize potential is heavily dependent on factors which may or may not be the control of the employee. For example, a potential linguist will only be able to develop their talent if they are placed in an environment where they can hear and speak other languages. Even if an organization can accurately identify an individual's potential, these data are pretty useless unless they can also define the conditions where that potential is most and least likely to be released.

- *Potential is often confused with competency.* Competence is what someone can do; potential is what they may be able to do, by applying and developing competencies. As we have seen already, the competencies required for a specific role may change substantially. Moreover, competencies come in many sizes and styles. Is the competency set with which potential is associated in this evaluation specific to the role? Is it generic to a certain level of management? Built around meta-competencies? And what evidence is there to support these conclusions?

- *Who judges potential?* Line managers are not generally reliable as sources for evaluating the potential of direct reports. Assessment centre data may be valid, but it is an expensive way to build evidence and its shelf-life can be limited.

An alternative view of potential

Another pragmatic way of looking at potential is the equation below:

Potential = Ambition + learning orientation/maturity + self-awareness − fatal flaws

Ambition on its own is not enough. Yet for many leaders, the concept of the thrusting young manager is highly appealing and carries considerable weight in the judgements they make. The television programme *The Apprentice* typifies this overemphasis on being both self-motivated and self-centred. Said Lord Alan Sugar of contestant Melody Hossaini: 'She's ruthless. She'll walk over anybody. She'll eat them up and spit them out... that's what I like about her.' Shortly after, she was fired, having failed to demonstrate that she

TABLE 4.2 Opportunities for learning

Learning opportunity	Characteristics
From others	For example observation, being coached or mentored, being shown how, job shadowing
With others	For example in classroom situations, action learning sets, new project teams
Self-study and reflection	For example reading, e-learning, thought experiments, learning logs
Teaching others	For example tutoring, coaching, mentoring

could also be a team player. The assertive, determined behaviours which many leaders admire are often not combined with the broader qualities that make a rounded leader.

Learning orientation and learning maturity are two connected concepts relating to how people approach their personal development. Orientation refers to willingness to engage in learning – in particular, focusing on specific learning tasks, making time for learning and seizing opportunities for learning, as shown in Table 4.2.

Learning maturity relates to how open we are to being challenged in our assumptions and ways of thinking. The more mature we are as learners, the deeper and more transformational are our reflections on experience, and the more capable we are at both achieving insights and translating them into behavioural and cognitive change.

So should we abandon the nine-box grid?

The conclusion I draw from these data is not necessarily that the nine-box grid is valueless, but that, while it is seriously flawed as an instrument of decision making, it has value in stimulating a structured conversation about an individual – as a vehicle for stimulating dialogue. And yet few organizations invite candidates and their direct reports to take part in this dialogue.

One way to lessen the dead hand of the nine-box grid model is to present an individual employee's position as a circle, which may overlap several boxes. This gives a much more accurate picture of where the employee is in terms of current ability and performance, and of potential. Psychologically, it also gives them greater freedom to break out of the box. If the circle is conceived as a bubble, there is an inherent assumption that it can rise. Even this, however, can be dangerously confining in the thinking of both the employee and those responsible for managing talent, if it is used as a decision-making tool rather than a guide to development. Moreover, a person may be at very different places in terms of different aspects of leadership capability. To be truly useful, the grid also needs to recognize when an individual has strengths which are relevant to roles more than one level of responsibility above their current role. In other words, context is all!

It's also important to recognize the negative side of putting people in boxes. It's easy for the box to become a cell from which it is difficult to escape. Even if people aren't told which box they are perceived to be in, they will intuit it, and the Pygmalion effect will kick in, in respect of how those in the know behave towards them. Labelling people may prevent them and other people from seeing them differently in different circumstances. It is remarkable, for example, how many apparent middling performers, perceived to have low potential for promotion, become different people under a different boss who offers different beliefs about them. The same principle may also apply to star players who wither on the vine when they move out from the protection of a powerful boss. Charan and his colleagues recommend investment in coaching as a pragmatic way to overcome some of these problems, but this ignores the reality that the boxing process is helping to create the problems in the first place.

One practical application of the grid is as a support for employee-driven development planning. The employee and their manager identify a small number (maximum six) of core competencies required in both their current role and the roles they aspire to. They then try to explore as dispassionately as possible where the employee is on the grid in respect of each competency, and where they could realistically aim to be in six months, with appropriate application and support. This journey is represented with thick arrows. (For some reason, thick arrows appear to be more motivational than thin ones!) The benefits of this approach are that:

- It is more clearly developmental than judgemental.
- It is consensual (sometimes the employee may be asked to gather their own evidence about where they are).
- It is specific and therefore actionable (as opposed to a generalization that doesn't lead to obvious ways to improve).
- The employee and the line manager are jointly responsible for both the evaluation and the learning journey.

The 'other' talent

The preoccupation of talent management with high fliers can divert attention from other employees who may be equally vital to the organization's continued success. For leaders to be able to implement plans and strategies, there have to be many people who, while lacking potential to rise to greatly higher leadership positions, possess difficult-to-replace skills and social networks. McKinsey estimates that these employees typically account for between 30 per cent and 45 per cent of the workforce (Cosack *et al*, 2010).

LG Electronics has identified some of these people in relatively lowly positions – and invested in both retaining and supporting them. For example, really good call centre staff are both hard to find and hard to retain. An outgoing personality and intuitive listening skills are important, and these qualities are often found amongst actors. So LG's call centre contracts with talented employees to let them go for auditions at short notice and do acting jobs as they get them. They then return to the call centre when free again. It's a great example of adapting HR policies to meet the needs of talented people, instead of expecting talent to conform to HR policy.

Summary

The evidence that we can gather about talent, performance and potential does not provide much confidence that we can identify or measure them with any credible level of accuracy. Like leadership itself, they are ephemeral dynamic concepts, not easily pinned down. For a reality check on how perverse talent recognition can be, I recommend going to an alumni gathering from your undergraduate university or school. Who were the people who seemed sure to make good? And who actually did so? It's often a sobering experience!

CASE STUDY Nuclear Decommissioning Authority

David Reay, former Head of HR

Our organization was established in 2005. Succession planning was not a priority in the first place, but as the organization matured, we realized that people view their careers with three years as quite sufficient to stay in one organization. So now succession planning is one of our main focuses, not least because, in the nuclear industry we are dealing with things 50–100 years old, so we can't afford to lose the knowledge. We recognize that succession planning is not just leaders; it's for everyone, and particularly everyone at critical pinch points in the business.

We've had a mind change away from the idea that succession planning is just for our top 10 per cent and hypos. It used to be behind closed doors and about putting people in boxes. We've realized that you have to be transparent to talk to people and involve them in the overarching strategy. Now, when it comes to succession issues, because we have been developing people in line with business challenges, we have a plethora of candidates to draw on. Competition has become healthier, because people feel they have a fairer chance of getting a new role than if we were focusing on an elite. We are also attracting people into the organization, because they see more long-term opportunities.

There's a dilemma for HR between boxing people and thirsting for real data. We've found that succession planning can be less tangible, yet still work, because it's much more flexible.

Organizations – even large ones – need to get comfortable with empowering people to drive succession planning, rather than doing it to them. A large part of it comes down to the quality of people I employ.

Aligning careers and business needs

All the most difficult decisions are about people.

(Sir John Harvey-Jones)

Academics have been fascinated about careers for decades. We know quite a lot about how people make career decisions and about the changing shape of careers. What we know surprisingly little about is the interaction between the aspirations and career management systems of companies and the career behaviour of individuals.

The problem is largely one of uncertainty and time-frames. Uncertainty, because it's hard to predict specific career opportunities within a corporation even in the short term, and because many people don't have a clear idea of where they want their careers to take them. Many talented people either find themselves faced with an excess of choice (if they are well educated, visibly motivated and fit the mould) or a dearth of choice (if they are less privileged). Either way, serendipity appears to play a major role in career decisions. If I look back at my own career, although I actively sought to create opportunities, my decisions were based in the main on 'what came up at the right time'. With a different opportunity and choice, my career could have been very different.

Time-frame is an issue, because there is a conflict between taking a long-term view – ie plans extending five, ten or more years into the future – and the practical realities of the here and now. Strategic planning is no longer a relatively comfortable process of projecting from the present. For the employer, changes in markets and technology make large-scale investments increasingly risky, the farther out they stretch in time. For employees, the danger is that whatever job they set their sights on in the long term may not be there by the time they are ready for it – or may be much less attractive. In the world of science and technology, for example, we can observe a repeated pattern of evolution. At the birth of a new technology, there are few people with the requisite expertise. Those involved at the start and over the next three or four years are greatly sought after and rapidly obtain management roles. Their perceived talent is to a large extent their specialist expertise and knowledge. As more people enter the field, however, their scarcity value falls and the senior jobs, in both academia and commercial exploitation, are now taken, with most of the incumbents young enough to have a long tenure in the role. The later they join the field, the tougher it becomes for talented individuals to rise through the hierarchy. It's not that these latecomers are less talented – the opposite may be true – but their timing is off.

Is career success dependent on luck? The answer has to be, yes, in part. But people and organizations can make lucky breaks more likely, by being smarter about the 'bet your future' decisions they make. Unfortunately, most of the time organizations and individual employees plan and make those decisions independently of each other.

So the critical questions for this chapter are:

- What do organizations and their leaders need to understand about careers, and what do talented employees need to understand about organizations?
- How can organizations and talented individuals develop realistic yet flexible and opportunistic career paths?
- How can the ambitions of the organization and those of employees be brought into closer alignment?
- How can organizations and employees recognize and make use of 'transition points'?
- How can organizations acquire and retain the talent they need to make succession planning viable?
- How can organizations create the environment for alignment?

What do organizations and talented employees need to understand about each other?

Although individual HR practitioners may have a clear understanding of how careers have evolved, the organizational leaders who make succession planning and career-supporting decisions tend to be much less aware. This in spite of the fact that they, their peers, or their children may have had career patterns very different from the traditional linear model of following a semi-defined series of upward steps through increasing levels of responsibility within a management silo. The leadership pipeline, as it is often interpreted, tends to reinforce this linear model.

Careers researchers identify a much more complex picture of career paths, showing that they are frequently non-linear and discontinuous. (Sullivan and Baruch, 2010). Four descriptions of alternative particular career patterns predominate in the literature: boundaryless, protean, post-corporate and kaleidoscope careers. According to Sullivan and Baruch (2010: 1542), societal change is driving major shifts in how people view and manage their careers: 'Individuals are driven more by their own desires than by organizational career practice. Thus while organizational leaders are struggling to identify positive strategies and practices to tackle the changing work environment and workforce... individuals are adapting to a more transactional employer–employee relationship and taking more responsibility for their own career development and employability.'

In the *boundaryless* career (Arthur and Rousseau, 1996), people feel independent of traditional organizational career arrangements. Their allegiance is to their career and their personal stakeholders rather than to the organization. However, inertia and psychological barriers, such as fears about learning to work in new teams and with new colleagues, tend to reduce their actual mobility.

Protean careerists are flexible people, who value freedom. They believe in continuous learning and seek intrinsic rewards from work. Rather than seeing job insecurity as a threat, they regard it as an opportunity to take charge of their own careers. They look to their own, internal values for guidance and in measuring their own career success. They are also self-directed – they adapt what they do and how they learn to the environment around them, and they welcome challenge – and they are more likely to feel true to themselves in their career roles (Briscoe and Hall, 2006).

Postcorporate careerists Peiperl and Baruch (1997) integrate protean and boundaryless concepts. 'Postcorporate careerists are self-directed, take responsibility for their own career management, perceive a variety of career options, and are willing to cross multiple boundaries to fulfil their needs for intrinsic job satisfaction as well as financial rewards. [They] tend to be those individuals who voluntarily or involuntarily leave large organizations to work in a variety of alternative employment arrangements, including working as independent contractors and temporary workers or working for a small firm that provides professional services to large organizations' (p 8).

The *kaleidoscope* career model (Mainero and Sullivan, 2006) is based on the concept that people change their career patterns from time to time by rotating various aspects of their work and non-work lives, their relationships and roles. The kaleidoscope of their careers is based on three key aspects:

- authenticity (making choices that allow you to be true to yourself);
- balance (trying to achieve an equilibrium between work and non-work);
- challenge (need for stimulating work, as well as career advancement).

What do talented employees need to understand about organizations?

It's a truism that organizations don't care, but that the people within them can. Career self-management is essentially about building reputation and relationships with people who have influence on how you are regarded – how you 'fit in', how you contribute, whether you have significant potential and so on. It's also about being perceptive and realistic about how the organization actually works, as opposed to how people project it as working. Some of the common assumptions which the talented employee might challenge include:

- *The myth of the leadership team.* It's rare, for example, for the leadership team to exhibit many of the characteristics of a team. In reality, they are more of a group, who collaborate when they have to, but are also pursuing their own, independent agendas. The kind of roles that can open up when there is a genuine team at the top, and those that arise when there is not, can be very different. In general, the more of a team there is, the more opportunities for broader, more cross-functional roles.

- *It's important to have a sponsor.* True, to a point, but a single, powerful sponsor (as often found in US corporate mentoring programmes) may be a liability if they leave or have a setback in their own career. It seems that having a network of sponsors, at various levels, is more useful in the longer term (Thomas and Gabarro, 1999).

- *Stretch goals work.* Stretch goals are goals that seem impossible, but which galvanize people into radical new thinking. The classic example is President Kennedy's promise to put a man on the Moon within 10 years. The idea is highly seductive and a handful of well-publicized corporate examples suggest that this is a recipe for success – and hence that talented employees should seek out stretch goals for themselves and join projects based on stretch goals. The reality, however, according to recent analysis by US academics (Sitkin *et al*, 2011) is that stretch goals – as typically created and managed – often don't deliver and are more likely to result in disappointment and derailing. (Although see the end of this chapter for a case study where they have been made to work.) It seems that the conditions in which organizations are most likely to make stretch goals work are when they are buoyed up by previous success, and when they have sufficient slack in terms of resources to invest in pursuing unconventional ideas. Unfortunately, say the researchers, organizations that fulfil these criteria are typically the least likely to be motivated to set stretch goals, and those that are most likely to set stretch goals can least afford the associated risks. So, whether a stretch goal relates to a wider project, or only to their own role, employees should be wary of embracing them without clarity around commitment and resources from the stakeholders.

Some of the career-critical knowledge about the organization that talented people can benefit from includes:

- *Both the formal and the informal structures and how they interact with each other.* Who are the key influencers and holders of power, by virtue of position, knowledge and – increasingly important – connectedness?

- *The explicit and implicit cultures: where they are mutually supportive and where they diverge.* In particular, how these affect perceptions of performance and potential, and how they influence decision-making processes generally. Interestingly, organizational culture can have a significant impact on how people manage their careers. People in low-power-distance (less authoritarian) cultures tend to be more self-directed in their personal career management (Segers *et al*, 2008) than those in authoritarian cultures, who tend to be more reliant on the organization to manage their careers for them.

- *How strategy is created and implemented.* In many organizations, leaders struggle to define the decision-making process, if the question even arises. In practice, different approaches may be applied in different circumstances. These may be:
  - top-down or bottom-up;
  - caucus (strategy is the job of a chosen few at the centre) or broad church (with contributions from lots of people);
  - ends-directed (emphasizing vision and results) or means-directed (emphasizing how);
  - unified (leaders want everyone to understand the strategy) or fractured (people are only expected to understand the bits of the strategy that relate to them).

  Insight into such information about how the strategy is created and disseminated can be invaluable in creating personal career management strategies. Understanding who creates the strategy and who is tasked with working out its implications allows talented people to engage in conversations that contextualize developmental and career choices.

Developing realistic yet flexible and opportunistic career paths

In a complex, adaptive system, scenarios can play a significant role by focusing attention on opportunities. If the organization and talented employees are both mindful of a particular scenario, or set of scenarios, it creates an attractive force: both are drawn towards the same place on the map. Broadly speaking, what you are attentive to is more likely to happen than what you are not attentive to, because you see and act upon many small enabling opportunities that bring that scenario closer to reality.

At the business level, scenario planning is a well-established and essential element of the strategic process. Scenario planning:

- uses creative thinking to identify a range of possible futures;
- applies value judgements to differentiate between them in terms of desirability;
- applies rational judgements to establish the level of probability that they will come about;
- establishes what practical actions will be needed to increase the chances of achieving the most desirable scenarios and avoiding the least desirable.

In simple terms, it creates a matrix as in Figure 5.1.

The desirable, high-probability scenarios are those that have greatest magnetism and, in theory at least, should be easiest to bring about. Undesirable but highly probable scenarios demand a high level of avoidance effort, or creative ways to reduce negative impact. Desirable but improbable outcomes require a greater level of investment, in terms of practical action, but people's motivation may be lower because they perceive that their efforts are likely to be wasted. Low-probability, undesirable scenarios need to be monitored, but require only a low level of avoidant activity.

FIGURE 5.1 The desirability/likelihood matrix

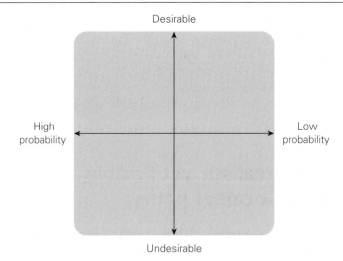

For an organization, this kind of planning is (or should be) routine. It helps in deciding which markets to be in, what products they should be developing and how to balance risk and innovation. In the talent arena, a range of scenarios might apply to, for example:

- the risks that talent will be tempted away by competition;
- the risks of skills obsolescence;
- the opportunities to capitalize on unique combinations of skills sets to create new products and services or competitive advantage;
- the opportunities to make the organization an employer of choice – either in general or for specific key groups of potential employees.

For the talented employee, a similarly wide range of scenarios is available, even if they are not necessarily aware of them. These might include:

- opportunities to develop skills sets and combinations of skills sets that would open doors to different or more senior roles;
- emerging markets, either within their current company or elsewhere, where their strengths and experience would be valued (for example, launch of a major new product or division);
- opportunities, perhaps arising from restructuring, to create new roles where they could make a difference;
- threats to their existing job role or the logical next-step job, arising from changes in technology or market, or from organizational restructuring, as in a merger.

Nonetheless, in my conversations with thousands of talented employees at all levels of management, I have been struck by how few adopt a genuinely systemic, scenario-based approach to their career self-management. Some have relatively linear career plans, which they track and pursue assiduously. For example: 'I am going to spend two years in this role, learning project management and building a reputation for getting things done. Then I'm going to transfer into a role that gives me wider visibility across the organization and greater visibility to top management, say on the change team, or in corporate communication. Then I want to move into a role that will let me demonstrate my skills in turning around a problem unit...'. But many have plans that are totally opportunistic ('I'll take the next promotion that offers me more money and more responsibility'), or fatalistic ('I'll do a good job in my current role and hope I get noticed. If not, I'll leave') or simply unimaginative ('When my boss moves on, I'll move up'). It seems that people can be highly talented in how they address issues in their work, yet fail to apply their talents to their own career management.

Herminia Ibarra, at INSEAD, has spent many years exploring career self-management (Ibarra and Lineback, 2005). Her work shows that people who focus narrowly on a small range of career options are typically much less successful than those who create and are aware of a much wider range of possibilities. It seems that the former miss out on opportunities because they don't see them or dismiss them as irrelevant.

An effective approach to using scenario planning in career self-management would start with defining a range of relevant scenarios, over perhaps a five-year period. Practical approaches include:

- Benchmarking against other organizations or other parts of the same organization. What kinds of roles and structures do they have to tackle similar business processes?

- Following major market and technology trends – how might they change this sector and the managerial or professional roles within it?

- Understanding organizational ambition – where does the organization aspire to be in five years' time, and what critically needs to happen to make that aspiration come about? Is it likely to acquire or to be acquired and will that open up more or fewer opportunities?

The key to all of these activities is information. Some of this information may be published on the web or elsewhere; some may only be gleaned through the quality of networking (see Chapter 12) and the conversations people have with organizational leaders.

Having decided which scenarios are most probable and why, the talented employee can test which are most desirable, by comparing them with their core personal values. Other aspects of desirability include whether the role would open up or close down the range of next steps open to them; how stretching and fulfilling the work would be; the extent to which it would play to their strengths; how it would affect their reputation; and the risks associated with it. Risk can be crucially important to assess: in a large information technology (IT) company, for example, HR had such a poor reputation that managers saw a transfer there as a sign that their career was no longer going anywhere. When the CEO persuaded a high flyer to take on the role of head of corporate learning, he removed this risk by giving very public support to the new appointment and by agreeing that the manager could opt out back into a line role at an equivalent level, after 18 months. In the event, the new manager was able to use the CEO's support to transform the role and the function, and stayed there for several years before returning to a more senior line role.

Next, the talented employee can identify practical steps that they can take to put themselves in the right place for the most desirable and most likely scenarios. Who do they need to build their reputation with? What competencies and experience do they need to demonstrate? How can they use their current role as a stepping stone to the next? At the same time, it can be helpful to look at some of the highly desirable but moderately unlikely scenarios. On the basis of 'having to be in it to win it', what relatively low level of effort could they undertake to ensure that they are positioned to take advantage of the scenario, if it should come about?

In Chapters 11 and 12, we will explore in more detail the kind of conversation that organizations and talented employees can have to share their respective scenarios. Clearly, such conversations need to be relatively frequent, to keep pace with change in individual and organizational circumstance. Clearly, too, the more open these conversations are, the easier it will be for both sides to adjust to continuous change, modifying strategy and tactics to maximize the level of alignment. One of the significant benefits of such an approach is that there will be a much higher level of employee engagement and a stronger psychological contract between the organization and its talent.

Equipping employees with the *skills, incentive and information* to create, share and follow through practical scenario planning for their careers should not be particularly difficult, so why doesn't it happen more often? When I have asked this question of HR professionals, three answers recur frequently:

- Although it wouldn't be difficult technically, or even especially expensive, it would take time and effort to establish the skills base; and a lot more time in holding frequent and meaningful career conversations.

- HR and line managers lack the skills and information to assist talented employees in their career scenario planning.

- The commitment to creating genuine partnerships between HR and employees, or between organizations and their employees, is insufficiently strong.

None of these barriers is insurmountable!

Creating alignment

What so often happens in organizations is that employee and employer interests become 'contested terrain... in which organizations pursue strategic advantages and individuals personal advantages' (Inkson and King, 2011). An alternative, more productive approach is to recognize the potential for concealed conflict and create dialogue around how employees and employers can best invest in each other for the long term.

Shared scenario planning provides a pragmatic framework for building alignment. At its simplest, alignment is about shared goals and shared values. By shared I mean not that they have to be exactly the same, but that they are congruent, mutually supportive and mutually transparent – that is, openly discussed without hidden agendas.

Shared goals begin with a sense of purpose. Both the organization and the individual employee need to be aware of and articulate 'What am I here for?' In a medium-sized financial services company, for example, there is a strong shared purpose that 'We are here to create wealth'. For the organization, ostensibly at least, the purpose is to assist developing economies to grow; for employees, the wealth creation is a bit more personal. The purpose of a police force might be to protect people from harm. People often select into and out of organizations, at least partially, on their sense of alignment with the organization's purpose.

To fulfil the purpose, organizations create goals that effectively relate to 'how' – the kind of products they produce, the kind of culture and technology they focus on, and so on. So, for example, electronics company Dyson has a long-standing goal of creating innovative products. That leads inevitably to subgoals that relate to hiring and maintaining a workforce of highly creative people and creating an environment where they can flourish. The goals alignment between companies such as Dyson and their employees is very strong. The conversations that people have day in, day out constantly reinforce the goals. In career management terms, continuous discussion of business plans, sharing of technological insights and a commitment to promotion from within combine to create a constant dialogue that links individual and company goals.

In my work on the psychological contract, I identify three meanings of the word 'value'. Value can mean *worth*. In the social exchange between employer and employee, the employee contributes to the share price or other measurable outcomes of the organization; the organization provides salary, benefits, opportunities for advancement and development that increases the employee's worth on the job market. Value can mean *respect*, in the sense that 'I value your opinion'. Here the social exchange involves behaviours by the organization, such as listening to employees and recognizing their contribution, and the respect (even pride) the employee feels towards the organization. Value can also mean *beliefs*, as in 'We share the same values'.

When people feel that the social exchange in all three of these areas is positive, there tends to be a strong psychological contract. If the psychological contract is strong, people are more willing and able to align their own ambitions with those of the organization. In the context of career planning, greater explicitness about each of these facets of value should have a major, positive effect upon how aligned employee and employer's interests and ambitions are. From a worth perspective, a conversation might begin with the recognition that good pay and benefits are, in career terms, largely a hygiene factor for the talented employee. They may even be willing to sacrifice these for the right learning opportunity. What counts more is the investment the organization makes in developing the employee's talent and the employee's willingness to reciprocate by using their talents to help the organization deliver increased value to its stakeholders. I am not suggesting here that this exchange needs to be a transactional, numbers-based exercise; rather, that talking about the exchange allows both the organization and the employee to be more attentive to each other's needs.

From a respect perspective, the conversation might look at what the employee is valued for, by colleagues and stakeholders. This is about more than acknowledging strengths. It is also about how the person uses their strengths in support of shared objectives. (By contrast, the typical appraisal process focuses attention on weaknesses.) Part of the respect exchange is also the sharing of confidence, in two senses. First, in having open dialogue and revealing concerns and fears – a climate where mistakes are valued for their learning potential and people are honoured for the quality of their sharing of lessons from mistakes. Second, in the sense that employees' self-belief is nurtured by the quality and depth of the belief which others express in them and their potential. This is particularly important for many people who come from minority backgrounds, are strongly introverted or who simply don't have a confident personality.

From a beliefs perspective, the career conversation might explore how the employee's personal values might impel them towards particular types of role within the company and away from others. Equally, it could examine opportunities for creating new roles, based on a combination of particularly strong values held by the employee and emerging market opportunities. Sometimes, too, it may become obvious that the values of the employee and those of the organization are so unaligned that this is the wrong place for them to work. Having an open conversation that articulates the mismatch and makes it explicit helps to avoid the path of conflict and psychological disengagement, which leads inevitably to physical disengagement and recrimination.

Recognizing and using 'transition points'

Transition points in this context are occasions when the status quo is about to shift. For the organization, this might be the launch of a new product platform, loss or gain of a major customer or a change in strategy – anything that will have a potentially significant impact on roles, structures, systems, or any combination of these. For the employee, a transition point might arise when an opportunity arises that offers them greater status, or access to new learning and experience. Or it may arise from a sense of mismatch between their role and their capabilities. Career transitions are often triggered by transitions in non-work life and vice versa (Latack, 1984). Organizations are not noted for helping people manage these transitions, with the result that employees often make important career decisions prematurely or on flawed thinking, or become locked into linear career paths (Louis, 1982). In theory, every career transition point should be an opportunity for reflection and personal recalibration, but only a small proportion of employees have access to appropriate coaching, mentoring or counselling in these circumstances.

A tool I use a great deal in coaching and mentoring is 'learn–exploit–coast'. When in learn mode, people feel positively stretched. The tasks they are doing are sufficiently challenging to engage them and give an overall sense that the work is contributing to the development of their expertise. In exploit mode, they apply this new learning to other situations, extrapolating and adapting as needed. There is still an element of learning here, but the main intrinsic reward relates to satisfaction in how they use their existing expertise. In coast mode, the work holds few challenges – except perhaps in terms of volume overload.

Having frequent career conversations, where both employee and the organization are well informed and well aware, makes it possible to recognize and prepare for transition points before decisions are made by either the employee, the organization, or both. Using the learn–exploit–coast model is one way of giving people a language to discuss these issues.

Honest conversations in this mode help to overcome another major problem in manpower planning. People are generally reluctant to admit to their boss or to HR that they are thinking of leaving. It is embarrassing, perhaps threatening, to do so. The subtle (and sometimes not so subtle) downsides of letting other stakeholders know that you are looking to quit and move on are also a deterrent; for example, being given less interesting work, or not being chosen for an overseas trip or to attend a training course.

Acknowledging transition points happens more easily, when the employer recognizes that it doesn't own talented employees; it just borrows them for a period in their careers. Focusing on achieving the maximum alignment between organizational and employee aspirations while they are there is much healthier than focusing on how you are going to keep them. Better to have high career alignment and a strong psychological contract with employees, and accept that they will move on, than to have mediocre alignment and psychological contract with people who are persuaded to stay, but who are not motivated or committed to perform at their best.

Identifying emerging transition points gives the employee and their manager the time and impetus to search for opportunities to enlarge current roles or investigate alternative roles that will maintain alignment. If these opportunities don't emerge, then a positive and gradual planned disengagement reduces the impact on the team and allows for a replacement to be found and take over. Over the years, I have employed a stream of young aspiring journalists to work with me as researchers. When hiring them, I would discuss the expectation that, at a point perhaps two years in the future, they would have developed their writing skills sufficiently to want to do their own thing. I contracted with them that they should tell me when they were feeling this way and that I would then help them, first, to adapt their role to meet their needs to the limited extent possible, and second, to make the transition to a more self-sufficient role elsewhere – for example, to a position on a newspaper. Their move to a new job elsewhere became a joint project for manager and employee.

How can you identify transition points? Some of the signs in an organizational context include:

- a shift or predicted shift in the market growth rate (growing, plateauing or declining);

- a sharp rise or fall in profitability;
- talk of stretch goals for the business or for particular areas of the business;
- change of leadership;
- technological pressure from competitors;
- a change in the organizational language (often a sign of a major shift in the way people think).

In each of these cases, there are threats for individuals, but also opportunities for talented employees to seek out or create new roles (or for the organization to create new roles) that will offer them new learning, or career advancement, or both.

Transition points for employees may be related to a wide range of factors, but triggers identified in research around this topic include completing a professional qualification, conflict with a work colleague, change in partner circumstances (such as having a baby), missing out on a promotion, a poor performance appraisal, and uncertainty in the employer organization (Mitchell *et al*, 2001). Signs of a transition point for a talented employee include:

- A sense that the learn–exploit–coast equation is out of balance for them
- Dissatisfaction stemming from peer comparison either within the organization or amongst colleagues outside the organization (for example, when friends who graduated in the same year appear to be making faster career progress than they are).
- An increasing sense of values conflict, or that the psychological contract is weakening.
- A sense of imbalance or dissatisfaction with regard to how their strengths are being applied; for example, 'What I'm really good at is working with people, but I'm spending most of my time on spreadsheets and dealing with numbers'.
- Having good ideas, but no opportunities to put them into practice (knock back an intrapreneur enough times and they will either quit to become an entrepreneur, or find another employer, which will value their ideas and give more opportunity to pursue them).

A McKinsey study (Baumgarten *et al*, 2007) found that executives on average experienced five significant transition points in their careers. Both men and women said the most significant of these transition points occurred at the age of about 30 and for 40 per cent of executives, this involved or resulted in their taking a new job in another industry.

It also seems that many employees are working to a personal career script (Allen *et al*, 2010), in which they link specific events (such as completing a course of company-sponsored study, or having gained a year's experience working in a cross-functional role, or being with the organization long enough to qualify for full maternity benefit) to a decision to move on. For obvious reasons, these scripts tend not to be shared with the organization. Opening up conversations around these scripts is a challenge for HR, but one principle seems to be fundamental: the more open and honest the organization is towards the employee, the greater the likelihood of the employee opening up in turn!

Retaining talent

As one head of talent at a multinational company expressed it: 'It's not much good if you have a succession plan and the talent you need has left.' Recruiting people who are likely to stay helps, so hiring should be less about whether a person will fit a particular role as it is, and more about how well they will be able to adapt with the role as it evolves, and about how many likely future roles they might fit.

Once you have recruited, however, given that talented people are only on loan, understanding the dynamics of how long they are likely to stay is pretty important. When an employee quits, the costs associated with recruiting, selecting, and training replacements often exceed 100 per cent of annual salary – some estimates double that figure (Cascio, 2006; Mitchell *et al*, 2001). The US Bureau of Labor Statistics reports that the national annual voluntary quit rate in the United States typically approaches 25 per cent, which adds up to a substantial drain on employer resources. Usually not taken into account in the costs of employee turnover is the impact on succession planning. Employers naturally tend to invest more in people who they see as having the potential to make an expanding contribution, than in employees in general. It's not just the cost of training, or of selection processes such as assessment centres. It's also the leeway they give talented employees to learn by making mistakes and the fact that managers tend to spend more time cultivating talented employees than they do less able ones. Talented employees are also more likely to be people with extensive relationship networks in the organization; losing them has a particularly strong negative impact on the business (Shaw *et al*, 1998; Shaw *et al*, 2005). Moreover, talented employees who leave and rise in other organizations are likely to recruit from amongst like-minded people who they respect in the organization they have left. It's hardly surprising, then, that according to some of the HR professionals I have asked, the costs of losing a member of the talent wave can be 10 times or more their annual salary!

So what makes talented people quit? There are, of course, many reasons, but it does not seem that pay is anywhere near the top of the list (Griffeth *et al*, 2000), nor job dissatisfaction (Lee *et al*, 1999). But having a sense of decreased opportunity is. So it makes sense for employers to try to identify and promote opportunities to employees. One way of classifying opportunities is:

- Blue Sky – medium to distant future, dependent on a platform of changes, not directly applicable to individuals as yet.
- Medium-term – emergent from existing plans and strategies, relevant to employees with specific aptitudes and track record.
- Short-term – known changes of role or position, for which candidates will be sought in the next few months.

Research into employee retention tells us that people who stay tend to be those who are most embedded in their organization (Mitchell *et al*, 2001). Embeddedness in turn is related to three kinds of connectivity: links, fit and sacrifice. Links are the connections we build with colleagues in the workplace, both within the team and more widely. Mentors have a particular role in helping people build strong co-worker networks. Fit is the values match or psychological contract we have explored above.

Sacrifice concerns the employee's perception of what they would have to give up if they left their job: perks, pension entitlements, status, promotion opportunities, convenience of work location, and so on. The greater the connectivity, the more likely people are to stay.

So how do you create such strong connectivity? Practical solutions include:

- Build the sense of community, especially between talented employees.
- Create opportunities for dialogue – both face to face and through social media – and encourage peer support networks.
- Enable people to challenge openly and without fear when they feel the organization is not living up to its values. Nobody's perfect, but discussing failings without resentment or blame helps people develop less of a 'them' mindset and more of an 'us' one.
- Establish what talented people value most about working for the organization, and make sure that that is what they continue to receive. Look for 'unique staying points' (USPs) which this organization can offer better than others.

Creating the environment for alignment

Many of the companies I have talked with in my researches had produced or aspired to create career road maps – guidelines and examples of career and role options and what employees had to do to work their way to each destination. The attraction of this metaphor is partly that it gives a sense of a continuing journey and partly that it allows for side roads and scenic routes as well as the trunk roads of obvious career stages. As a means of changing perceptions about career paths, emphasizing flexibility, diversity and ingenuity, this can be a helpful approach.

The problem with the road map metaphor is that road maps are flat and two-dimensional. Careers, however, have three dimensions: time, vertical movement and horizontal movement. It's easy to think in two dimensions if you assume that spatial movement is always onwards and up and that the terrain is fixed. But that's not the reality of many modern career paths, which are topographically much more complex and take place in an environment which is constantly shifting. In this complex, adaptive environment alignment and realignment needs to be a continuous activity. Employees and the organization need to recalibrate their career and succession planning GPS systems whenever they reach a point on the terrain where they can take a new bearing, discuss the next steps of the journey and, where appropriate, adjust course.

Among the practical steps organizations can take to build an environment where honest, well-informed and continuous conversations about career opportunities can take place, are:

- Make it the norm to take risks with people, by giving them opportunities and encouragement to take on roles and projects for which they may not be obvious candidates. When taking a risk on a new technology or new products, a typical process is to:
  - Assess the potential benefits (in this case, to both the organization and the individual).
  - Articulate and assess the risks.
  - Provide support mechanisms to ameliorate risks and help the individual succeed.
  - Have a back-up plan, if things go wrong.

- If you want to promote innovation, outlier employees – people who don't necessarily fit the competency spec drawn up to reflect the existing or previous incumbents – have great potential to introduce new perspectives and ways of tackling old problems. Sure, some of these risky appointments will not work out. Then much depends on whether this is seen as a personal failure (on the part of the employee and, perhaps also of the manager who appointed them) or as a learning opportunity for both the employee and the organization.

- Try to build into organizational structures and processes a greater balance between:
  - *Authority of expertise and authority of position.* Sometimes the best person to lead an initiative may be relatively junior. The more hung up people are on positional power, the less opportunities there are for those more junior to demonstrate their abilities and establish more innovative solutions to business problems. The less emphasis there is on hierarchy, the more encouragement there is for talented people to seize opportunities to lead – either as individuals or collectively as an informal team. The potential for networks of people with a common interest to lead change in organizations is often untapped or, worse, ignored and disparaged

by senior managers protective of their authority. For example, when working some 20 years ago with a large wholesaler, the biggest block on innovation and ideas from below was the head of operations and his staff, who believed that initiatives from other people should be discouraged, as innovation was their responsibility. The company's quality programme only really got off the ground when this manager was fired!

- *Reward for contribution and reward for seniority.* HR's love affair with pay grading systems has won it few friends. The rationale for paying people more on the basis of the size of office they occupy, and for the sometimes eye-watering differentials between pay at the top and pay at the bottom, is that basic salary should be based on the size and scope of the responsibility people hold. Bonuses should, of course, be based on contribution to the business, but inevitably the two issues get confused – for example, by tying bonuses to percentage of salary. Focusing reward on what people contribute beyond their job description (and assuming that they achieve at least acceptable performance in their core role), encourages innovation, delegation, networking and developing people around you to support challenging initiatives. It also means that genuine talent (people who can make things happen) has a greater chance of shining through amongst those people who just tick the boxes.

  In contrast, here's an example of what happens so often in large companies. Peter (not his real name) is a rising star in a retail company. Although nominally a junior manager, he is constantly acting further up, being given problem departments to turn around. Last year, one of these departments went from very poor performance to contributing 10 per cent of the company's profits. While Peter gets a lot of praise and non-monetary recognition from above, his salary is limited by pay bands that seem arbitrary to him, and his bonus by a formula that limits it to no more than 15 per cent of salary. The company has a limited period to prevent Peter walking – in this time, it must either find a way to promote him into senior management, at a time when there is pressure to reduce headcount at that level; or it must drive a coach and horses through the pay, grading and reward systems; or both. The worst thing it can do is nothing. Top management have maintained a constant dialogue with Peter and been as honest as they can, but the 'worth' dimension of the psychological contract is severely strained. It's a classic example of how HR structures and systems undermine key people objectives, such as retention and development of talent.

- *Recognition for your contribution and performance with regard to all the teams of which you are a member, rather than just the one you lead*. Agile organizations can't afford for people to work in silos. It's important for people to engage with multiple teams simultaneously, both for organizational cohesion and for developing personal capabilities and experience. In working with bright young employees, I find that a common complaint they voice is that having mastered most of their current role, they lose motivation because they are insufficiently challenged. As a mentor, I help them to look both for new challenges in the current role, and for opportunities to become involved with other teams and projects which will allow them to demonstrate or acquire new capabilities. However, 'what gets rewarded, gets done', and if rewards and recognition are focused firmly on the current role, people will tend to avoid challenges outside their main job role – especially if they are under time pressure. If the core role has relatively few opportunities to demonstrate their talent, then the organization's view of them (and often their own view of themselves) is likely to be much narrower and less holistic than if they are encouraged to link with and support other parts of the organization. For the organization, the risk of basing recognition and performance appraisal on behaviour in one role is that it rewards people, who are particularly competent in a narrow context, more than those who are more widely capable.

A handful of organizations have tried to formalize this principle by giving their high-potential employees both a core job and a secondary role, usually chosen to allow them to demonstrate and/or develop a different set of competencies. Both are considered in appraisals. This not only develops the employee more rapidly, but also provides a broader view of them and establishes whether there is consistency in their performance and behaviour in the two roles. If there is inconsistency, this initiates a dialogue around whether there is a skills deficiency or whether contextual factors in one role may be more constraining on their performance than in others.

- Develop the expectation of constant and honest exchange, and forums where it can happen.
- Invest in information, for example, by:
  - Making personal development plans (PDPs) much more dynamic documents than is usually the case. Put them online, make them transparent, and encourage people to both blog about their developmental experiences and make comments to help colleagues put their PDPs into action.
  - Creating an employee business plan at both corporate and business unit levels (and lower, if practical). These documents, pioneered by British Aerospace some 20 years ago, offer detailed descriptions of business strategy and its implications. Initial fears

that this would give competitors dangerous insights proved unfounded – it is at the product and technology level that the risk of giving away competitive advantage is greatest. This kind of easily available, annually updated information can be an invaluable resource in discussions about career options and direction.

- Transparency of information from working parties, such as change teams. Given that the greatest problems in implementing change come from people issues, rather than from technology, openness here can be intensely useful in exploring appetite for change. The talent pool (or as I prefer to call it, the Talent Wave, for reasons we will explore in the following chapters) can offer valid and insightful opinions. In return, they gain an understanding of the change team's thinking, which they can use in their own career planning.

- Encouraging talented employees to investigate areas that interest them and to share their learning. As already noted, a few companies, such as Google, give employees a percentage of their time to follow their noses on ideas they choose (Smith and Paquette, 2010). Although there is no empirical evidence about the impact on their core role, anecdotal evidence suggests that there is no negative impact on their performance in terms of either quality or quantity of output, and that there may be indeed an increase in performance, stimulated by the level of creativity that transfers from their time pursuing their own ideas into the time they spend on the 'day job'.

- Maintain a continuous dialogue around opportunities for promotion. The more opportunity talented employees perceive, the more likely they are to stay (Allen *et al*, 2010; Griffeth *et al*, 2000).

● Seek to understand and listen to Generation Y, or Millennial talent. Talentsmoothie's 'Tell it how it is' research (James *et al*, 2008) found that the Gen Y regard work differently to Baby Boomers – less as a means to live than as an important part of their social life. They expect to be trusted to work at home much of the time. They also place a high value on learning from peers and mentors. They expect to be valued for their strengths and given opportunities to use their strengths. If they don't feel aligned to the organization – for example, as a result of poor leadership – they are likely to quit. They are more likely to stay with their second employer than their first, because they use the first to work out more clearly what they do and don't want from their career. And, because they exert their own sense of individuality, they don't want to be categorized and stereotyped!

Against this background, HR and line managers need to cultivate the habit of listening. It may not always be possible to give Gen Y talented employees everything they want, but dialogue that builds the sense that the organization is listening and responding flexibly to them – that it wants to find the best way to use their talents – is the bedrock of career alignment with this growing and vital group of employees.

- Actively investigate the alignment process itself. In what circumstances is alignment between the employee's ambitions and those of the organization high and low? What barriers most commonly prevent people having in-depth, frequent and informed career conversations? Ongoing research (for example, through focus groups) can provide significant insights. Discussing those insights with high potentials and their managers can provide practical solutions for overcoming barriers and an additional motivation for people to engage more fully and more often in alignment conversations.

- Make succession planning as transparent a process as possible. The more that people understand the decision-making process, the easier it is for them to develop the skills and track record that positions them for opportunities. DHL (see case study below) provides a good example of how a company can educate people about what they need to do to achieve roles they aspire to. In many organizations, however, the process is quite obscure. Legal practices, for example, sometimes talk about the 'black box' of deciding who does and doesn't make partner. Mentoring helps, by illuminating the subtleties of behaviour, fit and performance that reassure existing partners that a candidate is suitable. But the more opaque the process seems, the more people are likely to feel that it is arbitrary and prone to favouritism.

CASE STUDY DHL

DHL's global strategy for talent management bucks a number of trends. For a start, it doesn't see great virtue in moving people around rapidly to gain broad experience. Instead, it puts greater emphasis in remaining in role long enough to gain depth (and for managers to live with and learn from their mistakes). It also aims (and largely succeeds in this) for 85 per cent of promotions at senior level to be internally resourced – partly because it has measured that productivity in a unit typically declines when senior managers leave, and partly because effectiveness as a leader in DHL is closely associated with scope and quality of networks, which take time to build and nurture. Human resources director (HRD) Steve Northcutt points out that 'you can hire brains, but not relationships' (Crush, 2009).

DHL also upturns the standard ratio of learning, with managers gaining only 10 per cent of their development through training, 20 per cent through mentoring and 70 per cent through stretch assignments, which are built into the personal development plans of all members of the Talent Wave and reviewed quarterly. Stretch assignments come in two varieties. One consists of projects lasting six to eight weeks, where the manager is acting further up by one level in their own country; the other takes three to five months and has to be located in another country. Assignments are selected to be tough, and managers are accountable for the decisions they make and the outcomes of those decisions. To get on this programme, they have to be nominated not only by their boss, but also by their direct reports.

To enable meaningful conversations about future job roles, DHL has produced detailed descriptions of every job role that show both what the incumbent needs to do, but also the kind of experience and track record that makes someone a potential candidate to step into that role. These become the basis of practical career and succession conversations between managers and HR.

The critical challenges: the maturity question

The Child is father of the Man.

(William Wordsworth)

At a conference in Sweden, a somewhat formidable female coach told me, in response to a question to the audience, that she saw her role as helping male executives to grow up. I responded by asking what made her think that these men wanted to grow up? A robust conversation ensued, in part about the respective qualities of Peter Pan and Wendy.

Although this exchange was at the surface level frivolous, it exposes a deeper, more serious issue. The behaviours which recur time and again in accounts of flawed executives and leaders are essentially immature responses to workplace situations: temper tantrums, unwillingness to hear bad news, demanding agreement, selecting direct reports who will not challenge their status as leader of the gang, and so on. In theory, the greater the responsibility a manager or leader assumes, the more mature they should be. Yet manifestly, this is not always the case. Maturity does not necessarily come with age ('There's no fool like an old fool!'), nor with the acquisition of skills and competencies. Maturity derives from a mindset that comes from gradually deepening understanding of oneself and how one relates to the world around us. Putting a person who is emotionally, cognitively or socially immature at the helm of an organization is not just unwise, it is a drastic failure on the part of Human Resources (HR) and the top team. It's also a negative advertisement for succession planning itself.

So how do people mature? It seems that the main ingredients are being open to a wide range of experience, engaging in reflection about that experience (both about how to use it and about what it tells you about yourself) and assimilating experience and reflection into a personal philosophy and sense of identity. Higher levels of maturity are often associated with qualities such as gravitas and authenticity, which are usually very apparent to others, but hard to pin down.

There are a number of different theories of adult maturity, but all have similar basic assumptions – in particular, that it is essential to pass through one stage of maturity before reaching the next. It is typical for someone to have a range of reactions to events, across several levels of maturity. On some occasions, they may operate above their current 'centre of gravity'; at others, they may regress to ways of thinking and behaviour associated with more childlike states. Personal development allows the centre of gravity gradually to move through the maturity levels.

Two of the best-known maturity models are those by Robert Kegan, and by David Rooke and Bill Torbert. As in all theories of human development, Kegan drew heavily on previous authors and in particular on the Swiss psychologist Jean Piaget (1985) who described a series of evolutionary stages in the development of a child's mind, from learning about their own body and senses, through understanding that other people and things exist separate to themselves, through visualizing external objects internally and imagining 'what if', to abstract thinking.

Kegan's book *The Evolving Self* (1982) is not the easiest of reads. Some years after its publication, he wrote in the foreword to another book: 'When I proudly told my father that it was being translated into German and Korean, he said, "That's great! Now when is it going to be translated into English?"'

Kegan uses Piaget's principles to develop a theory of social maturity, based on the premise that while the world around us is complex and dynamic, people's initial perceptions of themselves and how they relate to this world are simplistic and embedded in their own subjective perspective. People develop socially and emotionally as they enlarge this perspective. One of the limits of how far we can develop (how mature we can become) is the maturity of our peers – few people manage to evolve in maturity beyond this point.

Kegan identified the following stages of maturity:

- Incorporative: as babies we have relatively little self-awareness (sense of self) and little understanding that other people are different to us. This awareness only develops as they understand that there are things that are not me.

- Impulsive: the child becomes aware of its needs, arising from hunger, pain or discomfort.

- Imperial: the child learns to manipulate the external world to satisfy its needs.

- Interpersonal: the gradual awareness that other people have needs too.

- Institutional: acquiring personal values and rules.

- Inter-individual: recognizing that other people have different, equally valid value systems.

In a later book (Kegan, 1994), he claims that a half or more of people are not quite developmentally evolved or mature enough to meet the demands that societal institutions tend to place upon them.

Building on the work of Kegan and Ed Schein (1999), Otto Laske (2006, 2009) deconstructs the levels of human development in the context of the workplace and with particular emphasis on those that relate to adulthood. These levels differ in how people view others, how much self-insight they have, the nature of the values they hold, the predominant needs they feel, their need to control their environment, and how they perceive their roles in organizations. Crudely described, at Laske's level three, people allow themselves to be defined by others around them. So teenagers are heavily influenced in their values by peers, but also by parents and public figures such as rock stars and actors. Conforming to external expectations is important, so self-esteem is often bound up with group identity. Perspectives that do not agree with those of the group are rejected. In the world of work, says Laske, people at this level are unlikely to:

> think beyond the established operational principles and values of 'their' organization. Because their image is so caught up in the status quo, they will be unwilling to take the risks necessary to change it (*the status quo*), even if they can stand apart from their unit, group, or organization far enough to objectively assess what could make it operate more effectively... In a leader position, this person will follow whatever they believe the norms to be and will try to establish a climate accordingly.

At level four, described as self-authoring, people evolve their own values and principles (although these may be subtle borrowings from influential others) and assert their own identity. Laske describes them as 'highly, if not completely, identified with the value system that they have authored for themselves, yet they are very respectful of others for their competence and different values and beliefs. They find great difficulty in stepping back from themselves to discover their own voids but they will accept them when discovered.' While they can see the flaws in the organization, they are motivated to initiate change that fits their own world view, rather than in broader, more sustainable directions. 'Since they are caught in their own frame of reference, they fail to appreciate the value of other frames of reference just as much, if not more developed.'

At level five, they learn to take a much more systemic, fluid view of themselves and their relationship to the world around them. They accept other perspectives as having equal validity. Says Laske:

> They know that no matter what they do, it will be limited. Consequently, they have come to learn that learning-to-learn, lifelong learning, is not just a platitude – it becomes their life. Collaboration and collegiality become the means for exchanging frames of reference openly, where exposure of self-limitations is routinely accepted as the only means to learn more about the

self and others... Such a person is often highly self-critical, even humble... the climate they create will be the one that is open to exploration, risk-taking within reasonable limits and the emphasis, above all else, will be on promoting and sustaining growth and continued development of others and the organization as a whole.

Laske is not (necessarily) saying that leaders need to be at level five. But a major concern his analysis raises is that where the people who are responsible for deciding who is and isn't an appropriate leader have a centre of gravity in their maturity that is based in level four or below, they are unlikely to appreciate the value people at level five bring to leadership. Put simply, they are not mature enough to understand a higher level of thinking. Whatever words the frameworks of leadership competency use, the interpretation of these in terms of behaviour and mindset is likely to be different by people at different levels of maturity. Mature thinking may all too easily be confused with woolliness. Given that less than 10 per cent of adults ever reach level five, organizations may be weeding out the wisest potential leaders in the way that they identify talent and select for leadership qualities. This, in turn, makes it more likely that people who do get to the top may be relatively immature on socio-emotional terms – and this, in turn, will limit the sustainability of the organization long term. Alain Gauthier, co-founder of the Society for Organizational Learning, maintains that current global trends call for executive leaders who have reached later stages of development and demonstrate a high level of maturity in dealing creatively with increasing complexity, uncertainty, diversity and numbers of paradoxes (Gauthier, nd).

Another model of maturity comes from David Rooke and Bill Torbert (2005), who link maturity with different kinds of management challenge. They identify seven levels of maturity. At the lowest level, described as *Opportunist*, decision making and behaviour are driven by doing whatever it takes to win. These people are manipulative and self-focused, using and abusing authority to achieve their own ends. Their leadership style is characterized by focus on the short term and the concrete, doing what they can get away with, distrust and seeking personal advantage.

The second level is called *Diplomat*. As the title suggests, they tend to avoid conflict and have a strong need to belong. Their leadership style emphasizes conforming to the rules and to norms of behaviour, maintaining the status quo, and keeping everyone happy.

Experts are focused on logic and expertise. They see efficiency as a goal in itself. They assume that their personal systems of logic and beliefs are the only valid ones. Their style of leadership reflects consistency, certainty, continuous improvement and striving for excellence – but may also show obstinacy and dogged pursuit of the wrong goals.

Achievers are focused on achieving goals – usually goals set for them by others. Their leadership style emphasizes results, effectiveness and making things happen. They find ways to work around obstacles. They inspire others and set high standards for themselves.

Individualists focus more on themselves than on goals, but are sufficiently aware of the complexity of business and interpersonal systems that they can achieve goals through the quality of relationships. Their leadership style tends to be self-absorbed, questioning and innovative – they lean more towards change than stability.

Strategists are good at seeing and exploiting the links that others don't. They integrate principles and theories; are comfortable with paradox and contradictions; and are adept at managing both goals and the processes to achieve them.

The highest level of leadership style, the *Alchemist*, is about transforming oneself and others. These leaders are 'creators of events'. They reframe situations according to new metaphors, see both positive and negative aspects of issues, and are able to work with both order and chaos. They turn conflict into win–win.

Whatever the psychological model that is adopted, it seems clear that appointing someone to a role that requires a higher level of maturity than they currently possess is dangerous, possibly unethical, and highly likely to have medium- to long-term negative consequences, both human and commercial.

As with the Laske maturity framework, only a small proportion of people are estimated to have achieved the highest level of development – in this case, just 1 per cent, a very small pool to draw upon. Fortunately, Rooke and Torbert propose that each of these leadership styles has a place in an organizational context. Opportunists, they say (2005, p 3), are useful in a sales environment (though it's hard to see this approach being very effective in motivating a sales team!). Diplomats are good in situations that require bringing people together harmoniously. Experts are good contributors in their own right. Achievers are 'well-suited to managerial roles'. Individualists are 'effective in venture and consulting roles'. Strategists are effective as transformational leaders; and alchemists at leading society-wide transformation.

This analysis of thinking styles and resultant behaviours can be challenged on a number of counts. In particular, it's difficult to see the first three levels as relevant to leadership, other than that you wouldn't normally put anyone with those styles into any kind of leadership role. The principle of increasingly wider perception correlating with greater efficacy as a leader has not been empirically proven – but it's not hard to find examples of shallow maturity being associated with corporate short-termism and disaster!

The Leadership Pipeline, a concept which we will examine in the next chapter, is sometimes described as a maturity model, because it also proposes that different hierarchical levels in an organization require increasing breadth of perspective and understanding. However, the link with broader maturity is not clear and there is some doubt as to whether, as in an authentic maturity model, people have to move through one phase to achieve the next.

Managing the maturity issue

Organizations can assist employees to mature by:

- helping them recognize their current level of maturity;
- providing opportunities for experience which will assist them in moving to the next level of maturity;
- providing opportunities to reflect (and to become more skilled at reflecting);
- linking talented employees with more mature colleagues who can act as role models through informal learning methods such as coaching and mentoring;
- making appropriate maturity a key criterion in senior-level appointments.

Helping people recognize their current level of maturity

It can be difficult for someone at one level of maturity to imagine, let alone value, higher levels. And moving from one level to the next doesn't happen just because a person wishes it. Wisdom and maturity come gradually, through a combination of experience and reflection on experience. For many people, the most that can be accomplished is perhaps having the conversation that makes them aware that there are higher levels. It's important in having those conversations that they also understand that it is OK to be where they are and that being where they are is a necessary part of achieving greater maturity.

Removing taboos about discussing personal maturity and including maturity as an element within personal development planning, would help to identify and potentially remedy fatal flaws. And the earlier in a career this can be tackled, the more beneficial it is likely to be.

One of the problems for HR is that the executives who have to approve senior appointments may not be aware of their own level of maturity and/ or may not appreciate the perspectives and thinking patterns of someone at a higher level than themselves. It's not uncommon in coaching, for example, for an executive who is used to excelling in everything they do to dismiss the whole concept of maturity, if they are assessed at anything but the 'top' level. It takes time for them to understand that where they are is where they are, and that this is not about status or competency, but about mindset.

Providing opportunities for maturing experiences and reflection

This is not just about giving people developmental roles that will stretch and challenge them. It's about selecting tasks and roles that will require a more mature perspective, but not so much above their current level that they are likely to fail. One of the characteristics of Laske's work with executives and their coaches is identifying approaches that will take people to a higher level of thinking, but still within the range of their current centre of gravity. In other words, if someone has a centre of gravity just within level four, a sufficient stretch might be to move them to a point, still within level four, where they can envision the possibility of level five thinking. The same logic would apply within developmental conversations, where the learner is helped to reflect upon their experiences and gradually to widen the perspectives from which they view them.

Linking with more mature role models

Mentoring, in particular, is strongly associated with role modelling (Levinson, 1978; Kram, 1980, 1988). Conversations with a more mature mentor provide a safe environment for absorbing more complex, systemic and integrating ways of thinking. One of the themes of my studies in recent years has been the efficacy of different approaches to matching mentors and mentees. Learning maturity (how mature an individual is in the way they approach and manage their learning) of both partners in a mentoring relationship is potentially a significant factor in determining relationship quality and how much value the relationship will add. However, as Laske has observed with regard to executive coaching, too great a gulf in maturity can be an impediment to an effective learning relationship, because the more junior partner cannot fully associate with the more senior as a role model, and because the more senior may expect more comprehension than the coachee or mentee is able to give.

Maturity as a criterion for senior-level appointments

Higher levels of maturity don't necessarily correlate with more effective leadership behaviours. (But they do correlate with greater self-awareness of fatal flaws!) It all depends on the demands of the leadership role. With maturity comes greater reflexivity, but that can slow down decision making. An instinctive, activist style can be highly successful in an environment, such as retail, where rapid, mainly tactical decisions make the difference between profit and loss. At some point, however, long-term business development and survival depend upon deeper insights generated from greater maturity. Implanting a person at, say, Kegan level five into a sales team which is performing well in a level three environment, where peer pressure and extrinsic reward are effective, may simply create conflict. Yet helping the team as a whole become more reflective and extend its range of responses to include aspects of more mature mindsets might make it even more effective. Getting the balance right for the organization and its context is a tough challenge.

What should happen, I believe, is that any candidate for a seriously senior role should be interviewed by a psychologist or other professional qualified to assess their maturity level. The language people use when they talk about issues which are important to them, is very revealing in terms of their maturity; and maturity is relatively hard to fake. Talent development programmes should also provide a balance between opportunities to acquire skills and knowledge, and opportunities to mature.

When should you assess maturity? Sheer cost suggests that, for most organizations, it's not practical to do so for all potential leaders. One option is to insist on an evaluation for:

- appointments to all the most critical key roles;
- every transition involving a critical transition in responsibilities, as described in *The Leadership Pipeline* (Charan *et al*, 2001), ideally starting with managers of managers, but at a minimum for potential enterprise managers.

Of course, assessing maturity of the individual is only part of the requirement. It's also necessary to assess the relative level of maturity required for the role. That may not be simple, because there are likely to be differing opinions.

Assessing candidates in this way doesn't mean that you would always block the appointment of anyone who failed the 'maturity test'. For example, you might appoint someone relatively immature emotionally to a senior management team, but only if:

- They are balanced and moderated by more mature leaders of equal authority in the same team.
- They are not permitted to be a single leader (for example, when more mature colleagues move on).
- They are assessed as having the potential to acquire greater maturity within that role.
- Mechanisms are in place to support the development of their maturity (coaching, mentoring, psychological support etc).

Managing potentially fatal flaws

One thing I am most certainly not recommending here is that anyone who is psychologically different or unusual should be weeded out simply on those grounds. That would be a great way of removing a large proportion of the most creative talent! I am however arguing, first, that the risks associated with mildly abnormal personalities need to be managed; and second, that such people should be valued, because of their difference. Malcolm Davies (2009) points out that on the one hand, extreme strengths can easily become fatal flaws, and that 'dark side' characteristics including personality disorders can be drivers of very successful leaders – for example, under-pinning creativity, tenacity and persistence. Renaming these characteristics as 'exceptional personality' qualities, he quotes an Australian study of CEOs that found that most had 'two or three potential derailers, which, if well managed, can be great strengths, but if not well managed, can derail people, relationships and performance'. This reinforces the view expressed in previous chapters that effective leadership involves collective responsi-bility and authority which provides the checks and balances needed to harness the leader's strengths, while preventing or ameliorating their nega-tive expression.

Making the maturity dialogue happen

Maturity is about connectedness – the quality of how an individual con-nects with the world around them. As the world of business becomes increasingly connected and increasingly complex, the penalties for immatu-rity in leadership roles will become even greater than at present. Succession planning that ignores this is doomed to repeat the mistakes of the past. It is essential that HR engages the organization, but especially the talented em-ployees and the existing leaders, in thinking about maturity and ensuring that it becomes part of both the developmental language and the talent and succession agendas.

The maturity question is still one that is largely unconfronted in many organizations. If HR is serious about succession planning, it should at the very minimum reflect upon and try to find answers to these three questions:

- What is the collective maturity of current leaders at each level in the organization?
- What is the collective maturity of each level of identified potential leaders?
- What strategies do we have in place for when potential leaders are more mature than the existing ones? Or for when the socio-emotional or cognitive maturity of designated 'crown princes' does not align with the demands of the role they are in line for?

Pools, pipelines or waves?

> Metaphors are so deeply embedded in our language that it would be difficult, if not impossible, to think without them. And there's nothing wrong with that, as long as we keep a firm grasp – metaphorically speaking – on what they really mean.
>
> (Julia Galef, 2011)

This chapter starts with an acknowledged bias. I don't like the concepts of talent pools or pipelines. The reason is simple: for me, both metaphors have serious limitations or drawbacks. The word I most readily associate with pool is '*stagnant*'. Pools are contained, smooth and lack any sense of energy or dynamism. While that's a fair description of quite a few organizations' approaches to talent management and succession, it's far from ideal.

The pipeline metaphor does have a sense of movement. But again, it's confined and there is an assumption that people have to go through one valve after another, in the right order, at the right time. Pipelines have a habit of getting constricted, and when they are partially or fully blocked, pressure builds up until there is a serious leakage. According to Ofwat, the UK water regulator, 3.5 billion litres of water is wasted through leakage from the country's water supply system every day. For what actually happens in so many organizations, maybe it's not such a poor analogy at all – but is that what those organizations are aiming for?

Both pools and pipelines are metaphors based on assumptions of succession planning and talent management as simple, linear systems. What's needed is a metaphor that captures the complexity and dynamism of these activities. The best I've found so far is the *Talent Wave*. A wave is pure energy. When they see waves on the sea, people often assume that the water is moving. In reality, it is only the energy that is moving through the water. Waves constantly adapt to the terrain. As the terrain becomes shallower, they become larger and more powerful. They go round obstacles, or knock them aside, or simply wear them down. They interact and reinforce each other. They are constant motion.

In the modern organization, the Talent Wave is a force to be reckoned with. It is going places, and HR can either surf with it or get out of the way. Its members are interlinked and recognize each other's talent and contribution. They are impatient to make things happen. And they know that, behind them, is a whole succession of other waves.

Does it matter whether we refer to pools, pipelines or waves? I think it does, because the metaphors we use shape our assumptions, and our assumptions influence processes, expectations and behaviours. So the key question for this chapter is: 'How can we create and sustain succession planning and talent management systems that harness the energy of the Talent Wave?'

Dropping a rock in the talent pool

First, let's look in a bit more detail at the notions of talent pools and talent pipelines. The core proposition behind having a talent pool is that the organization has enough talented people to fill most or all of the key positions, should they become vacant. Leaving aside the arguments already rehearsed about what constitutes a key role, the proposition is flawed on several counts. Firstly, there is at least an implied supposition of interchangeability of role – that the members of the pool all have the right mix of generic leadership skills to slot into a range of vacancies. Inevitably, this tends towards a certain level of conformity and lack of diversity. This would be fine in a steady-state environment, but shifts in markets and trading environments may throw up a need for someone with radically different qualities. Looking outside the organization is a possible solution, but external appointments take longer to bring onboard and are much less likely to work out, especially the higher up the organization you go. An example of the problem is a large retail bank which was very proud of how many of the people in the talent pool scored highly on their framework of leadership competencies. Moreover, almost all had their formal bankers qualifications – a reward for years of study. As markets changed, however, a new critical leadership competency emerged – commercial awareness – that most of the talent pool significantly lacked! People who did have those qualities were at lower levels and/or not in the talent pool, and so were not considered. A massive, culturally disruptive influx of commercially minded people from outside was a temporary fix, but it demotivated the talent pool, who felt inferior and inadequate. The organizational immune system then got to work on the newcomers, swiftly diluting their numbers and their cultural impact!

Secondly, pools tend to have a high level of inertia, unless they overflow. They prevent overflowing, by restricting the number of people within them. If we mix the pool and pipeline metaphors for a moment, it might be helpful if a strong inflow from below were constantly forcing the stagnant layers at the top out of the pool. Companies justify not creating this kind of pressure on the basis that it costs enough as it is to develop people already in the pool, and on the grounds that they do not want to raise expectations of advancement among people who are going to be disappointed. A problem with this inertia is that it prevents HR and top management taking a regular, serious look at how the criteria for being in the pool need to change.

A number of other issues emerge from a recent study of talent pools for the CIPD (McCartney, 2010), which found that:

- There is much confusion about what being selected for the talent pool is for (is it to prepare them for promotion, or to help them perform better in their current job, or both?).

- Unsuccessful applicants are less likely to see a future with the organization. They are also more likely to say there are fewer career opportunities open to them and feel less in control of their careers in general.

- Line managers are inconsistent in their support for talent management initiatives.

The two issues around selection are directly related to the concept of the pool itself. For all the talk of 'co-opetition', companies and their leaders still think largely in terms of win or lose. For example, it's no good coming second in a pitch for business. It's not surprising, therefore, if the win–lose mindset also permeates talent management and succession planning. Metaphors such as 'the rat race' or 'the War for Talent' subtly reinforce the notion that success is about being accepted into the exclusive club of the talent pool.

When people outside the talent pool peer through the windows, what do they see? Do they say to themselves: 'I can see why these people have earned a place inside. I would like to learn from them and use them as role models'? Or do they wonder what makes these people special, or worse, say to themselves: 'If the price of entry to the talent pool is being like that person there, I'm not sure I want to play this game'? It is the mistakes in selection to the talent pool that outsiders notice. It doesn't need many psychopaths in the mix to poison the perception of the talent pool by employees in general, and this in turn will affect who aspires to acquire the talent label. Having even a small number of highly visible 'wrong' people in the talent pool may actually deter genuine talent from engaging in the process.

The line manager issue may relate to a wider problem of talent management programmes generally. When more and more is being asked of line managers and when it becomes increasingly difficult for them to spend sufficient quality time with their teams, it's hardly surprising that consciously or unconsciously they should ask, 'What's in it for me?' Equally, when they are being assessed personally on output of their team, it takes a substantial dose of altruism to encourage your best performers to move on. The practical solution is to link line managers' rewards, status and recognition, and their own promotion prospects generally, to people development criteria, with sufficient 'bite' to maintain their attention. In essence, that means that delivery of short-term results and medium-term development have to be of equal weighting – but that isn't easy to accomplish in a performance culture, unless we redefine what we mean by performance.

The perils of pipelines

The issue with pipelines is more complex, because the concept has gone well beyond being a metaphor, evolving into a detailed theory of talent management and succession. In my conversations with academics, managers and HR practitioners, it's clear that the phrase Leadership Pipeline has become a grab-bag for a variety of concepts, which can be divided into two categories. The first is the core concept that 'what it takes for managers to succeed differs for different jobs at different levels in the organizational hierarchy' (Kaiser, 2011: 71). Evidence to support this has until recently been thin – Kaiser points out that neither book *The Leadership Pipeline* (Charan *et al*, 2001) or *What Got You Here Won't Get You There* (Goldsmith and Reiter, 2007) references a single empirical study or formal theory and that 'there is not a single predictive study in the published literature that demonstrates different relationships among the managerial behaviours, skills and competencies related to effectiveness at different organizational levels' (p 72). However, studies published alongside Kaiser's critique do provide a level of confidence in the broad principle of differences in leaders' required competence in supervisory, middle-managerial and executive roles (Kaiser and Craig, 2011; Kaiser *et al*, 2011; De Meuse *et al*, 2011).

What's more in question is the paraphernalia of assumptions, processes and purported good practice built around this basic phenomenon – what I have sometimes described as HR bling – much of which we have explored and found wanting in the previous chapters. So what can we usefully extrapolate from the core concept, based on evidence?

The first thing to make clear is that the pipeline metaphor is an overlay upon previous work that talked of pathways and crossroads – a bit of creative packaging around a metaphor that worked pretty well already. Charan *et al* (2001) expanded the number of organizational levels and crossroads or transitions, on the 'great fleas have lesser fleas' principle.

Arthur Freedman (1998) found that managers making a significant shift from one level to the next were often ill-prepared for the corresponding shift in mindset demanded by the new role. They often needed help in letting go of perspectives, values and skills that were no longer relevant or helpful in their new role; they needed to refine and strengthen those that were useful; and they needed to develop new ones which had not been needed to any great extent in the previous role. Some of the skills on which they relied at the previous level may even become liabilities at the next; for example, micromanaging may work in some supervisory roles but will be disastrous in a middle-manager or executive role. If they encounter difficulties in making this transition they may revert to previous behaviours because these are comfortable, even though there is a negative effect on performance; and they may experience stress and/or derailment. Other research has suggested that higher-level jobs involve longer time horizons, or 'time spans of discretion' (Jacques 1964, 1978, 1989); different functional activities, with those at the top focused most on organizational structure, policy, strategy and culture and those at the supervisory level focused on applying standard operating procedures (Katz and Kahn, 1978); different levels of three types of skill – conceptual, interpersonal and technical – (Mann, 1965); and increasingly wider span of responsibility for other people and resources (Freedman, 1998).

A second important contextual factor is that there are two schools of thought about the competencies managers and leaders require as they progress up the hierarchy. The continuity perspective says that the same basic skills are needed at any level of leadership, but that people need to be more capable in each of those skills as they take on greater levels of responsibility. The discontinuity perspective says that people need to drop some skills and take on others as they transition through a career crossroads which takes them from one authority level to the next. The pipeline concept is firmly rooted in the discontinuity perspective, while the broad weight of the evidence tends to support the continuity perspective. De Meuse *et al* (2011) defuse some of the contradictions here by showing that while the importance of nearly 70 competencies rises from supervisor, through manager, to executive, the skills levels in many of these competencies changes. As might be expected, when supervisors become middle managers they improve in competencies related to people management; and middle managers transiting into executive roles gain greater skills ratings with respect to strategy and business acumen. When they become executives, however, there is a significant drop in people-related skills. They are less likely to show patience, to listen, to be approachable, to show they care about people below them in the hierarchy, to be seen as fair, to make personal disclosures or to use humour. Given that these are mostly qualities associated in other studies with highly effective leadership at the top, this is worrying. Say Kaiser and Craig (2011: 107): 'Middle manager effectiveness was a function of more directive and less empowering leadership. Whereas executive effectiveness was characterised by more empowering and less directive leadership.'

Fortunately, some competencies seem to be vital at all three levels of supervisor, middle manager and executive. Learning agility and adaptability are important in all leadership roles and Kaiser and Craig suggest (p 111) that these may be metacompetencies – an underpinning to the intellectual and emotional growth maturing of the manager. Integrity and trust also appear to increase in importance from supervision to executive roles, but the level of demonstrated competence in this vital area decreased as people became more senior.

Studies such as these indicate that there is indeed a discontinuity in leadership competencies and skills between organizational levels. But they also bring into question the whole pipeline metaphor. Is it any wonder that so many leaders and managers fail to make a successful transition, when they have been selected into previous roles specifically for qualities that are not wanted at the next level? If those competencies have been rewarded through recognition of performance, they will have been even more deeply ingrained. So the most suitable candidates for roles at the next level are likely to be people *outside* the pipeline – those who are *not* necessarily the most effective middle managers.

These studies also raise the question: *What is it about the way we develop talent in organizations that makes them become less competent in areas critically associated with the higher roles they aspire to?* This is unlikely to be an outcome of formal training and more likely to be a result of subtle acclimatization – role modelling and both intrinsic and extrinsic reward systems. In addition, where is the evidence that people *need* to progress through each level of the pipeline to be considered for the next? Many of the most successful entrepreneurs would struggle to demonstrate competence at lower levels of the pipeline. Many of the entrepreneurs I have interviewed have been stimulated to launch their own businesses in part or whole because the large organizations for which they worked did not recognize and appreciate their talent mix.

The overall lesson to be drawn from this discussion is yet again that the simple, linear approach doesn't work. It may be convenient to assume that high performers in middle management will, with a little help and encouragement, make successful executives. But it is likely to ensure that candidates are limited to a smaller, less diverse pool, many of whom are doomed to fail.

Linear thinking says that people develop, for example, the skills of strategic thinking by being exposed to roles which require progressively wider contextual understanding and increasing competence in using planning tools. That may be one way of achieving the objective, and certainly coaching and mentoring provide a pragmatic and effective way of supporting these transitions. But strategic thinking is as much a mindset as a measurable skill. Some people have it at a remarkably young age. However, organizations prevent them from becoming involved in and contributing to strategic thinking, because they are at the wrong level in the management hierarchy and leadership pipeline.

An alternative approach, practised for example by Welsh Assembly Government, is to appoint young high-potential employees onto a 'shadow board'. The shadow board meets about a week before the real board or top team and considers the same papers. Each of their meetings is chaired by a different director. They make recommendations and comments, which are fed to the real board or top team. One of the shadow board members may also attend the real board meeting as an observer and to elaborate on the shadow board thinking. The outcomes of this approach include developing the strategic awareness, skills and confidence of the shadow board, constructive challenge to assumptions the real board or top team make about how proposed changes will be perceived further down the organization, and insights into potential implementation problems. The shadow board also become ambassadors for the top team. In terms of the pipeline theory, these junior managers are taking a mindset bypass around middle management competencies!

The concept of a pipeline assumes that people will follow a set path, growing into new levels of leadership step by step and branching from one pipe to another in an ordered procession. But that linear model of career progress won't work in some of the new models of organization that are emerging. For example, lattice organizations permit job moves in any direction. What you do is far more important than what level you are in the hierarchy, and people at relatively low levels can take authority for projects where they have the requisite expertise, with teams including people much more senior than themselves.

Harnessing the power of the Talent Wave

Some practical ways in which to move to a Talent Wave mindset and away from pipelines and pools, include the following:

- Identify cross-functional, cross-role issues that need to be addressed – things that don't fall neatly into a single silo. Open up opportunities for people to put themselves forward to work on these – individually or collectively, as appropriate – and support them by allocating time away from their main job. But keep a wary eye out for the person who wants to do anything but attend to their core job!

- Have a resource fund (time and money) for people to propose initiatives that both interest them and will develop their leadership capabilities. Base allocation of this resource on the quality of the case they make in terms of both benefit to the organization and benefit to their personal development. Open up this opportunity to anyone who has the drive and insight to take it.

- Learn to distinguish between people who simply ride the wave, and those who provide its energy. The principal energizers are those who initiate ideas, those who seize on ideas and make them work, and those who build and sustain the networks that impel innovation.

- Build links between senior leaders and emerging talent. The leaders can feed off the energy of the younger generation; the emerging talent gets to understand how to use the system to achieve change.

- Look at role evolution as an effect of the wave. Give people lots of opportunities to seize new responsibilities, and create opportunities for them to move their role in line with their new capabilities. So promotion becomes a continuous, gradual process, marked occasionally by recognition in terms of organizational level, rather than a series of discontinuous jumps.

- Talented people are not there to step into roles as they become vacant. They are there to question and change roles as they advance towards them. Make job shadowing an element of talent development: expect every member of the Talent Wave to spend at least two or three days a year shadowing roles in the layer above and making suggestions as to how they might be managed differently. This is not about critiquing the competence of the role incumbent, but about questioning the purpose and scope of the role.

- Recognize that the scarcity model of development practised by many companies (development is a privilege, it's costly and rationed – so partly a reward, too) is no longer tenable. Development opportunities are part of the psychological contract with talented employees, as important as or more important than regular pay cheques. To make development more affordable, many companies are already shifting to much greater reliance on online training (and increasingly emphasizing quality in e-learning), and to making coaching and mentoring endemic.

- Expect jobs to evolve constantly. Think in terms of a core role, with medium-term sustainability, and adaptable, optional roles. The former will tend to be set by the organization and measured in terms of relatively short-term 'hard' outputs; the latter negotiated between the organization and the employee, and measured in terms of 'soft', medium-term outcomes.

- When a member of the Talent Wave moves into a job role, recognize them less for how they *perform* the roles than for how they *transform* it.

- Question all the HR bureaucracy. What is it there for? To control or enable? What evidence do you have that it is delivering choice for the organization and employees? That it's retaining talent? Explore what HR policies are helping and hindering the progress of the Talent Wave. Instead of relying on traditional top-down perspectives, place at least equal reliance on the perspectives of Gen Y employees. Task some of them with exploring how procedures such as induction, performance appraisal, work assignment, workforce planning and so on could be made more relevant and more responsive.

- Move away from seeing progress as an upward movement. Create expectations of horizontal moves that offer learning. Be flexible in allowing people to move into roles where they are half in the company and half out (for example, to go take a course of study).

- If there is spare energy, it will leak away. Talent will out – which often means that unused talent will walk. Look for ways to harness it creatively. Some Japanese companies, for example, cope with severe market downturns by loaning talented employees to customers and suppliers, to help build their businesses. When the employees return, they have created a wealth of goodwill that leads to further business for their own company.

At the risk of mixing metaphors, another concept which I have found to resonate with line managers and HR alike is that of the 'talent node'. Talent nodes are job roles where you grow talent faster (eg in a hothouse environment), and need to have particularly talented people.

Examples of talent nodes include new product teams, change management teams and teams tasked with developing a new venture. Often these teams need to be protected from the main organization, because they are to some extent countercultural – and that is part of their value. The node analogy implies that they have the potential to influence the future direction of the organization more widely and, at the same time, to influence the direction of their own careers. Talent nodes work because intelligent, motivated people stimulate each other. Here's how one CEO describes a talent node that was a start-up within a larger organization:

> It was exciting. We'd come in at seven o'clock and not notice the time until it was late. Nobody complained about long hours because we were all caught up in the act of creation. The project belonged to all of us and we were all learning from each other as we built on each other's ideas to make the project work.

Talent nodes are important for organizational creativity and flexibility. They provide opportunities for talented people to demonstrate aptitudes that may not have been apparent in previous roles. They also provide a reason for talented people to stay with the organization. But they come with risks. People in talent nodes may make more mistakes as they experiment and learn. They can also become more aware of the contrast between their current hothouse environment and the more plodding, bureaucratic culture of the larger organization, so transition back into the organizational mainstream poses major retention challenges. The solution is often to move them to roles where they still have a high level of freedom to operate in creative ways.

Summary

As I write this chapter, by coincidence I have on my side table an article examining a range of new solutions for improving the efficiency of generating electricity from wave power. The conclusion is that solutions based on simple up-and-down motion have limited potential to deliver energy at anywhere near the cost per megawatt of traditional land-based power generation. Fortunately, this rather staid and unexciting area of technology is being addressed by radical innovations, some of which are designed to operate under the surface. The comparison is apt, I suggest. If HR and the senior leadership want to tap into the creativity and energy of talented people, they must find radical solutions in place of limited-efficiency up-and-down models. Part of the return on this investment of creative thinking will be that, just as waves tend to drag along anything in their way, so the Talent Wave will impart some of its vast energy to other, less talented people and increase their performance too.

CASE STUDY Tetley

Tetley is a UK subsidiary of India's Tata Group. It takes a very pragmatic perspective on its talent development and succession planning processes. Says head of learning and development Alison Jenks:

'Succession planning here is bottom up, not top down. We focus on talent, not on jobs. The idea is for the Operations Board to surround themselves with people better than themselves. Each talent pool member owns their own action plan and development plan. They are encouraged to shape jobs around themselves – their talents and their development needs.

'The Executive Board challenges and signs off on each others' nominations for the talent pool – it's a form of peer appraisal for them, as well. For everyone on the list, we ask "What's the key development need for this person?" For example, are they interested in achieving a leadership role as well as being good at their job? Or, can they continue to develop their influencing skills cross-functionally? We have the advantage that we are small enough to know our talented people well.

'We've also defined what our talent pool is not: Going to drift into increasing numbers; dull; cumbersome; or creating prima donnas.'

Critical conversations

08

> In a very real sense, a business is the sum of a thousand everyday conversations.
> (Winter and Jackson, 2009)

In the previous chapters, my focus has been largely on the problems with traditional approaches to succession planning and talent management. However, I have at the same time hinted at potential solutions, lying in the nature and quality of the conversations that take place. In the majority of organizations, the greater part of activity is not about making things, but in having conversations. These conversations may take many forms. They may be easy or difficult; shallow or deep and meaningful; highly focused or wide-ranging and exploratory. They may involve debate (a win–lose, or lose–lose option), discussion (which leads to compromise) or dialogue (which tends to lead to discovery, new meaning and unexpected solutions).

In my work on coaching and mentoring, a useful framework has been the seven levels of conversation. Not included in this definition of a conversation is the transactional task of just giving instruction – to be a genuine conversation, there must be a two-way exchange and some level of either debate, discussion or dialogue. The first level of conversation is *social*. Social dialogue is vital for building all the elements of rapport, and particularly trust, which in turn depends in large part on a sense of shared values and mutual positive regard. *Technical* dialogue is built around sharing information needed to get tasks done. It requires clarity, asking questions and checking understanding. *Tactical* dialogue is more complex, requiring participants to examine and evaluate different options. *Strategic* dialogue explores a wider range of options and develops scenarios around them. Dialogue for *self-insight* shifts the perspective from the external to the internal and addresses issues such as being aware of personal values and understanding one's strengths and weaknesses. This insight is essential for effective dialogue about *behavioural change* – making and implementing plans for personal evolution. Finally, *integrative* dialogue (sometimes called transpersonal) examines deeper questions about personal identity and awareness of one's role as part of the human system.

All of these dialogues are important in succession planning and talent management. Social dialogue is essential for building connections and relationships. High performers tend to have much wider and higher quality social networks than their peers. HR can encourage and assist people to build and maintain social networks; for example, in several companies I have worked with we have created informal market spaces, where new recruits can develop their social networks and learn about jobs elsewhere in the organization. HR can also use the scope and quality of an employee's social networks as an indicator that they are a potential member of the Talent Wave.

Technical dialogue is essential in acquiring skills and expertise. Some companies, such as IBM, support their talented employees by rewarding knowledge holders for transferring their expertise. One of the observable characteristics of highly effective managers is that they are precise about the skills and knowledge they need to acquire and they aim to acquire it in the most efficient way. Talking to someone who knows is a lot more efficient in most cases than going on a course, much of which will not be immediately relevant.

Tactical dialogue plays a significant role in career conversations. What projects will help me gain the specific experience and track record I need? What's the best time to move employer, if I want to have a baby in the next two years? What specifically can I learn from my current boss? Will the job with less pay in the short term give me better prospects in the medium term? The problem for many employees is who they can have this conversation with. Their boss may or may not be helpful, but tactical decisions often require perspectives from people who are knowledgeable but not involved.

Strategic dialogue comes much closer to our recurrent theme of aligning employee and employer ambitions and needs. The more uncertainties there are in the system (and, as we have seen, succession planning and career management are full of uncertainty), the more important strategic dialogue becomes. But strategies need to be grounded in relevant data and perspectives. The term 'strategy' derives from the Greek for a general – someone who sees a situation from a vantage point (ie a perspective from which an advantage can be gained). Succession planning and career management both suffer from lack of information. The more that dialogue can inform employees about scenarios of potential opportunity and inform employers about shifting capabilities and aspirations of employees, the easier alignment becomes.

Dialogue for personal insight is equally important for career management and succession planning. Raising people's awareness of their strengths, weaknesses, values and motivations helps them make better career choices. When they are able to share these insights, it helps the company determine what roles will allow them best to express and develop their talents.

Behaviour change is a necessary precursor to a shift into the next layer of the leadership pipeline. If the person still thinks and behaves the way they did in a lower level role, they have probably carried fatal flaws into their new role. For behaviour change to take effect and be sustainable, it's important that both the individual and those around them adapt – and that requires continuing, honest dialogue. A while ago I started collecting personal cases of managers, who had been on a 'sheep-dip' (two- or three-day course) to learn coaching skills. Most had been keen to try out these new behaviours on their direct reports. Most also reverted to their old behaviours within three days. The problem was that they and their teams were a system, and systems respond to change by trying to return everything to the way it was. The solution was to replace the manager as coach programme with one to build a coaching culture within the team as a whole, where everyone was switched on to making coaching work. If the manager needed subsequent coaching skills training, it was much more specific and was accepted by the team system as reinforcing behaviours.

Integrative dialogue becomes increasingly important as the person gets closer to the top of an organization. It supports their maturing and the development of more perceptive, holistic ways of thinking and behaviours. The question, 'What is your life purpose?' seems to have more power and relevance (and urgency!) as people mature.

By and large, conversations in organizations tend to place more emphasis on technical and tactical dialogue than on any other form. Yet all are important in making the most effective use of the people resource and especially in retention, employee engagement, performance management and, of course, succession planning.

The importance of good questions

When I encounter an organization in difficulty, I rarely find that people have a shortage of good answers to the problems it faces. What are mostly lacking is good questions – questions that stimulate insight, provoke reflection and lead either to better answers or, more often, to a clearer understanding of why a particular answer is better than others. A standard coaching question, of course, is: 'So what's the question you know you should be asking about this issue, but haven't?'

In succession planning, charts and forms can be very helpful in focusing thinking, but the downside is that they tend also to limit thinking and hence the kind of questions that are asked. There is a strong role to play in the succession planning process for the person, who – in true coaching style – can interject the kind of question that opens up the conversation. Consider, for example, the contrast between:

- 'Is he ready for promotion?' versus 'What would allow her to contribute much more where she is?'
- 'Who could fill this role in six months time?' versus 'Why do we need this role at all? Is it time to rethink it?'
- 'Which box does she belong in on the grid?' versus 'Why would anyone that talented stay with this company?'

- 'What's the next stretch role for this person?' versus 'What will they leave behind for someone else to clear up?'

The challenge imposed by good questions can transform conversations about careers and succession planning, from the discourse between a mentor and a mentee about career choices, to strategic manpower planning.

Critical conversations for succession planning

Having good questions isn't enough, however. They have to be offered at the right time, in the right environment. Or to put it another way, they belong in the context of critical conversations.

By critical conversations I mean dialogues that have the power to create radical shifts in understanding. For many HR professionals, I have found that this concept of critical conversations resonates well with the shift that they see is needed in the mindset for succession planning. From dozens of interviews with HR professionals a picture has emerged of four critical conversations, which play a role in the engagement between company and employee, in the context of career management and succession planning (Table 8.1).

TABLE 8.1 Four types of critical conversation

	Internal dialogue of employee	Systemic dialogue of employee with immediate stakeholders	Employee/ organizational dialogue	Social networking dialogue
Process	Self-reflection: - Connection with personal values - Creation of sense of personal direction and momentum - Expressions of aspirations - Identification of roadblocks	- Reflective conversations with the work team - Reflective conversations within the family	- Macro-conversations (with employees generally) - Micro-conversations (with employees individually)	- Conversations within the profession - Conversations with peers in other professions - The organization and the individual have separate conversations with the external world

TABLE 8.1 *continued*

	Internal dialogue of employee	Systemic dialogue of employee with immediate stakeholders	Employee/ organizational dialogue	Social networking dialogue
Support required	• Self-development training • Coaching/ mentoring	• Time and space for reflective dialogue	• Career forums • Formal annual or bi-annual development/ career management conversations	• Encouragement to make wider, more creative links with the external world
Critical issues	• Level of self-awareness • Level of ambition	• Psychological safety	• Psychological safety • Changing business strategy/priorities • Business agility vs employee agility	• Organizational boundaries • Loyalty • Redefinition of employee engagement • Linking the organization's and individual employee's dialogues with the outside world

Critical conversation one: internal

The first of these conversations takes place internally, within the individual employee. This internal dialogue is about working out what the person wants from their working life, how they plan to achieve it, what they value, what they are drawn to and what they want to avoid, what gives them a sense of self-worth and what doesn't, what plays to their strengths and what renders them ineffective, and so on. It's not about defining a specific, narrow career path – therein lies disappointment, especially in working environments where the rationale for job roles may change almost overnight. It is more about achieving a sense of self, of clarifying both work purpose and life purpose, and how these can be aligned in terms of a 'best practical fit'.

This kind of intimate, self-aware dialogue requires a high level of reflection and introspection, which may be outside the experience or competence of many employees. One of the most valuable resources in this respect is the availability of skilled coaches or mentors, who can help the employee to develop career-related self-awareness by providing a role model and through the use of penetrating questions, such as:

- What is your contract with yourself?
- What is the critical, benchmark question you use to test difficult alternatives in work and career decisions?
- When new job opportunities arise, what values will you apply to assess whether they are right for you at this time?
- Are the career options you envisage likely to open up horizons of opportunity or narrow them?
- Who do you want to become?

A particularly valuable transition, with which coaches and mentors can help, occurs when the employee learns to distinguish between those inner voices that are truly themself, and those that belong to childhood authority figures. Choosing their own values provides employees with a more balanced and emotionally intelligent foundation for their ambitions.

An aspect of the internal conversation that has received relatively little study is ambition. A brief search on Google Scholar leaves the impression that most of the literature on ambition: (1) sees ambition as a negative trait; and (2) is concerned with politics. Yet ambition is a necessary element in the make-up of a leader. The most effective leaders are not so much ambitious for themselves as for a cause, a group or simply an idea. A working definition we have created is that ambition is the 'concurrence of enthusiasm and will to achieve'. Organizations need to encourage employees to sculpture and shape their ambitions, in a context of self-awareness. Rather than attempt to subordinate individual ambitions to an organizational goal, employers should seek ways in which the organization can become exciting opportunities for talented individuals to express and pursue their ambitions. In this symbiotic relationship, the organization seeks less to exploit than to create the conditions where it can be exploited to mutual benefit. This is simultaneously the epitome of the entrepreneurial society and the antithesis to the rapacious organization.

People differ widely in the extent, nature and focus of their ambition, with culture and gender playing a significant role in these variations. The typical succession planning scenario sees ambition in a very constrained context (onward and up) and from a top-down perspective. Tomorrow's succession planning will need to encourage people to develop and express their sense of personal ambition according to their own values and rules; and to recognize and value and seek to integrate corporate ambitions with this much richer and more varied menu of ambitions.

Critical conversation two: employee and their stakeholders

The second conversation or dialogue takes place between the individual employee and the people around them. These might be their boss, their spouse, their colleagues, and so on. Each has a stake in the employee's success and how they achieve their personal goals. And each can be instrumental in helping the employee do so. However, these conversations often either don't happen at all, or can be stilted, unproductive affairs.

While attention in career planning tends to focus on the big changes, such as promotions, or being given new significant responsibilities in the current job role, the micro-changes and micro-opportunities also have a role to play. Small tasks, such as deputizing for a colleague at a meeting, or observing the team leader working with more senior managers, have a massive cumulative effect in making people promotable. In a study of career pathing I carried out in the early 1990s, one of the observations was that people's progress into the next level of the hierarchy was often very gradual. In general, they had absorbed and demonstrated competence in most of the additional skills needed for the next job role before a position at that level was offered to them.

The implication of this in terms of succession planning is that there should be clarity within the work team and between the team and its leader about the ambitions and broad career direction for each employee. Rather than annual or six-monthly performance and career discussions, there should be continuous dialogue around core questions such as:

- What will take this team closer to where it wants to go?
- What will take each employee closer to where he or she wants to go?
- What can we do together to ensure an appropriate mixture of routine tasks and stretch tasks?
- What learning can each team member assist colleagues with?
- What opportunities can we identify that will assist any (or all) of us to build career-relevant experience and expertise?

A pragmatic process that can support this is the Team Development Contract. Everyone in the team, including the leader, shares his or her career ambitions. Regular team conversations – perhaps once every two months – examine the detail of the learning and experience each team member needs to acquire, to progress towards their career and personal development goals; and what opportunities might arise in the foreseeable work tasks to support them.

Unfortunately, conversations about career issues don't happen anywhere near as often as they should. A study by Winter and Jackson (2009) found, for example, that a third of employees didn't have any conversations with their manager, or HR or anyone else in their company, about their future development and that there were significant 'conversation gaps' on a number of other areas of importance to employee sense of direction and engagement. The study concludes that annual or six-monthly appraisals are ineffective in this context, saying: 'It is not reasonable to rely on a single formal process at a fixed time to close the conversation gap.' It also found that the conversation gap was associated with a threefold increase in intention to leave.

Critical conversation three: wider organization and employees

The third set of conversations occurs between the wider organization and the employees. Employees in the 'Talent Wave', particularly at middle and senior management levels, tend to be regarded as belonging to the organization rather than to a department or division. Regular conversations with 'godfathers' (more senior managers, out of the reporting line, who take a long term responsibility for steering the careers of a group of more junior managers)[1] are a pragmatic way of ensuring that the Talent Wave members have the opportunities they require to move around and build a track record. A downside is that when godfathers leave, they are excellent recruitment officers for their new employer. An alternative approach is to build the quality of conversation with the Talent Wave collectively. For example, the company can expose them to thinking about the psychological contract and how the organization can capitalize on the talent within it.

Like societies in general, organizations are influenced by 'memes'. (A meme can be described as 'an idea with attitude' – a concept or theme that spreads and stimulates change without necessarily being promoted deliberately.) Memes may originate within or outside the boundaries of the organization. They affect how the organization allocates resources, what skills and experience it values in the moment and what leaders perceive to belong to the past, present and future. These powerful ideas only gradually become apparent, even to the leaders. To most people in organizations, including the Talent Wave, emergent memes are fleeting shadows until someone in authority captures and formalizes them. By that time, career-critical decisions are likely already to have been made and the meme may already be at or past its peak of influence.

An alternative approach is to engage the entire Talent Wave in searching for and identifying memes and making them relevant, at both an individual and organizational level. Leaders and followers – particularly if they are from different generations – will see emergent ideas from different perspectives, so conversations between leaders and the Talent Wave that simply share ideas and explore their potential career developmental implications have the potential to make the organization and its people far more agile in their response to change. Forums for these conversations may include online communities of interest, 'ideas fairs' or regular 'what if' breakfasts. The key is that they open up new thinking about opportunities (and traps) for both employees and the organization.

But why stop at the Talent Wave? If the organization and its needs for talent are constantly evolving, doesn't it make sense to engage *emergent talent* in these conversations as well? Emergent talent is the reservoir of able people in the organization who have either not declared their ambition, or who have not yet been recognized as being in the Talent Wave. Figure 8.1 suggests two places where such talent may be hidden: people who have high but narrow performance; and people who perform less well but have greater breadth. Either may be motivated to become a 'star', with the right opportunities, support and encouragement. Given that the greatest impediment to an employee's performance and motivation may be their line manager, this third level of conversation becomes massively important in sustaining and expanding the Talent Wave – especially in the context of diversity.

This reasoning suggests a very different perspective on how the Talent Wave might be defined and supported. Agile organizations have much in common with self-organizing systems (think ant colonies or the internet). Rather than expend vast amounts of energy trying to identify who the most talented individuals or 'high potentials' are, often with questionable results, organizations might do better to create the conditions and support structures where talent can emerge – in the quirky, often surprising and unpredictable way that seems to be so much more effective than systems based on rigid frameworks or rules. If everyone has roughly equal opportunity to

FIGURE 8.1 Breadth versus quality of performance

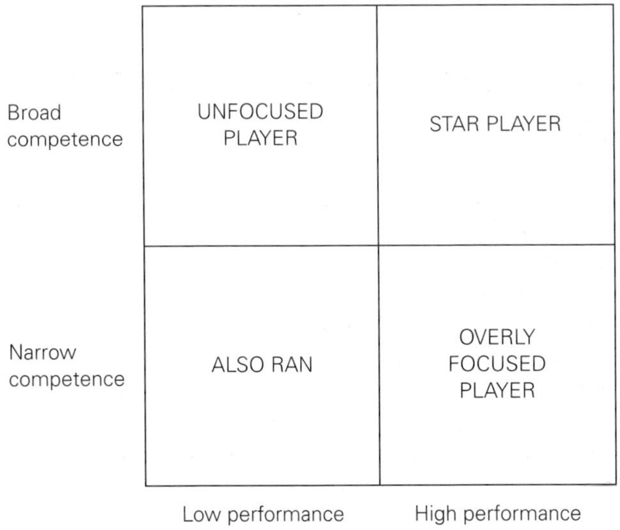

	Low performance	High performance
Broad competence	UNFOCUSED PLAYER	STAR PLAYER
Narrow competence	ALSO RAN	OVERLY FOCUSED PLAYER

access support and build a track record (defined as experience, expertise and reputation), then what counts is what they do with the opportunity. One way of establishing the Talent Wave is therefore to distinguish between those employees who seize and shape opportunities and are instrumental in the creation of career and succession planning strategy (who engage with the dialogue and act upon it); and all those other employees who are simply beneficiaries of the first group's initiative. What happens currently, in most organizations, is that high potentials are identified through a variety of more or less arbitrary methods, before being exposed to a higher level of opportunity than other employees. This not only creates a self-fulfilling prophecy in terms of track-record-based succession planning, but also raises an additional barrier for emergent potential. Anecdotal evidence suggests that much emergent potential responds to being left out of the talent pool by using the very initiative and competence they are not perceived to possess – in finding jobs elsewhere, where their talent will be appreciated!

Simple changes by an organization can have a remarkable impact in engaging the 'non-hypos' in the career and self-development dialogue. A financial services organization, now absorbed into one of the mega-corporations to the extent that its identity and individuality is entirely lost, encouraged every employee to talk about their dreams. Through workshops and structured conversations, employees articulated a wealth of ambitions in both their work and private lives that the company was unaware of. Everyone received a 'dream catcher' at the end of the workshop, to remind them of their dream and to question themselves from time to time: 'Is this helping me fulfil my dream?' The idea that the company genuinely wanted to help them achieve these ambitions was an eye-opener to many employees. Helping them to establish 'What's stopping you?' and giving them permission to build their ambitions into their personal development plans freed up employees to reveal and exploit latent talent.

Critical conversation four: between social networks

The fourth area of conversation bridges two social networks: that between the organization and the outside world; and that between the individual employees and the outside world. Organizations talk to each other, to professional bodies, and government agencies exploring macro-issues of technology, labour markets, globalization, competition, and so on. What seeps through to conversations with employees is typically filtered, anodyne and of little practical use in career management, other than as a very broad backcloth. Individuals talk to peers in their profession, to social networks and to other employers. Again, what gets shared with their employer is heavily filtered.

Some years ago I asked UK and European HR directors what proportion of their employees who left had actively looked internally for their next job. Most had no idea, but the handful of companies that did some rough and ready investigation produced estimates ranging from one in three to one in seven. The exceptions were companies which had enabled employees to register an interest in jobs outside their department without the knowledge and approval of their current line manager, and which actively encouraged moving around within the organization. In the 15 or so years since, the opportunities for people to look externally for their next job have increased greatly. Employer organizations, in general, have failed to keep up. Knowledge workers, in particular, may belong to a wide range of networks – communities outside the organizational boundaries – that open up direct and indirect links with many potential employers.

Bringing these two conversations together can be highly beneficial for both organizations and employees. For example, Cancer Research has found great value in expanding its concept of employee from people currently on the payroll or under contract to anyone in the medical research profession, including alumni (people who used to be employed there) and potential employees of the future. Whenever existing staff travel, they are encouraged to meet and engage with this wider circle of colleagues. This builds Cancer Research's brand as an employer and encourages potential employees with good ideas to bring them to Cancer Research, if their current employer is not interested.

Contrast this with what happens in so many other organizations. The employee who quits – especially to join a competitor – is cast as a traitor both to the organization and to their colleagues. HR's role becomes one of damage limitation. A less paranoid reaction may be to regard defections as a mutual opportunity. If employees learn new skills and gain different or wider experience elsewhere, they are potential future valuable rehires and it makes sense to keep in touch with them. (A cynic might also say that companies should encourage their least effective employees to seek jobs with the competition. If the company's evaluation of them was accurate, that is a source of competitive advantage; and if they really were talented, and the new employer can bring that talent to the surface, then they are also a potential rehire.)

Some other ideas for improving communication between employee and organizational social networks conversations include:

- Virtual symposia on careers in an industry or profession. By making these open access, the company can educate its own employees, identify potential talent elsewhere and adapt people strategies to take advantage of the wider employee resource.
- Second Life and similar virtual environments. Encouraging current employees and outsiders to come together in virtual project teams, where they can combine expertise to create and exploit new ideas and products.

Other practical approaches include building communities of practice: networks specifically aimed at building individual and organizational competence in areas where the business's and employees' interests align, or can be *imagined* to align. (Although I was once a strong fan of the dogma 'Make the business case', it has become increasingly obvious to me that, in some circumstances, seeking a clear business outcome tends to weed out radical ideas and block the progress of beneficial memes. When we lose the capacity to support and explore what is merely interesting, we limit our capacity to respond to environmental change in a timely manner.) Letting these communities and the people within them follow their instincts and interests, on the basis that ideas of commercial and career interest will emerge and converge, creates environments where resourceful employees will find ways to exploit them to corporate advantage. Communities of interest can also be valuable resources for career mobility by providing the seeds of new projects and initiatives. A key role for HR is to facilitate the creation of such learning communities, and to equip people with the skills to use them. Indeed, it can be argued that a core competence for all leaders and Talent Wave members in organizations of the future is to lead in these virtual communities as well as in their own relatively narrow areas of responsibility.

Open dialogue, which crosses the boundaries between the organization and the outside world, has its risks, of course. But it also has tremendous advantages – not least that it increases organizational agility. And it reflects the reality of career related conversations in a wired world.

A strategy for career and succession planning conversations

Whatever approach a company takes to succession planning or an individual takes towards their career planning, it becomes in the end an exercise in balancing risk and opportunity. For organizations, the more they emphasize the risk management perspective, the more they attempt to control and the less honest and meaningful the conversations that take place, at all four levels. For individuals, the more risk-averse they are in career choices, the narrower the range of opportunities that open up for them. In the medium to long term, the greatest risk lies in the failure to have sufficient conversations about career and succession planning issues. The greatest opportunity may lie in linking these conversations into a coherent strategy, which enables companies and their employees to coordinate the evolution of their thinking and planning about career management.

Unfortunately, organizations in general aren't particularly good at dialogue. Discussion, debate and transactional communication skills are much more deeply embedded into day-to-day practice. Over four decades of exploring dialogue in the workplace, my personal observation is that there are several reasons why there is so little emphasis on dialogue:

- lack of skills (dialogue is more intellectually and emotionally demanding);
- lack of opportunity (meeting schedules and processes typically preclude dialogue); and
- fear (because dialogue stimulates insight and change).

Some of the practical ways which our research so far suggests may increase the quality and quantity of dialogue include:

- greater emphasis on coaching and mentoring, both internally and externally resourced, which builds the skills of dialogue and raises all sorts of career-related issues (both specific to the individual and more general to groups within the organization), that might otherwise remain hidden;
- building on 360-degree feedback to engage a wider audience in the developmental planning and support for managers and leaders;
- creating forums where the organization and groups of employees can explore openly the succession planning processes and their impacts – making the succession planning process something that is done *with* employees rather than *to* them.

I am not suggesting here that increased dialogue on its own will be a panacea for organizations' succession planning woes. We need in addition better systems of talent identification, support and reward; and more effective links between succession planning and the day-to-day functioning of the organization. I am encouraged, however, by the increasing willingness I find to discuss these issues, and that leads me to believe that better ways to align organizational and employee career ambitions will emerge over the next decade.

Note

1 Godfathers are different from mentors in that they are tasked with taking action to free up members of the Talent Wave held back by line managers who don't want to lose a valuable resource from their teams. They are much more akin to sponsors, although they may also be expected to operate impartially, and their primary responsibility is towards finding the best solutions for the business, rather than for the employee.

Conversation 1: the inner dialogue

09

We understand that you can't transform people, who don't have internal drive and desire to create. But we also know it doesn't work to urge people to think outside the box without giving them the tools to climb out.

(Laurie Dunnavant)

This chapter seeks to address two questions:

- What kind of conversations do people need to have within themselves (internally) to be well equipped to navigate careers in a complex, adaptive system?
- How can organizations help them to have these conversations?

In a structured and ordered society, where everyone knew their place and little changed over centuries, people had a relatively clear sense of where they were, where they could go, who they were and even why they were. In a society that is mobile in almost every way imaginable, that certainty is absent.

In career terms, there has never been so much choice for talented people. But choice brings its own problems. For some people, who researchers label maximizers, making the right choice is of great importance and they invest much time and emotional energy in considering, or agonizing over, many of the choices they make, both before and after they make them (Simon, 1993; Schwartz, 2004). In contrast, satisficers are content with solutions that are 'good enough'. They make choices and move on without regrets. Maximizer mindsets are associated with increased stress and risk of burnout at work.

In career terms, maximizers tend to compare their own career progress against that of people they see as peers; satisficers are more likely to use internal benchmarks of progress. Most of us have a little of both in our personality, and the side we emphasize may vary according to situation. For employers, it is beneficial that talented employees have healthy, balanced and insightful conversations with themselves about career issues. Otherwise it is difficult, if not impossible, to have open, honest and informed career conversations between employees and the organization.

Given that people differ considerably in their ability to have these inner conversations, and that the kind of inner conversation they have will be influenced by their existing mindset, it's important that organizations both recognize and try to capture the diversity of such conversations taking place. How does the way people think about themselves and their careers vary? Are there clear subgroups of employees, which have a distinctive mindset about these issues? What mindsets are likely to be most helpful in career self-management, within the culture of this organization?

Equipping people with the skills to make their inner dialogue more effective seems an obvious step, but it's far from normal practice. Even better is to have a coherent strategy for raising the quality of the internal career conversations. Such a strategy would include training, monitoring and practical support. Some existing processes may already provide aspects of this strategy. For example, coaches and mentors support the quality of thinking in employees' inner conversations, and provide perspectives and information of which they may not have been aware – although this may not be a core expectation of the developmental relationship.

Managing the inner dialogue

One of the downsides of the electronic revolution is that it has reduced the time and opportunity people have for quiet reflection. In many organizations, it is only the most senior employees who are trusted to work at home, free from interruptions and free to step back and observe. An exercise I have undertaken in hundreds of workshops and seminars is to explore with people where they do their real thinking. People talk of thinking when, for example, they drive home, walk the dog or are preparing to sleep – but hardly anyone expects to do any deep, significant thinking at work!

When people do have time to think, it tends to be about relatively urgent issues. Longer-term issues, such as personal career planning, by their nature are not urgent. Only when the person approaches a career transition point – for example, rising dissatisfaction with their current role, or a new opportunity, such as a call from a headhunter – do they turn their minds to thinking about career planning; and by then it is too late to undertake the depth of reflection needed for quality decision making.

But it's not just the lack of time that impoverishes people's thinking about their careers. It's also lack of skills – skills of reflective practice generally and skills more specifically in how to structure the inner dialogue on career planning. For the Talent Wave especially, it must pay to equip them with these skills, and some organizations, such as Atkins (see the case study at the end of this chapter) are doing just that. But anyone can become more effective in career-related reflection, if they have:

- Reflective space – not just quiet time, but a quiet environment, in which they can concentrate. Energetic activity, such as being on a treadmill at the gym, is not a bar to reflection. For many people, this is one of their most productive times for thinking about what we call SUIs (Significant Unresolved Issues).

- The right powerful questions to stimulate creative thinking.
- 'Authentic intent' – the willingness to address issues openly, to learn about oneself and to challenge one's current assumptions.

In my work with people at all levels in organizations, I have found that three foci are particularly helpful in the inner conversation:

- Self-awareness (this includes reflection on identity and values, self-belief and self-motivation).
- Environmental awareness (What is going on around me and how do I relate to it?).
- Purpose (What do I want to achieve for myself and others? Who do I want to become?).

Together, these three foci create a rounded picture of the person, their perception of their own potential and how they wish to contribute.

The self-awareness conversation

The words 'Know Yourself' are inscribed on the walls of the Temple of Apollo at Delphi. What they specifically meant originally, we don't know, but many martial arts traditions take the view that understanding yourself is as important as understanding your enemy. Being self-aware provides more options in addressing challenges from our environment.

Some practical ways to know yourself better include:

- Set aside quality time for quiet conversations with yourself daily. Don't confuse this with meditation, which involves clearing your mind of conscious thought. If it works, close your eyes and imagine that a younger or older you is in the chair opposite you. Start a conversation and see where it goes!
- When you have a setback or make a mistake, instead of feeling sorry for yourself, spend the time and energy analysing what happened, with a view to learning from it. Ask yourself questions such as:
  - What was my intent?
  - How prepared was I?
  - What was my state of mind?
  - What happened before the setback that made it likely (or inevitable)?
  - If this were a script, what would I change the next time a similar circumstance arises?
- Keep a diary or learning log. What did I learn about myself today? One of the tools I often guide people towards is a frustration–elation

log, where you record weekly a description of the times you have felt most in flow, and those where you have felt most frustrated. After a few weeks, you begin to notice recurring patterns of thought, behaviour and outcomes.

- Take any of the validated personality tests and aptitude tests, but don't take them too seriously. The more generic they are, by necessity the cruder they are; and the more complex a person you are, the less likely they are to represent the holistic you. The value of these instruments lies in the insights they give you into how you tend to think – and hence how you tend to behave.[1] But don't become boxed in by them (for example, 'I'm an INTJ so I'm not good at...'). You still have lots of choices in how you behave in different circumstances.
- Find powerful questions – resonant and insight-provoking – that oblige you to look internally. Consider how you answer them. Are you avoiding being honest with yourself?
- Watch and listen to videos of yourself in action.

So what do you need to know about yourself to manage your career better? Amongst the most important sources of self-insight are your strengths and weaknesses. Actually, it's more helpful to think of them as a spectrum, as in Table 9.1. Some useful questions to reflect on include:

- When do I demonstrate my strengths best? (What am I doing then that I could do more of?)
- What roles enable me to apply my strengths?
- What coping strategies do I have to compensate for my developed and emergent weaknesses? How could I improve these strategies?
- What evidence do I have for my assumptions about my strengths and weaknesses? What contrary evidence is there, which I might be ignoring?

TABLE 9.1 A spectrum of strength and weakness

	Strengths eg	Weaknesses eg
Developed	Where you are already a high performer	Fatal flaws eg self-destructive tendencies; arrogance
Emerging	Where you have some successes, but need greater knowledge, skill or consistency	Strengths you tend to overuse or use in the wrong places
Embryonic	Where you feel drawn to, but have not had opportunity to develop capability	Things you feel averse to, but have not had great exposure to

- In what ways could I reframe my weaknesses to become strengths? (For example, if I am risk-averse, in what roles would this quality be valued?)
- How would I need to change my analysis of my strengths and weaknesses, in the context of a different role? (The strengths that serve you well in the current role may be inadequate – or even a liability – in the next!)

Identity and values

Who are you? It's a simple question, but one that people find very hard to answer from an internal perspective. We tend to describe ourselves in terms of profession, nationality, ethnicity, gender, religion, family relationships, and so on – but these are essentially *what* responses, defining ourselves in the context of the external world. To begin to address *who*, we have to dig deeper, into the values that underlie our beliefs and behaviours and which shape our sense of identity.

Establishing who you are is important in deciding who you want to become. Otherwise, how do you know what you want to change?

Identity

What defines you? Who or what do you *allow* to define you? Table 9.2 is a simple way of creating an identity narrative for oneself. The words and

TABLE 9.2 Defining one's identity

I am a/the person who...	About...	With the intention/ potential/result to...
Believes	Other people	Achieve
Likes/ enjoys	Myself	Contribute
Values	Society	Make others
Aspires to	Family	Help
Desires	Friends	Influence
Thinks	Colleagues	
Impresses others as	Roles	
Supports	My team	
Is excited by	This organization	
Is drawn to		
Is good at		

phrases in each of the three columns are just suggestions – you can add others or ignore the suggestions as you wish. The key is to develop a number of sentences that capture the essence of you. As presented, the table describes current identity, but it can also be used to examine the identity you want to acquire and what that would mean in terms of relationships and outcomes.

Many people have both a personal and a professional identity. Professional identity is defined as one's professional self-concept based on attributes, beliefs, values, motives and experiences (Ibarra, 1999). An important part of the inner dialogue is to recognize and explore these identities. If there are differences between the two, what are they and what do they say about your overall identity? How do they support or undermine each other and how? Can you be truly authentic in both your personal and professional identities? Who are your role models in your personal and professional identities? What is it about these people that makes you see them as role models?

The more you understand who you are in and out of work, the more you can align your identity and your job role, and the more firmly you can ground your career and personal development strategies. Given that 'a good career allows us to attend to meaning and mattering in our lives' (Amundson, 2009), positive interaction and alignment between personal and work lives is a powerful source of self-esteem and general well-being. And the drive to create such alignment is especially strong in Gen Y. Says Christine Lloyd, former HR director of Cancer Research: 'Identity is critical to them. There's a shift towards searching for meaning in what they do. We are a major recruiter of Oxbridge graduates who want to work in social entrepreneurship. People today identify a lot more with causes rather than organizations and they are clearer about their career identity a lot earlier now.'

There are lots of ways to think about what we value and what motivates us. Most managers have come across Maslow's hierarchy of needs, for example. The Reiss Motivational Profile is a very practical way of analysing personal drives, with 16 dimensions that help to define what is important to an individual. Another, simpler approach comes from US self-development promoter Anthony Robbins, who proposes six basic needs:

1 Certainty/ comfort (comfort often comes from certainty).
2 Variety (a relatively safe antidote to certainty).
3 Significance (the search for personal meaning).
4 Connection/ love (wanting to be accepted and cared for).
5 Growth (a sense of personal progress and betterment).
6 Contribution (what we put back into the world around us).

My own work in work–life balance has focused on six life-streams (Clutterbuck, 2003):

1 Work (the job that you do now).

2 Career (which may be loosely or strongly connected to the current job – for example, an emerging author might work at a check-out to pay the bills, while he spends his spare time writing a novel).

3 Close personal relationships (friends and family).

4 Physical well-being.

5 Intellectual self-fulfilment (what we do to keep ourselves intellectually stimulated outside of work and career).

6 Spiritual and community (what we do to feel we belong and are contributing to the greater good).

Personal development planning tends to encompass only the first two of these six dimensions – at most. Bringing some or all of the other lifestreams into the development planning processes helps to create a more balanced, healthier individual. It also helps to head off some of the myopic behaviours that permit apparently normal leaders to accept or ignore corrupt behaviour in themselves or others, by giving them a wider range of contexts against which to judge behaviours and attitudes (Ermann, 1987).

The utility of all these approaches is that they provide a framework for reflecting on who you are and want to be (your identity), and what you want to achieve in your career (your purpose). There is another major upside, too. Knowing yourself – and even better, liking yourself – helps you avoid one of the major causes of becoming the wrong person at the top:

> Many leaders... develop an imposter complex, caused by deep insecurities that they aren't good enough and may be unmasked. To prove they aren't imposters, they drive so hard for perfection that they are incapable of acknowledging their failures. When confronted by them, they convince themselves and others that these are neither their fault nor their responsibility. Or they look for scapegoats to blame for their problems. Using their power, charisma, and communications skills, they force people to accept these distortions, casing entire organizations to lose touch with reality. At this stage, leaders are vulnerable to making big mistakes, such as violating the law or putting their organization's existence at risk.
> (George, 2011)

Cultivating the habit of self-honesty helps build emotional resilience and maintain authenticity.

Self-belief and self-motivation

The more confident we are in who we are, the greater our sense of self-belief and self-efficacy. Mentoring, for example, is closely associated with helping people discover and reinforce their self-belief. But while conversations with others can help us grow in self-belief, the critical conversation is internal. Table 9.3 is a very simple way of reflecting on the state of our self-belief. Once you've answered the questions honestly, you can use your reflections to have deeper conversations with a coach or mentor.

TABLE 9.3 Self-belief

I value myself for...	Other people value me for...	What prevents others valuing me in the way I want them to?	If I want to change how other people value me, how can I do that?

Self-esteem is also linked with stress (Bramston, 2008: 95), with people under 35 being prone to higher levels of esteem-reducing stress. Reflecting on the sources of stress in our lives and how we can develop more effective coping strategies can raise both ambition levels and our attentiveness to opportunities to achieve our ambitions.

Another useful framework for self-awareness is career anchors, originally proposed by Ed Schein and Thomas de Long some four decades ago. Anchors are traits corresponding to situations and roles where people feel most comfortable (ie that play to their strengths and interests). The main career anchors are:

- Technical or functional competence – most suited for people who like to become experts. They seek to be challenged to demonstrate their expertise and to do a job 'properly'.

- Managerial competence – suited to people who want responsibility, like to take charge, and enjoy problem solving and dealing with people. Emotional intelligence is an essential component (though also a capability that some people who have other aspects of managerial competence lack – making them less effective in management roles).

- Autonomy or independence – working best in situations, where they set their own standards, work pace and routines, and can get on with tasks without 'interference' from others.

- Security/stability – people who avoid risk, resist change and seek continuity.

- Entrepreneurial creativity – people who like opportunities to innovate, start up new products or businesses, and engage with others, who can help them make things happen, and often see success in terms of personal financial return.
- Dedication to a cause – motivated by being able to help others.
- Pure challenge – easily bored and often restless, these people seek constant challenge and novelty; they welcome stretch tasks.
- Lifestyle – aiming to integrate work and life, people with this trait may take large chunks of time to pursue non-work activities, such as sports or travel.

Sometimes criticized for lacking empirical support, psychometric tests based on career anchors nonetheless have a strong following and, in recent years, have been validated as a practical tool for exploring career aptitude (Steele and Francis-Smythe, 2007). However, as with most generic personality tests, they are best used as part of a portfolio of insights into individuals.

Environmental awareness

External awareness involves what might be described as external identity – how people define themselves by their social networks. It encompasses being aware of what is happening in the world around that may affect a person's well-being, status or opportunities to use their talents. And it includes having a realistic perception of one's own value.

Purpose

When we set goals for ourselves (or allow others to set them for us), what gives them meaning is a sense of larger purpose. So, for example, gaining a professional qualification is a means to achieving greater responsibility, status and more satisfying work, as well as increasing earning power. So purpose can be defined as the practical vision of achieving what we value. Purpose is also closely related to identity. It is about how we become the person we aspire to be. Purpose gives us something to focus on and against which to test alternative courses of action: will they help or hinder in achieving my purpose?

When coaching a deeply religious person a while ago, they kept avoiding the issue of purpose by returning time and again to the statement that their purpose was to serve God. What moved the conversation on was the question: 'What talents have you been given that would enable you to contribute most to that purpose? And what could you do to use those talents most effectively?'

A pragmatic way to capture your purpose is to imagine you are looking back on your career from 10 or 20 years in the future, having achieved everything you wished. What would you be most proud of? What would you have contributed for others, who you care about most? What would you have learned that gives you particular satisfaction? Then:

- What would I have to change in myself to bring this about?
- What will I have to change in the world around me (eg my support networks)?
- What can I do today to make this future more likely to happen?

Taking responsibility for your own career planning

William Rothwell (2003) suggests seven key questions that employees should ask themselves to take greater accountability for their own role in succession planning:

- What are my career goals, and how committed to them am I?
- What characteristics are necessary for success now?
- How well am I presently performing?
- What characteristics are necessary for future success?
- How can I tell what my future potential is?
- How can present and future developmental gaps be closed?
- How can I evaluate the relative success of my efforts?

There is nothing greatly original about these questions, but they provide a useful framework for structuring that part of the inner conversation which aims to convert self-knowledge, environmental knowledge and purpose into practical plans for the future. A point to note is that except for the first question, which is essentially affirmative and focusing on purpose, all these questions need conversations with others. The individual has to do some thinking and observing themselves, but a comprehensive answer can only be derived with the help of people, who can give feedback and/or provide wider sources of contextual information.

A recent *Bottom Line* programme on BBC interviewed three CEOs about the role luck had played in their success. All agreed with Thomas Jefferson's famous quip that the harder he worked, the luckier he became. All said they felt lucky and that they deeply enjoyed their work.

The CEOs presented various theories or ways of interpreting their own experience, but all amounted to either the level of attentiveness or the level of flexibility they displayed. On attentiveness, they painted a picture of constantly thinking about where they and their businesses were going. Said one: 'Work is like music that's always in your head'. On flexibility, they talked about pursuing goals obsessively for a year, then stepping back and completely remaking their plans, if needed, for the coming year. Said one: 'You have to keep your ear to the ground and seize opportunities as they arise.'

These themes are very similar to the evidence David Megginson and I have been gathering about goals within coaching. It seems that goals need to be neither too narrow nor too broad; and that a combination of attentiveness and flexibility help raise awareness of opportunities and create the will and initiative to take advantage of them.

Capturing the inner conversation

People tend to be biased more towards action than reflection, or vice versa. But both are equally important in the effective inner career conversation. Writing the inner conversation down is for many people an important step in moving from reflection to action. The three headings of self-awareness, environmental awareness and purpose make a good starting point. They provide a context against which the individual can establish a career development plan (CDP) that is relatively highly likely to be put into action, because it is embedded in their values and priorities. The CDP then addresses questions such as:

- What additional skills, knowledge and experience (track record) do I need to acquire, over what time period, to give me the career options I seek?
- What other resources do I need, such as wider or different networks, and sponsors?
- What choices am I likely to encounter over the next year, and how might these affect my career?
- How will I prepare for these choices?
- How will I measure progress?
- What are my tactics for coping with setbacks?
- Who do I need to make aware of my progress, and how will I do this?
- What else can I do to create my own luck?

Of course, the CDP is not a static document. It needs constant revision, in the light of change within the individual and their circumstances. Sharing it with other, trusted stakeholders, such as a mentor, will refine it in the light of new information and insights. As a dynamic, evolving document the CDP doesn't need to be highly detailed, with moves set out as if in a chess game. It is most effective when it is less like a road map and more like a wave front – a rolling energy surge that adapts constantly to wind and terrain. Indeed, as Herminia Ibarra at INSEAD has shown, being overly specific about next career moves is not a particularly effective strategy, because it deflects awareness away from other possibilities and opportunities (Ibarra and Lineback, 2005). The key is to ensure that you regularly evaluate and adjust the CDP in the light of your reflections in the context of self-awareness, environmental awareness and purpose.

A useful exercise is to undertake a regular SWOT analysis (Strengths, Weaknesses, Opportunities, Threats) of oneself under each of the headings of the internal dialogue.

Social context

Social context also plays a significant role in how people think about themselves and their careers. We tend to assess how well we are doing by comparing our progress against those who we regard as peers, either inside or outside an organization. People who see themselves as ahead of schedule tend to have more job moves and more positive attitudes towards work than those who feel they are falling behind. The sense of having succeeded in the past gives greater confidence in their career future (Lawrence, 2011). Other relevant aspects of social context discussed by Lawrence include that people's sense of career satisfaction is linked with how they perceive the status of their co-workers and how well networked they are (Forret and Dougherty, 2004); and that career and pay expectations are associated with how valued they think they and their work are. For the talented employee, being aware of these influences is valuable in injecting a healthy dose of realism into their career thinking.

Green, amber and red zones

Another useful way to take stock is to think of your current life and career in terms of green, amber and red zones. In the green zone are the things that are going well for you. Useful questions to consider include:

- How well do I understand why they are going well?
- What can I learn from these that will help me do better in other areas?

Amber zones are those where there are warning signs – or simply a sixth sense – that things are likely to go less well in the future. Useful questions here include:

- What are the real or potential risks here?
- What can I do now to avoid those risks?
- What would shift these things into the green?

Red zones are those where there are clearly problems now or on the horizon. Useful questions include:

- How can I prevent the worst happening?
- What can I learn about how the red situation occurred, which will help me avoid the same mistake in future?
- How can I find opportunities in these situations?

Expertise versus experience

All job roles need both expertise and experience. As they involve more and more senior levels of leadership, the breadth of both experience and expertise required widens. Failure to achieve appropriate breadth creates narrow perspectives that tend to be partial (towards what the leader is familiar with) and insufficiently linked with the external environment.

Gathering the 'right' expertise and experience requires constant openness to opportunities. It's a bit like sailing a yacht: you need to be constantly watching the wind, the waves, the sky and the horizon, but you also need some kind of compass to keep you heading in roughly the right direction. So an important part of a personal development plan is mapping current and future expertise and experience against a range of possible future job roles or career paths. It helps in this context to be clear about what expertise and experience are. Expertise is a specific combination of skills and knowledge that can be applied to definable tasks or categories of task. Experience is a combination of exposure to specific tasks or environments, and the resulting learning that you have acquired. Track record is your professional reputation as demonstrated through outcomes of your combined expertise and experience. In building this part of a personal development plan, it helps to consider questions such as:

- What additional experience and expertise can I obtain in my current job?
- What expertise and experience could I gain by joining a task force or engaging in activities outside of work?
- What experience and expertise is likely to be valued most in other roles I might aspire to?
- What expertise and experience will it be valuable for me to 'nail down' now, so I don't have to backfill from a more senior role later in my career?
- Who do I want to be noticed by, and what for?
- How can I make sure that my reputation is well founded on genuine achievements?
- How will I make sure I find time and energy for these personal development activities?

How the organization can help

There are at least three practical things that the organization can do to promote the inner dialogue:

1 Provide feedback and other opportunities for increased self-understanding.
2 Help people acquire the reflective and analytical skills required to become more self-aware and manage their own career planning.
3 Encourage and support mentoring to enhance the depth, breadth and quality of the inner conversation.

The term 'mentoring' has been co-opted to describe a variety of helping relationships, some of which overlap with 'coaching' and/or 'counselling' – both of which have a similarly rich diversity of definitions. Two models of organizationally supported or structured mentoring are particularly represented in the practitioner and academic literature:

● Sponsorship-based mentoring, which originates in and is most common in the United States, tends to be relatively directive and about gaining access to influence. Learning tends to be mainly one-way and the mentor provides protection (the recipient is referred to as a protégé). Specific expertise in a task or profession is core to the relationship.

● Developmental mentoring, which originates in Europe, is much more about helping people do things for themselves, and the quality of their thinking. It tends to be much more of a two-way learning experience, and contextual awareness is more important than awareness of a specific role. The recipient is usually called a mentee.

It can be argued that sponsorship mentoring has particular application within linear assumptions about careers and succession planning. It emphasizes following in the mentor's footsteps, opening doors, and adopting the mentor's values. Knowing the career moves a person is likely to make, a mentor can help them prepare, share learning from their own successes and failures, and help the protégé make the right connections to maintain their career progress.

Perceiving this as a somewhat anachronistic model, some organizations now separate out the mentor role from sponsorship. The modern version of a sponsor is an informed senior manager who takes on the long-term responsibility for balancing the career needs of talented individuals against the evolving needs of the business. They ensure that an appropriate range of moves is available for the individual and that the person's progress is not obstructed by line managers who want to hang on to their best people.

Developmental mentoring, under the same argument, is more readily adaptable to complex, adaptive systems. It emphasizes mutual learning, creating new, unforeseen career pathways, self-knowledge and ambiguity.

Rather than focusing closely on set paths, it is opportunistic and concerned with aligning the developing self with the developing environment.

One of the ways to describe developmental mentoring is: 'helping someone with the quality of their thinking about issues that are important to them'. Succession planning can be similarly (if more long-windedly) defined as: 'helping people with the quality of their thinking about their careers; helping organizations with the quality of their thinking about how they make best use of people resources over the medium to long term; and helping both organizations and the people in them to have constructive dialogue, with the aim of aligning aspirations'.

Mentoring currently plays a mediating role in helping the organization overcome each of these problems. The positive impact of mentoring, in particular, on retention is well documented. Developing learning relationships with role models who have achieved both senior status and a fulfilling non-work life both demonstrates what is possible and opens the debate within the organization as to how it can support different lifestyle needs of people with leader potential. The quality of dialogue in developmental mentoring permits at least some senior managers to get to know talented individuals in real depth, and to avoid superficial judgements. And some organizations which have made significant steps towards becoming coaching and mentoring cultures have begun to weed out from their talent pools those who are either not interested in developing themselves or not interested in developing others.

Mentoring has a major role to play in making succession planning deliver real value for organizations. It creates or supports conversations about careers and personal ambition that are difficult to encompass elsewhere. It broadens horizons, by helping people recognize options they had not previously considered and raising the level of their ambition. It opens windows, by helping people gain an insight and feel for functions and roles, which they have little experience of. And it opens doors, by connecting the mentee to other people and resources, potentially influential in achieving their career ambitions.

Mentors have a role in each of the four succession planning conversations. At level one, they can help the mentee better understand themselves and their motivations. As role models, they can explore what it's like, for example, to be in a more senior management role and transfer some of the thinking patterns necessary to operate at that level. By expressing belief in the mentee's ability, they also help them to set their sights higher and to achieve more, faster. At level 2, a mentor can help the mentee work out where they can find challenge in their current job role, and act as a sounding board for conversations the mentee needs to have with their boss about the work tasks they are assigned and how these can be made more stretching.

At level 3, the mentors collectively can influence how the organization understands the talent it has. Bringing mentors together to share experiences and perceptions can be a powerful way to identify issues which are blocking the effective use of talent. In one case, it led an organization to remake its succession planning strategy completely, to create two career streams. Until the feedback from mentors, the organization had not listened sufficiently attentively to a large group of employees in specialist roles, who did not want to progress through a managerial route. Other organizations have taken the path of regularly briefing mentors about how the internal career market is developing, so that mentors can use this information in helping the mentee think through their career strategy.

Engaging the mentors in this way also helps the organization think more strategically about its use of talent. Rather than focus solely on fitting talented employees into pre-set roles, the organization can also consider how it might capitalize on the qualities of the talent pool, designing job roles to fit the talent resource.

At level 4, the informal network between mentors and mentees who have now moved on to roles in other organizations is a powerful resource that deserves a lot more attention than it usually receives. One use of this resource is re-recruitment – enticing back talented people after they have added to their experience elsewhere. Maintaining the mentor–mentee relationship informally makes it easy for either party to open a conversation about new openings in the organization. Another use is to tap into former employees' social networks: who do they know, who is acquirable and has talents and experience the company needs?

The key roles a developmental mentor can play include:

- *Getting to know talent at an intimate yet objective level.* Particularly if the mentor is two or more levels more senior, their knowledge of the mentee can be invaluable in gaining a real understanding not just of what talent there is, but how willing it is to be employed in different ways. Too much succession planning assumes without evidence that employees will want to take the promotions offered to them – but if the planned move does not align with the employee's own career intentions, it can have the negative effect of either causing them to fail, or encouraging them to leave. Even if a mentor only knows a few people at lower levels with this degree of insight, collectively it helps to bridge the gap between the top-level perception of the talent pool, and the perceptions of the talent pool members themselves. Organizations where mentoring is widespread tend to have much richer conversations about how they allocate, use and develop their talent.

- *Focusing mentees' attention on internal career opportunities.* It's common for people to look outside their current organization for their next job, partly because it's easier (especially through social networking and job search websites) and partly because it avoids letting your boss and/or colleagues know that you are thinking of moving on. In the non-threatening environment of a mentoring conversation, however, it is much easier to open up about such issues. Moreover, the mentor will typically have a different and often wider perspective about opportunities for job moves than would, say, the mentee's line manager.

- *Addressing diversity issues.* Case study data reveal that having a mentoring programme, which people from minority or disadvantaged groups are encouraged to join, has a remarkable impact on the perception that people in those groups – whether mentored or not – have about their potential to advance in the organization. This has several beneficial effects. One is to encourage them to put themselves forward for promotions and projects that enhance their track record, and hence get themselves noticed. Another is to motivate them to take a stronger commitment to their own development, because the ratio of perceived effort to perceived likelihood of reward has become more positive.

- *Influencing the systems that influence succession planning.* With help and encouragement from a mentor, mentees learn how to work with, rather than in conflict with, systems such as appraisal, access to learning resources and how work is allocated. For example, mentors often help mentees identify and recognize the value of horizontal moves that build breadth of experience and expertise.

- *Managing reputation.* Sponsorship mentoring typically involves some form of active promotion on behalf of the mentee (or protégé). While this isn't encouraged in less directive forms of mentoring, there is still a great deal of room for helping the mentee acquire the skills of managing both politics and their own reputation. Given that much talent in organizations goes unnoticed, because it does not self-promote, mentoring can provide a practical way of helping people become visible and, at the same time, authentic.

- *Portfolio mentoring.* Rather than confine talented employees to just one mentor who is expected to meet all their needs, portfolio mentoring recognizes that the most talented people have the greatest need to be challenged. So they are encouraged to develop a number of simultaneous mentoring relationships for different needs. Some of these relationships may be long term, others may involve no more than two or three meetings over a relatively short period. Success factors for portfolio mentoring appear to include:
  - strong expectation of two-way learning;
  - high initial clarity of purpose for short-term relationships; moderate initial clarity for longer-term relationships;
  - a variety of distance in terms of mentor job role vis-à-vis mentee job role;
  - feedback from the mentee to the mentors, both individually and collectively;
  - recognition and articulation by the mentee of the value of the mentors' help.

One of the side-benefits of portfolio mentoring is that it builds the mentee's networks across and sometimes outside the organization; and hence facilitates cross-functional communication more generally.

- Helping the talented individual identify unconventional, less obvious moves and make the case for these. Rather than always promoting people into positions where they have strengths, it may be a much better solution to place into the position someone who has identified a weakness, which they are working on with proactivity and commitment. Again, a systemic approach is valuable here. The newly moved manager does not work in isolation. Making their success and their learning a *team* responsibility changes the whole dynamics of the situation. The coach or mentor can help them plan how to engage the team in this way; but equally, there is a requirement for the organization to create appropriate expectations in the team before the manager joins.

- Assisting the talented individual to establish better and wider networks inside and outside the organization; and to manage those networks effectively. More a mentor role than a coach role, network development can be both passive and active. In the active sense, it involves making introductions and suggesting people who the talented individual should contact. In the passive sense, it involves working with them to develop the skills of networking and managing personal credibility. Some organizations have specifically introduced mentoring programmes to help bright but unnoticed people become known, and therefore to enter the running when new opportunities arise.

- Providing a resource to reflect upon wider issues of identity, personal values and personal goals. The keys here are a safe environment in which to open up this dialogue, and the skills to maintain dialogue at a much deeper level than in most other working conversations. The payback from this investment of time is that the individual has a much deeper understanding of their motivations in taking on a new role.

- Helping the talented individual extract more value from their current role. It's very easy for the coaching or mentoring conversation to concentrate on the next job the person wants. Yet there is usually a great deal of learning in the current job, if the person knows how to look for it. It is not uncommon for mentoring to help someone who is desperate to move on recognize 'unfinished business' in their current role, and take an extra six months or so to consolidate a skill, which will prove invaluable to their subsequent career as a leader. (It also helps to prevent them gaining a reputation for always leaving their mistakes for someone else to clear up – a charge frequently lodged against fast-moving high flyers!) One of the key roles a mentor can play in helping employees think more clearly about themselves and their careers is to challenge their assumptions. In part, this is about widening their horizons and sense of self-belief, where needed. In part, too, it is about helping them recognize how unconscious biases may be holding them back. Five biases that have a major impact on leadership and decision making are:

- *Negative bias*. Negative experiences tend to have a larger impact on memory. This can lead people to avoid whole career areas on the basis, for example, of having worked alongside a really unpleasant person who had that job role.

- *Frequency bias*. The more often you hear or read something, the more likely you are to believe it is true. So 'being in sales is the route to the top' might be no more than a myth based on the career paths of a handful of individuals in the distant past. Mentors can help the employee focus on the evidence for such beliefs.

- *Recency bias*. Something you learned a short while ago will often carry more weight in decision making than information you learned long before. It's easy for people to be seduced by a novel opportunity!

- *Attachment bias*. People often opt for the status quo when they make decisions, because it feels safer and because they have emotional attachment to what they know. Employees often dismiss imaginative career moves on the basis of 'better the devil you know'.

- *Escalation bias*. When people embark on a career path, the investment they have made tends to blind them to evidence that it was a poor choice.

Because these biases are largely unconscious, it often takes someone else to point out how they are distorting our perceptions and hence our choices. The dialogue between mentor and mentee begins the process of self-challenge where the employee, having identified biases they have been applying, can choose to adopt new perspectives and beliefs which will lead to better performance and career outcomes.

Helping the employee plan their learning journey

It's a characteristic particularly of Western organizations that they invest heroic qualities in their leaders. Leaders are expected to be heroes, and when, as happens so often, they do not demonstrate heroic qualities, the sense of disappointment and disillusion can be extreme. The great mythical stories of all civilizations, from the *Odyssey* to *Star Wars* and *Lord of the Rings*, appear to follow a classic pattern of stages (Campbell, 1949) and some of these have direct relevance to the development of leaders. Joseph

Campbell's original analysis had 17 stages in the journey, but a simplified version, as presented by Simon Edwards of the Mowgli Foundation, consists of:

1 *The normal, orderly, predictable world.* For potential leaders, this includes the comfortable job and routines they know and the beliefs they have about themselves and their place in the world ('the natural order'). But this ordinary world is subject to change.

2 *The call to change.* A threat or opportunity arises that would mean discomfort and disruption. A new job opportunity or a new learning opportunity arises.

3 *Refusing the call.* 'I can't do that.' An inner conflict arises between listening to the call and stepping into the unknown or blocking it out and trying to ignore it. In Marshall Goldsmith's insightful book, *What Got You Here Won't Get You There* (2007), a recurring theme is the resistance of talented managers against even thinking about radical change in the way they think and behave. It often takes a perceived catastrophe to shake their complacency – for example, being turned down for promotion, or losing their job.

4 *Meeting the mentor.* (Surprising how often we keep coming back to mentors, isn't it?) The mentor raises their hero's level of curiosity and instils enough self-belief to encourage them to look again at the journey opening before them. They see, says Edwards, a glimpse of the person they were meant to be.

5 *Crossing the line.* Taking the step from which there is no going back. For example, agreeing to a new job role, or asking people around you for 360-degree feedback. Simon Edwards speaks of 'stepping into the real you' – a sense of leaving behind the world that you knew and stepping into the unknown that has the seeds of greater authenticity – and leaving your self-limitations behind.

6 *Trials, allies and enemies.* The hero does not know what setbacks lie ahead, though their mentor may give them some clues. Enemies are likely to arise in the guise of people who feel threatened by the changes the hero brings with him, or who resent their leadership. Enemies can also lie within, in the form of the inner voice that expresses self-doubt. Unexpected allies may also appear.

7 *Facing the darkness.* The low point, where everything is all too difficult or, worse, the hero's followers begin to despair. This is when self-belief and the support of others (such as a mentor) provide the stamina to keep going. For many would-be leaders, this is the point at which they lose heart and give up. This is especially true of those who suffer from 'imposter syndrome' – a much more common problem than is generally thought. These managers typically have a strong track record of success, yet each success heightens their sense that they have got away with it, that they

didn't deserve the praise or recognition they have received, and that they will be 'found out'. This fear of discovery can be paralysing. If these potential leaders are to realize their potential, the organization needs to recognize their symptoms and support them in developing a more 'heroic' mindset. This often requires a low-intensity psychotherapeutic intervention. In facing the darkness, heroes learn to forgive themselves, to accept and learn from their mistakes.

8 *The journey.* Change doesn't happen overnight. Even if they don't physically wander, potential leaders need time to let their conscious and unconscious minds reflect and ruminate – to wander metaphorically. In conversations with themselves and other people who exert a significant influence on their thinking, they explore new landscapes, redolent with new possibilities.

9 *A new perspective.* The result of the journey is a radical shift in perception of who you are and how you relate to the world around you. Frequently, this means re-evaluating what is important. For example, in the story of Odysseus, the hero's great learning is that honour and glory are less important than home and family. For potential business leaders, the journey may provide a new perspective on their identity, that gives them greater authenticity.

10 *The return.* A perhaps inevitable dilemma for the hero is that, while they have changed, the world they left behind may not have. Perhaps the greatest challenge facing leaders is often enabling others to share their journey and the lessons from it, but without the pain that they have endured.

Of course, the hero's journey is only a metaphor, but it does have relevance to how organizations recognize and support leadership talent. Heroes don't emerge from neat structures of management development programmes and appraisal systems; those belong in the structured, *ordinary* world and they produce managers who belong in that sheltered, unchallenging environment. Generic development programmes can't imbue people with courage, authenticity and the other critical attributes of the heroic leader. They are instruments of the status quo, not of change. So one of the fundamental challenges in the design and implementation of talent management and succession planning approaches is: 'How do we ensure that our potential leaders discover and set off on their own hero's journeys?'

A danger in taking this metaphor too far is that we forget that the heroic leader is mostly a myth. As we've explored elsewhere, effective leadership is much more a collective activity than the preserve of a single, charismatic individual. Indeed, when we follow the heroic stories, in most cases there is a band of heroes – the story simply follows from the perspective of one of them. So members of the Talent Wave and their supporters need to be mindful that great things are accomplished when many energetic people work in concert.

Summary

The internal dialogue is an essential precursor to effective career management. HR can't have this conversation for people, but it can help them by giving them skills of reflection and information to build into their understanding of themselves and their context. It can also encourage conversations, such as in mentoring and coaching, which stimulate reflection. The result should be that the Talent Wave are better equipped to engage in dialogue and negotiation with their bosses and other people who have influence over their careers.

CASE STUDY Interview with Brian Fitzgerald, HR Director

Atkins is a UK-based multinational engineering company, specializing in large-scale civil and mechanical engineering projects. 'Conversations in development' have been a core feature of the company's talent management and succession planning processes for some years and are perceived by top management to have played a substantial role in a consistent above average score in the annual employee engagement survey and a prominent place near the top of the UK 100 best companies to work for. They also appear to be behind positive feedback to HR about the quality and appropriateness of new appointments to key positions.

Nonetheless feedback, recognition and involvement – three indicative measures for coaching culture – remain the three lowest scores out of the 10 measures of engagement, (albeit that they are also higher than for the majority of comparator companies). The problem, says HR director Brian Fitzgerald, is that 'managers don't naturally confront in developmental conversations. We've been addressing this through a course at Henley, focusing on the quality of these conversations. It's also asking a lot of a typical manager to spot talent – it's not what they've been trained to do.'

Mechanistic methods are out

Atkins has rejected many standard talent management and succession management tools on the basis that they don't work. For example, says Fitzgerald: 'We don't have talent pools or a leadership model. Talent pools aren't helpful. You have to tell one employee they are in and their colleague they are not. This creates a divide and expectations that may not be fulfilled – so you lose both those who are disappointed at not being selected and those who are disappointed at not progressing fast enough. Then you also find that the qualities of the people in the talent pool meet changes in what the company needs... The only benefit of a talent pool is that it helps you focus expenditure.

'I don't have in my top drawer a picture of what Atkins' leadership will need to be like in the future. I don't measure people and put a template of them over that picture. Because I don't know what those needs are going to be.

'We've almost banned the word competency. When you produce a large matrix of competencies, it's out of date immediately; it requires an army of people to maintain it; and when you have measured everyone against it, you are left with the problem of what you are going to do with that information.

'I have a nightmare in which there's an orderly queue of people outside my door, saying "I've ticked all your boxes, now promote me!" And I have to look them in the eye and tell them they are still not suitable for the next job.' Instead, a 'career framework' with links to a training portfolio provides guidance around indicative skills, and the basis for a much broader, individually customized developmental conversation.

'For me the best appraisal conversations are without any paper at all. But our managers needed a scale of some sort. So now our performance and development review form has a three-point scale. Some managers want it to be five or seven points, so I ask them "What will you do with that information?" and they can't tell me. They want it because it makes them feel comfortable and because they wouldn't have to think or have a really open conversation with the direct report.'

Development centres as a source of dialogue

Atkins divides its leadership and professional staff into three broad strata for development and succession planning purposes: senior management; middle management; and graduate recruits and junior managers. For the middle level, management development centres provide valuable information about the individual employee's qualities and aptitudes. The process includes relatively standard assessment exercises, an interview with an occupational psychologist, 360-degree feedback and help in creating a personal development plan. Participants then have to present their plan to a senior management audience of their choice as a draft bid for developmental support and engage in a dialogue around the findings.

This element of dialogue is critical in gaining buy-in from both the participants and the organization. 'Some of those nominated don't receive as good a report as they expect', says Fitzgerald. 'So we wanted to see if that was having an effect on retention. Only two per cent of the 2000 people who have been through the development centre have left the organization in the subsequent year compared with double digits turnover for employees in general. The reason the process works is not the content of the development centre, nor the process, but the quality of conversation and engagement between the employee and the organization.'

Developmental dialogue for senior managers

With development centres working so well at middle and junior levels, the contrast of opportunities for senior managers was stark. Fitzgerald found himself having frequent conversations with senior managers about whether or not they were considered for particular promotions and what they would have to do to be considered in the future. He explains: 'We needed to give people time to reflect, to teach them to have in-depth conversations with their bosses about their own careers. And, of course, to have similar conversations with their direct reports, about their careers and development. We also needed to stop having developmental conversations in business silos. These conversations needed to result in mutually agreed personal development plans that emphasized the importance of stretching experiences rather than training courses. They needed to involve forcefield analysis, to help people understand why they are where they are; and to engage people in discussion about reputation and their current standing in the organization.'

Facilitated by Henley Business School, the intensive two-day events for cohorts of 10 to 12 senior managers begin with 360-degree feedback and psychometrics. Each participant receives two coaching sessions during the workshop, to help them develop their personal development plan, and two subsequent sessions as they try to implement it. The executive team provides an overview of where the company is going and the kind of career opportunities which might result.

Breaking the career silos

A continuing problem for Atkins has been that talented employees pursue moves to other parts of the business for which they are not suited, because they perceive that these provide faster routes to the top. The result has been that appointments fail or people struggle in roles that do not play to their strengths. The solution, at least in part, has been to establish three distinct career routes: project management, technical and business management. Developmental conversations increasingly focus on what contributions people can make in specific roles and on how to help people navigate across the three streams, or up the stream they are in. Equalizing recognition and reward at the same point in each stream reduces the motivation to take on inappropriate roles, just to get higher pay.

Note

1 A personality type from the Meyers–Briggs inventory.

Conversation 2: stakeholder dialogue

> Change happens by listening and then starting a dialogue with the people who are doing something you don't believe is right.
>
> (Jane Goodall, scientist and author of *My Life with the Chimpanzees*)

The environment in which an employee works has a major impact on their intention to stay and how they approach their career self-management. It shapes their ambition by raising their self-esteem and sense of self-efficacy; their choices, for example in terms of seeking or avoiding risk; their performance, and hence their reputation. The organization and the employee have a shared responsibility to engage in conversations, which will enable the employee to contribute to their full and to grow.

This chapter sets out to answer two questions:

- How can employees and their line managers have open, honest and informed conversations about issues such as potential, performance and careers?
- How can employees build and maintain networks of career support and personal growth more widely amongst colleagues and other stakeholders?

Dialogue between the line manager and the employee

It's one of the bizarre side-effects of the IT revolution that people who sit at adjacent desks often communicate far more frequently with each other through e-mail than they do through spoken conversation. Whether we are truly losing the power of conversation is debatable, but workplace surveys repeatedly find that lack of dialogue between line managers and their direct reports is a common problem. Two conversations have particular significance in the context of talent management and succession planning: those relating to performance appraisal and to personal development.

It's not surprising that managers who see their role as creating order out of chaos tend to see their ideal team as a static environment. Knowing how each person fits in, what they can be relied on for, and where they are best and least able to contribute is comforting, because it is predictable. The trouble is, stable teams (where the task and membership remain the same over long periods) are only one of many types (Clutterbuck, 2007). In most team types, either the membership or the task change rapidly. And even in stable teams, stability is largely an illusion. While it is common for stable teams to be unobservant or ignorant of change happening in their external environment, they are even more prone to ignoring change in their internal environment. It is analogous to what happens in families: sometimes it is hard to acknowledge that children have become adults in their own right, for example. Within the team, subtle changes are happening in terms of:

- the skills, knowledge, experience and maturity of team members;
- the relationships between people;
- how members relate to their own tasks and the overall team task;
- how the team manages its interface with the external world, and especially with other teams.

The formal appraisal and development systems aren't very efficient ways of recognizing and adapting to these changes, especially if they take place only every 6 or 12 months. So many times I have heard managers complaining that they are under pressure from Human Resources (HR) and their own bosses to carry out appraisals, which are interrupting other urgent tasks they have to do. If managers see the process as a chore, it's not surprising that employees do not approach the conversations with great enthusiasm.

Much the same is true about developmental conversations. A CIPD survey published in 2010 shows that only two in five employees say that their boss 'discusses my training and development needs with me'. And if we look at the level of senior management, the position is equally depressing. A study conducted by Ashridge, Career Innovation, Clutterbuck Associates and the Talent Foundation (Clutterbuck, 2010) found that a third of top teams rarely or never discuss their personal or their team development, and for most others it is an annual formality. Less than one in five top teams has a top team development plan, and less than half of top team members have a budget for their own development. Less than half of developmental conversations for directors differentiate between directorial and managerial roles and competences. It all suggests a general inability or unwillingness to address developmental issues, whatever the level in the organization. Another study, examining experiences at a wider spread of organizational levels, found that: 'In every group of ten talented employees, on average four have an issue they wish to discuss with their manager, but feel unable to do so' (Winter and Jackson, 2009). Lynda Gratton and Sumantra Ghoshal

(2002) also reveal a depressing picture of appraisals and development discussions, describing them as 'dehydrated rituals', and call for improvements in the depth, quality and frequency of developmental conversations.

If succession planning and performance management are to be integrated in a really useful way, then it's important to ensure that performance and developmental conversations are a continuous, evolving and dynamic process. If the annual appraisal is simply a means to capture the content of a series of informal, helpful and just-in-time conversations, it matters a lot less that it is little more than a formality. (A bit like an annual report.)

The line manager as coach

A lot of money has been spent in recent years on trying to make managers coach their teams. There's not much evidence to say that it has had a significant effect. Coaching conversations frequently don't happen, or are ineffective, according to research by Philip Ferrar (2006), because there is an inherent role conflict between being a manager and being a coach. Among the issues he identifies are the following:

1 *Trust.* The manager is often seen as having his or her own agenda, in parallel with or, worse, overlaying that of the learner. Moreover, the fact that a manager gives one employee more coaching than another can be interpreted as a lack of trust in that individual.

2 *Confidentiality.* Employees do not always believe that the discussion with their line manager will be kept confidential. (Indeed, some organizations are explicit that the content may be shared with HR and/or the manager's own boss.)

3 *Openness.* For the line manager, there may be a significant conflict of loyalties, as the following quote illustrates: 'How could I tell him his job was likely to be the victim of a restructure? I did my best to steer the coaching with this in mind, but there was no way I could hint at what was going to happen, let alone open up on the subject. It was like working with one hand tied behind my back.' Equally, it can be hard for the direct report to be fully open with someone who has a major influence on their pay, work allocation and career.

4 *Solutioneering and short-term imperative.* The manager's need to demonstrate short-term gains to his bosses can easily overshadow the learner's longer-term objectives. This puts increasing emphasis on quick-fix solutions, rather than addressing issues and their root causes in depth.

5 *Linear processing.* Says creativity guru Edward de Bono (1985): 'The way managers think can be a hindrance to the creative process. Managers are taught analysis, to evaluate and use judgement.' As a result, the line manager coach may become enmeshed in the

numbers and in the 'hard' part of performance change, to the extent that he or she pays inadequate attention to the human factors.

6 *Groupthink*. People who work together tend to adopt the same filters on the world around them and have the same blind spots. Paradoxically, the better the relationship between line manager and learner, the more likely this is to be the case.

7 *Power pollution*. Managers may experience a conflict of role between being a trusted friend in the coaching relationship, and the guardian of team discipline outside of it.

8 *Word–deed misalignment*. 'Do as I say, not as I do' isn't a healthy basis for a learning relationship. The problem becomes much more obvious in a relationship where people work in the same team, than where they meet only for the purposes of coaching.

9 *'Parent–child gravitational pull'*. Having adult-to-adult discussions around critical feedback can be difficult when both parties are emotionally bound up in the work task in question. 'Putting on my managerial hat' tends to result in a more authoritarian tone by the coach/manager.

10 *In-groups versus out-groups*. If one subgroup perceives that another receives more coaching (or less, if coaching is seen as remedial) than another, it may breed resentment. It can be hard for a manager to be equitable in dividing out their coaching attention. Should they invest mainly in those who are performing poorly, or in those who are performing well? Can they overcome the natural reluctance to coach less those people whose response is least enthusiastic?

11 *'Set up to fail' syndrome*. The other side of the coin is that individuals who are singled out for coaching as poor performers may avoid the manager to protect their own ego. So their chances of improving performance are yet further reduced.

In recent years, I have gathered the experiences of large numbers of people who have either been line managers on coaching programmes, or whose manager has been through such training. In very few cases has there been much in the way of significant behaviour change. Typically, the manager returns to the team energized by the training and a little apprehensive about putting it into practice. The team's reaction is confused and also apprehensive. After a little while (often no more than a few days) everyone breathes a sigh of relief and goes back to normal. The problem is partly that coaching is an uncomfortable experience, when done well – not least because it makes people think harder than they might normally do and about things they might otherwise avoid! It's also partly that the team and the line manager form a system, and change in one part of a system tends to create a reaction that tries to restore the status quo.

So is open, developmental dialogue between line managers and direct reports a lost cause? Fortunately, it seems not. The key lies in the team environment.

Where there is a high level of psychological safety, the foundation is laid for positive challenge and mutual support between team members and the team leader. Characteristics that we see in such teams include: openness by the team leader with regard to their own developmental needs and objectives; encouragement to share and learn from mistakes; and active seeking of feedback by all team members, including the leader. Add to this positive developmental climate the skills of *being* coached and an expectation that people will ask for coaching when they will benefit from it, or offer it (including coaching from the team to the leader) when they perceive a colleague needs help, and the majority of problems described by Ferrar are greatly reduced. New team-based learning tools built around these principles have proven that it is practical to create a coaching culture at the team level.

For the line manager wanting to create more effective career and developmental conversations with talented reports, the following thoughts may prove helpful:

- Annual developmental discussions rarely work and may actually be a demotivator. The problem with any kind of ritual is that the process tends to be more important than the content. Both manager and direct report may see this conversation as something they are obliged to do, according to HR's timetable. Better to align developmental conversations with what is happening for the employee, so that they occur just in time and so that they can focus not on past half-forgotten events, but on current, live issues.

- Appraisals need to be genuinely two-way. Seek regular feedback from direct reports about how you helped or hindered their performance – perhaps twice as often as you give feedback to them. Try to avoid the corrosive language of so many appraisal processes – 'met expectations' or 'met requirements' is almost guaranteed to undermine people's motivation. In one company which I chaired, employees chose the language for appraisals. Being mostly young people, the highest level of appraisal was 'respect'!

- Be attentive to the employee's transition points: demonstrate interest in their evolving perceptions about their role and their career progress, and seek to use their frustrations productively by finding new outlets for their energy and their newly acquired skills.

- Talk with talented employees about your own role. This helps them to understand the constraints you have to operate under, while giving them an insight into the thinking patterns of the next layer of management.

- Look at your own role with a view to what you could delegate and would be a developmental opportunity for direct reports. Don't assume they will see it that way, though. Let them pitch for new responsibilities, from their greater understanding of your role. Draw-down is generally better than pour down!

- Encourage them to find mentors and sponsors who can provide additional perspectives and help with their career self-management. Mentors tend to be more experienced colleagues (often but not always more senior) who assist with learning and development; sponsors tend to be very senior, long-term supporters who ensure that hypos are given appropriate career moves and act as advocates for them. While the two roles are sometimes merged in the United States, in most countries they are separate and to some extent incompatible roles. Both mentors and sponsors can give the employee additional perspectives, which can feed back into the conversation with you.

- Think about what you can do to make it easier for them to be honest with you. If appropriate, contract with your team, or with individual hypos, about just how open you and they can be. For example, you might say: 'There will be times when I have career-relevant information which I can't share, in the same way as I am not going to share things you tell me in confidence. But what I will do with that knowledge is make sure that you aren't wasting your time pursuing dead-end paths.'

Becoming a learning team

In my researches into how teams manage their learning, I identified nine key characteristics of a learning team – one that generates learning and supports the continued development of its members. These characteristics were:

- A common sense of purpose – shared expectations of what the team was there for and how it contributed to its stakeholders.

- A common sense of priorities – close agreement about what was most important to accomplish (and along with this a willingness to subordinate one's own priorities to the collective priorities).

- Willingness to speak openly – feeling psychologically safe.

- Awareness of each other's strengths and weaknesses, interests and disinterests; knowing what tasks will engage colleagues and bring out the best in them.

- Valuing differences – recognizing the differences in knowledge, personality and approach that each team member brings, and embracing this diversity for the flexibility and creativity it brings.

- Willingness to share knowledge and expertise – the opposite of 'knowledge is power'.

- Knowing how each other thinks – a heightened level of awareness of how colleagues approach issues.

- Trust in colleagues' ability and goodwill – confidence that they can and want to do a good job.

- 'Fizz' (the pleasure that comes from the work itself) and 'buzz' (the enjoyment that comes from working alongside colleagues you respect.

- Help direct reports manage their reputations. Talented people often get overlooked because they are under the radar. Highly extrovert, perhaps aggressive executives tend to equate talent with characteristics and personalities like their own. Assist 'quiet talent' to develop and pursue reputation management strategies that align with their own values.

- Look at the developmental climate in your team. How conducive to learning is it? How close is your team to being a learning team, as described in the box? If any of these characteristics is absent, or at a low level, discuss with your team what you can do together to change it.

- Look at how your team reacts to mistakes. Do people cover mistakes up and hence learning to fail or do they learn from failure? What can you do to make it safe for people to share their learning from mistakes?

- Engage the team individually and collectively in open conversations about performance and potential. For many people, the distinction between these two concepts is far from clear. They assume, for example, that good performance in their current role is an indicator of potential, and wonder why they don't get promoted. Help them to understand that potential is about demonstrating that you can do the next level of job, while you are still in this one.

- If you haven't got one, build a team development plan – one that integrates the business goals for the team with the evolving collective and individual needs for skills and knowledge. Include in the plan opportunities for team members to support and coach each other.

- Look at the processes for work allocation. Do you tend to give tasks to the usual suspects, because they can do them, or to team members for whom they will be developmental? Is allocating work a productive use of your time or could you leave it to the team to sort out among themselves? (If the latter, there is likely to be much less tolerance of 'social loafing' – people not pulling their weight.)

- Look at yourself as a role model for self-development and career self-management. If you don't take these issues seriously, why should you expect your team to do so? Share with your team your own ambitions, the learning journey you are on, and the lessons you have learned. Legitimize conversations about their careers and self-development by disclosing about your own.

The common thread to all these ideas is that they involve conversations with, and sometimes between, team members that don't typically happen. The reasons they don't happen are many, but the most common seem to be time, skills and confidence, and the manager's beliefs about the team. The time issue is endemic and relates to almost any non-urgent but important task in a manager's responsibilities. Making time for developmental activity is closely associated with high-performing teams (Wageman *et al*, 2008), so managers who don't create the time tend to be in avoidance. Lack of skills or confidence in being able to manage these sometimes complex conversations is a development issue for the manager. The manager's beliefs about the team, however, comprise a much more subtle and difficult barrier to open conversation.

Part of the problem is that we perceive people as being less capable, or less appropriately motivated, when we see them as different or if we don't particularly like them. (It is worse if we actually dislike them.) We also tend to confuse context with capability. A good example of the latter is the special issue of plateaued managers. Plateauing in performance, or in career progress, happens to many people and is not necessarily a sign that they have peaked. Research in the mid-1980s identified that the causes and remedies for plateauing are partly personality dependent and partly an outcome of failings by the employer (Souerwine, 1985). Effective plateaued managers have the following characteristics:

- They had clear and generally positive feedback on their work.
- They felt they did a quality job that was of value to the company.
- They still aspired for promotion, while recognizing their limitations, and were motivated by being able to apply the talents they did possess.
- They had the skills of managing their career paths and took responsibility for doing so.

Ineffective plateaued managers, on the other hand:

- are seen as constantly scheming to gain more control over their work schedule;
- rely on politics and inside knowledge to get on;
- regard promotion as a mark of status;
- put their failure to progress as fast as they'd like down to malice or incompetence on the part of more senior managers.

Broadly speaking, these two personality types fall into the descriptions of people who are inner directed (look to themselves for the explanations of what happens to them) and outer directed (perceive what happens to them as caused by external factors – 'not my fault'). Commenting on Souerwine's research, John Foden, a consultant with PA Consultants, identified four key periods when talented employees commonly hit career plateaus:

- three years after they are appointed to their first managerial position;
- at around 40, when they need to make major decisions of career direction;

- between 40 and 45, before it is too late to move voluntarily;
- after 50, when moving employers carries additional risks of not finding a role elsewhere.

Souerwine found that companies frequently create an environment where talented people are driven into plateauing. One factor he observed was that a culture that emphasized youth and 'energy' often created an environment where older employees felt devalued and where both top management and HR saw a lot more dead wood than was the case in reality. (Being active and enthusiastic does not necessarily equate to effective management!) Another was that roles tended to carry career status, so someone appointed into a role where the previous incumbent had plateaued was more likely to plateau in turn, while other roles were noted by the rapidity with which people passed through them. One of the routes by which effective unplateaued managers were unfrozen in their careers was giving them responsibility for mentoring younger colleagues. This tended to refocus their attention on their own careers.

So a challenge to all managers is: 'To what extent are my own biases and assumptions getting in the way of my recognizing and developing the talent in my team?' Reconfirming bias – placing greater weight on evidence that reinforces a pre-held opinion and less on evidence that contradicts it – is a common human failing. So other useful questions managers can ask themselves are: When is this person at their best? What am I or other people doing then that allows them to perform well? What opportunities can I create, which will allow them to demonstrate their potential?

Another challenge is: 'To what extent am I preparing members of my team to progress into more senior roles?' It's useful from time to time to question one's own motives: are you to some extent trying to hang onto talent, rather than let people move on within the organization? You may initially cause some concern by encouraging direct reports to try for jobs they had not considered, but one of the most valuable things a manager can do for talented employees is to give them opportunities to gain experience of being interviewed for higher level roles. If appropriate, you can help them prepare for and subsequently deconstruct the interview.

Yet another challenge is how the manager can equitably manage their own succession. As we have seen in earlier chapters, the best candidate to take over a role may not be someone like the incumbent. So how can a manager recognize the talent in their team?

Looking for talent

We've already seen that line managers, in general, aren't particularly good at recognizing talent. It requires them to abandon stereotypes and accept that what got them to their current role isn't necessarily what will help tomorrow's leaders succeed. In my correspondence with other people around the world, exploring this issue, I was struck by this comment from Rob Kaiser, of US consultancy Kaplan DeVries, who says: 'One of my key messages when speaking or consulting on high-po identification is this: First, whatever you are doing to identify high-pos now, STOP! Second, look at your current high-po pool. Which handful of people scares the hell out of you? Half of them are your high pos.' Although his comments are intended to shock leaders and HR out of their complacency, rather than present empirical data, the gist of his message is echoed by many others who have taken an objective view of the talent identification process.

Here are some other practical guidelines for taking the blinkers off talent identification by line managers:

- Talent may not be like you – in fact, given that talent is creative and self-authoring, it is almost certainly not like you.

- You may be the biggest barrier to people in your team showing their talents. If you don't believe in their potential, you will discourage them from showing what they can do. If you create an environment where mistakes lead to criticism or even punishment, then the people who will shine through are those who are talented at conforming and not innovating.

- Spend more time identifying strengths and less time trying to correct weaknesses. That's not to say that you should avoid working with direct reports on their weaknesses; rather, create an appropriate, confidence-building balance and focus on weaknesses *they* are emotionally and intellectually ready to address. Don't think about correcting weaknesses; think instead of helping them in developing coping strategies that will enable them to be at least 'good enough' for the role they are in and the role they aspire to.

- At the same time, be alert for fatal flaws – personality traits or mindsets that are precursors to derailment. Don't rely on your own judgement here; seek professional help before you place such people in positions where their fatal flaws might break out.

- Recognize that talented people are likely to respond better when you help them approach developmental tasks in their way, rather than yours. A leader I was coaching expressed deep frustration that one of his team kept avoiding a confrontation with one of her direct reports about a performance issue. What would happen, I asked, if she were given a free hand to work out her own approach to the issue, rather than follow his solution? Given the opportunity, she laid out an approach in which she helped the direct report confront himself. As this approach showed results, the leader was honest enough to say to her that while he had originally begun mentally to write off her leadership potential, on the basis of being insufficiently tough, he now recognized that her approach was in reality a lot tougher – but much more subtle – than his own.

- Look for people doing things well. Tom Peters famously talked of 'catching people doing things right'.

- Listen to what each person's peers and direct reports say about them; place more emphasis on this than on your own observations. Remember that sociopaths are very good at smiling upwards and showing their less attractive side downwards. (Think of a tree full of koalas and compare what the ones at the top see, compared to those at the bottom!)

- Contract with your direct reports about how you will recognize progress against their developmental goals. This gives encouragement to the less self-promotional to make you aware of their successes and learning. It also increases your mindfulness: you are much more likely to notice improvements if you are specifically looking for them, than if you are not.

- Examine your own stereotypes and biases.[1] Take an implicit bias test to reveal the level of instinctive, unconscious bias you have towards people who are different to yourself (for example, in terms of race, gender, weight, or personality type). When you form a negative opinion about one of your team, ask yourself: 'What does this opinion say about me?' or 'How might my instinctive reaction to this person prevent me from noticing or undervaluing the talent and potential they possess?' Simply accepting that we *all* discount other people's talent in this way is a good starting point to overcoming a built-in barrier to talent recognition.

- Be aware of the frequency and the quality of the conversations you have with each member of the team. It's natural for managers to spend more time on and be more open in conversations with people who we have greatest instinctive empathy with. We gravitate automatically towards people we feel common identity with and away from those we don't. In my work with police forces, it is evident that this phenomenon is a factor in 'institutional racism'. Try to make it easier for members of your team to talk to you at a human level and don't expect them to make the first step. Research by the Samaritans says that many younger employees have particular difficulty initiating conversations with their managers (Bramston, 2008: 94).

As with many of the checklists in this book, I hope that many of these are things you are already doing. The key message I hope you take away is that you, as a line manager, are the most influential opinion-former about who is and isn't a high-potential employee and future leader, and that your mindset and filters can either encourage a highly diverse explosion of talent, or nurture a culture of clones.

Finding development opportunities for the talent in your team

When someone is good at a task, it's tempting to give them more and more of the same. It's rather like an actor finding that he or she is typecast. And the better they get, the more reason there is not to take risks by assigning the work to other team members. If a manager takes a developmental mind-set, however, they will ensure that at least 25 per cent of the work given to each employee puts them in learn mode. But the manager can be much more proactive than that, by selecting assignments with high developmental potential. An increasing academic literature now links the developmental quality of job assignments with the acquisition of managerial competence. For example, McCauley *et al* (1994) define 10 dimensions of developmental quality:

1 Unfamiliar responsibilities – eg switching from line to staff, or changing employers – make managers think about what they do and how they do it.

2 Developing new directions – eg initiating a new strategy or creating a new department.

3 Inherited problems – addressing problems left by a predecessor.

4 Problems with employees – eg engaging with and developing the competences of direct reports, who may be resistant to change.

5 High stakes – eg high visibility, especially to senior management.

6 Scale and scope – eg responsibility for large budgets, a substantial number of people, and/or diversity of functions.

7 Influencing without authority – having to work through peers and more senior managers to get things done.

8 Handling external authority – eg dealing with suppliers and other independents, again through influence.

9 Managing work group diversity – eg managing and working with a range of disciplines, who need to collaborate.

10 Working across cultures – eg preventing intercultural conflict and using cultural difference to stimulate creativity.

Lisa Dragoni *et al* (2010) compare these environmental factors with the learning orientation of the individual. A key distinction here is between learning orientation and performance orientation (Dweck, 1986; Dweck and Leggett, 1988). People with a strong learning orientation view challenging tasks as opportunities to learn. They seek out stretching assignments, adapt their behaviour to tackle them and tend to be resilient in coping with setbacks. People with a high performance orientation view challenges as inherently risky, because they may be found inadequate. So they adopt maladaptive behaviours, avoiding challenge and showing little tenacity or resilience when they meet setbacks.

The conclusions Lisa Dragoni and her colleagues draw are that managers with strong learning orientation are more likely to be in developmental assignments (because they seek them out and because others recognize this), and that managers in strongly stretching assignments show higher levels of competence development. The stronger the manager's developmental orientation, the greater the learning they take from stretch assignments. All of this may seem somewhat obvious, but it seems to be rare for organizations to apply these insights other than very informally. In choosing new assignments for members of the talent pool, tasks and roles may be designated as stretching, but without any robust analysis of what will make them stretching, either in general or in the context of the particular learner's developmental needs.

Moreover, we can make a cogent argument that problems of talent retention may frequently be related to a mismatch between the amount of stretch people receive and the amount that they need. Negative stress is one of the factors that influence people to leave jobs; it is also associated with employee perception of lack of developmental opportunity (Bramston, 2008: 96).

Harnessing stakeholder goodwill in your career and personal development

The emphasis of this chapter has so far been on the responsibility of the line manager for developing talent. But of course the employee is equally, if not more, responsible for their own development. And a big part of this is recognizing and using the resources around us, to grow and progress. The stakeholder resource is often much wider than people think. In addition to the immediate boss, it includes peers within the team, peers across the organization, the boss's boss, customers, suppliers, HR, and direct reports.

In Chapter 12, we discuss the power of social media to support individual and collective development. One of the simplest and most practical ways to engage others in supporting your personal growth, and pointing you towards opportunities to learn new skills and behaviours, is to share your personal development plan and your planned career journey with them. Putting this information on your personal blog, within the company intranet, may seem like self-promotion, but if you emphasize that you seek help, encouragement and helpful feedback, it's unlikely to be taken that way.

Other practical steps you can take include:

- Identify tasks that will give you useful experience and offer assistance to the colleagues or superiors who have responsibility for those tasks. Don't expect them to spend a lot of time teaching you how to do the task (that makes it a chore for them), so select bite-sized activities that can easily be handed over, and work up to larger tasks. If appropriate, shadow them in the task so you can learn by observation.

- Offer the same courtesy to other people, who could learn from you. Having a reputation for helping others in this way tends to stimulate more positive reactions when you request a learning opportunity.

- Look out for project groups which would provide new learning for you. Make a clear business case for why you should be included, both for the project leader and for your boss.

- Do your current job well. Otherwise you have a credibility problem when you ask to get involved in other tasks.

- Get into the habit of talking with your boss about the things that are making his or her life most difficult at the moment. In fact, seize any opportunity to gain deeper insight into the thoughts and concerns of managers at a more senior level, because this will subtly influence your own thinking. Reminding your boss occasionally that you are willing to help increases the likelihood of being given developmental responsibilities.

- Take the time to look for the recurrent problems your department faces and work up potential solutions. This kind of proactive seeking and solving of problems is closely associated in managers' minds with leadership potential.

Dialogue with colleagues

By definition, a career conversation requires active participation from at least two parties. So employees have responsibilities to help the manager help them. Not least among those responsibilities is contracting with the manager about how they will together establish openness and authenticity in their conversations about career issues. While overformality isn't likely to be helpful, you can share with your line manager your expectations about frequency of career conversations, confidentiality of content and support in developing expertise, experience and track record. It's also up to the employee to take shared responsibility for arranging career conversations, to be honest in the feedback they give the manager about how he or she is helping or hindering the employee's performance, to prepare for career conversations and to reflect on them afterwards.

In the absence of a supportive manager, a mentor can be a partial substitute, but they can't have a detailed conversation about learning and progress within the current job role, both because they do not have direct authority there and because the line manager would feel undermined if they 'interfered'. A more pragmatic tactic is to use the mentor as a resource to develop strategies for 'manager engagement' (essentially employee engagement in reverse, driven by the employee!).

One of the most effective ways in which an employee can create a wider dialogue to support their career aspirations is to look beyond their own role, as defined in their job description, and look for ways to assist other members of the team and/or key stakeholders outside the team in achieving their priorities. There is always a lot more support for career progress of people who we see as helpful to ourselves, than for people we see as narrowly focused.

Rivalry becomes an issue most clearly when career progression is centred on a small number of particular roles, rather than on a wider range of role possibilities. Members of peer networks tend to be at their most reciprocal and generous towards each other at this level. The talented employee therefore needs to develop several sources of network capital:

- Information – passing on articles, linked-in conversations and other snippets that are relevant to issues of concern to a colleague (including opportunities for promotion or for getting involved with interesting projects).
- Influence – sharing useful contacts.
- Recognition – giving and receiving respect and praise for ideas, work outputs or support.
- Expertise – becoming known not just as someone who has specific knowledge, but also as someone who will respond promptly to requests for help in that sphere of knowledge.

The payback from this generosity is that the employee now has a whole network of others who are consciously or unconsciously a positive part of their reputation management. Sharing developmental and career aspirations with this network makes them mindful, in the sense that they will mentally connect you with relevant opportunities, which they encounter. This process is particularly powerful within the Talent Wave, where although everyone is aiming to reach the shore first, their impetus is bound to the energy in the talented peers around them.

Within the immediate team, the talented employee can enhance their self-development and career management by asking themselves questions, such as:

- Who in this team has expertise and experience I can learn from?
- Who in this team can I share networks with, to our mutual benefit?
- What would make my team colleagues ambassadors for my career ambitions?
- Would increasing my respect for my team colleagues increase their respect for me? If so, how can I bring that about?
- What could I ask my manager to delegate to me, which would help them and give me a learning opportunity?

- What is my line manager a good role model for? How can I use observation of my line manager to develop my own capability?

Of course, there is a balance here between being obsessed with one's career, and lacking proactivity. If people around you understand your ambitions, they don't need to be reminded more than very occasionally! The key for the talented employee is to aim for quality conversations: right person, right topic, right time. And a supportive line manager is the ideal place to start.

CASE STUDY Paul Venables

Paul Venables is group finance director of Hays plc. He takes a pragmatic view of succession management in his team, which is spread in some 30 countries around the globe. He uses a simple framework of observable meta-competencies to assess and categorize the team members and their own direct reports. Amongst those competencies are:

- Self-motivation (drive to achieve, for both themselves and their team).

- Resilience (how do they cope with setbacks?).

- Ethicality (do they demonstrate an appropriate sense of 'rightness' and imbue this in their own teams?).

- Working *with* their teams (do they delegate, provide opportunities for direct reports to develop, use the team intelligently to support them in their own areas of weakness?).

Through quarterly conversations, he explores both performance and developmental issues with each team member. Part of this conversation is an honest appraisal of where he sees each of them in terms of three categories, based on evidence provided by both him and the team member. The top category is the high-performer, high-potential group. Here the challenge is to provide sufficient motivation, in terms of stretch tasks and financial reward, to keep them in post until a promotion opportunity arises. Inevitably, some of these high flyers will be headhunted before that, so a recurring theme of these conversations is the development of their own potential successors. One of the most likely triggers to make these employees consider leaving, or to undermine their performance, is boredom. Hence a strong focus in the quarterly conversations about what else they can do in their role that will maintain their interest.

The second category is what some organizations call 'workhorses'. They are highly effective in their roles, but lack the hunger to achieve more. As long as they don't act as blockers to their own direct reports, these people are intensely valuable. The conversation with them is less about containment than ensuring that their more limited self-ambition is a conscious and positive choice. (Life style appears to be a significant factor in the approach to work adopted by many effective plateaued managers.)

The third category is the poor performer. Often the reason for poor performance is that they are in the wrong role. This may not be the result of ill-judged promotion or appointment – roles may change or the business may grow to the point where a person with a different set of skills and interests is needed. Here, the conversation revolves around a development plan (and the individual's willingness to implement it) that will redress the performance issue, as the maxim is improve or remove.

The keys to all of these conversations are their *honesty* and their *frequency*. Paul makes a point of spending sufficient one-to-one time with each person early in their appointment to build the mutual confidence that they can be open to each other, to create the trust and psychological safety that underpins open conversations. With the top category, the conversation may often turn around 'How do we get the maximum value out of you, before you move on, whether inside the firm or outside?' There is no pretence that they are hired for life. Frequent conversations mean that latent dissatisfaction usually surfaces early enough to be addressed. In the second category, honesty reinforces the employee's sense that they are valued and leaves the door open for them to seize developmental opportunities when they are ready to do so. Valuing them for developing their own direct reports reinforces this open exchange. In the third category, honest conversations avoid the painful dance that so often accompanies the 'managing out' process. 'Are you genuinely prepared to make these changes and what support do you need to do so?' If the answer is 'no' right off, then both sides can agree a smooth exit. If the promised improvements don't happen, then an open conversation allows Paul to help the person plan how to leave with dignity.

Note

1 Implicit bias tests are used to demonstrate how subconscious associations affect our thinking and decision making in a wide variety of areas of diversity. Harvard's Project Implicit offers free online tests as part of long-term research.

Conversation 3: between the organization and employees

> Learn from the people, plan with the people. Begin with what they have, build on what they know. Of the best leaders, when the task is accomplished, the people will remark, 'We have done it ourselves'.
>
> (Lao-tzu, *Tao Te Ching*)

One of the most influential career conversations I ever had was with an informal mentor, when I worked for an international publisher. I'd been with the company for nine years, gradually moving into more senior roles. We were sitting in the comfy chairs of his club in New York when he said: 'Son, you have to understand something about the way this company works. We don't take well to anomalies. We don't know what to do with them. You're an anomaly. You are one of the most senior people in the company, who isn't American and hasn't spent time in our US operations. If you want to progress in this company, you are going to have to move to a job here, at your own expense, and learn how to be an American.' That was the point at which I decided to become an entrepreneur and start my own business.

That information shared with me over the after-lunch coffees was not something that appeared in the employee handbook. It was probably hardly ever articulated at all, even amongst those who led the company and moulded its culture. It was the kind of information shared only with the privileged few and I was grateful, because I was able to make a clear decision about my future career direction.

It's a role mentors often play: lifting the veil on how the politics of careers and succession really work. In professional firms, for example, what's needed to make partner has been described as a 'black box': indecipherable if you haven't made the transition already or if you don't have someone to guide you through the subtleties and nuances of how existing partners decide who should and shouldn't join them. But not everyone has a mentor, and in an age of increasing transparency there is a strong case, I suggest, for opening up the black boxes wherever they occur in organizational structures, so that anyone who wishes to can shine their own light in.

More generally, organizations and particularly HR have a mass of data about employment trends and future skills needs which rarely sees the light of day. Perhaps it's understandable to be coy about sharing information on comparative pay unless, of course, the company is in the upper decile – though such data are relatively easy to gather through social networks. But wider trends, both within the company and in its sector more generally, can be tracked using workforce analytics, which gathers evidence to allow employers to develop realistic predictions and scenarios about how their needs for skills and knowledge will evolve. Workforce analytics uses both historic data and current data to put some discipline into planning. In most organizations employing these techniques, the data are primarily a tool for HR. However, an increasingly strong case can be made for opening up this data to the Talent Wave – or wider – so that people can work with identified trends in planning their own careers.

Add to this sharing of information opportunities for dialogue – for example, through online communities of interest built around particular areas of career potential – and the groundwork is laid for a much more dynamic interaction between employer and employees. For example, it's easy for HR to assume that existing employees will want the jobs that will evolve in the next five years, but that may not be the case. They may see emerging roles as lacking in attributes, which they see as essential to their job fulfilment and job engagement. With sufficient forewarning, HR can work *with* employees to redesign jobs and create workforce strategies that sustain the psychological contract between employees and employer. For example, where technology threatens to deskill a job role, the opposite effect may be achieved by *increasing* the amount of automation, by opening up time for other tasks the employee can absorb.

Creating a broad career management dialogue and supporting employees with tools and skills to manage their own careers and understand employment trend data should enable a much higher level of alignment between employee and organizational aspirations. The psychological contract between employer and employee now includes the question: 'How can we add future value to each other?' – which makes it much easier to refocus appraisal around mutual benefit, rather than mutual blame.

If we focus more narrowly on the Talent Wave, the challenging question to HR and senior managers is: 'Who do we want these bright people to be having this kind of conversation with?' If they are not having this conversation internally, they are likely to have it externally, which inevitably directs their attention to a wider range of possibilities outside the company. The higher the quality of the broad conversation between the organization and the Talent Wave, it can be argued, the more likely the employee's career plan and strategy will focus on opportunities within their existing organization.

So what do employees want to know from the company for their own career planning? Some of the answers I have gathered from individuals and groups of employees in a wide variety of countries are:

- Where does the business plan predict expansion and/or the creation of new roles? (A shrinking business can provide some of the best opportunities for advancement and personal learning, because reducing headcount almost always involves restructuring job content, giving fewer people wider and deeper jobs.)
- What skills and knowledge will become more important and more valuable in the future? What resources are likely to be available within the company and elsewhere to support us in developing these?
- What kind of track record will be valued in the future? For example, will a period in the field be regarded as essential in grounding a manager's experience and giving them credibility with the line?
- What constitutes a reasonable time period in a particular job? One of the classic problems with rapid rotation of Talent Wave members is that they stay just long enough to create problems, but not to resolve them. Yet talented people are keen to move on to new challenges. Setting some organizational expectations about depth of learning within each role can help them to be more realistic.
- What constitutes 'talent' in this organization? What can individual employees do to increase their chances of being included in the Talent Wave?

What do organizations need to know about employees' career aspirations?

Some of the most useful questions to address include:

- Which employees are genuinely ambitious to take on greater responsibilities?
- What kind of roles do they *want* to move into? Employees and managers will tend to think in terms of existing job roles, which is a very limited perspective. It makes greater sense to cluster job roles in terms of core characteristics, such as their requirement for knowledge, skills and personality attributes; whether they are customer facing or internal; whether they require creativity or following procedures; and whether they emphasize routine or initiative.
- What kind of learning do they want or need to acquire, and what is their preferred method of learning?
- How do they view their psychological contract with the company? An important issue here is their expectation of how long they will stay and what factors might influence their decision to bring forward or to delay moving on. Also important is how fair they perceive the talent management and succession processes to be.
- What barriers do employees perceive we place in front of people in terms of their career planning?

Addressing these issues through an ongoing broad dialogue with employees – through focus groups, intranet discussions and other media – also allows the company to initiate dialogue around potential solutions. For example:

- What generic and specialist new roles could we create that would bring together employee ambitions and business aspirations/needs?
- How could we remove barriers to career planning?
- How might we be more creative in managing predictable skills gaps?

The key here is that while HR has much of the expertise in these areas, it doesn't have all the expertise, and it certainly doesn't have a monopoly on creative thinking on such topics.

How to gather and communicate information about likely roles in the future

A practical way of making different likely scenarios accessible to employees is to explore the future under two headings: business as usual (BAU) and discontinuity. Both can be further divided into opportunities and threats, and into specific areas of stability or change. These areas will vary from company to company, but are generically likely to include markets, products, technology and skills. Discontinuity produces both the greatest opportunities and the greatest threats; for example, a skill can be devalued by technological change or by rising numbers of people qualifying in it. However, business-as-usual scenarios can also be fertile ground for talented, entrepreneurial employees, who see opportunities for creating constructive and planned discontinuity.

At a macro level companies can gather data, make predictions (with all the necessary provisos about reliability) and spell out some of the likely implications. Figure 11.1 is one way of structuring this information, so that employees and the organization alike can use it for planning.

Clearly, what happens at a sector level will impact upon the company, which may in turn need to restructure individual functions, which is likely

FIGURE 11.1 Scenarios for career development

	Sector	Company	Function	Roles
Business as usual				
Discontinuity				

to lead to changes in role. Turning the data into narratives brings scenarios alive for employees and allows them to associate these possible futures with their own dreams and aspirations. And, as the case study at the end of this chapter illustrates, with their own narratives.

Using the broader organizational conversation to support the Talent Wave

Five particular factors have emerged from my conversations with HR professionals about how to support this broader conversation with employees generally, and with the Talent Wave in particular. Sharing of information, aspirations and ideas in each of these appears to create high-quality career conversations between the organization and its people. I stress here that these factors are extrapolations – they are not supported by empirical research, but are fertile ground for study. The five factors are the following.

A sense of the possible

Ambitious visions of future possibilities create and focus energy. 'Big Hairy Audacious Goals' (Collins and Porras, 1994, 1996) are equally energizing at organizational and individual level. But how much overlap is there between the employee's vision and the employer's? Continuous dialogue with employees generally can help the organization constantly adjust and bring shape to its vision. Equally, helping employees see the possibilities open to them from pursuing the corporate vision helps them to adjust their own sense of the possible. It's important to recognize that this is not a once-a-year or occasional exchange. Possibilities on both sides are constantly emerging and adapting.

The more aware people are of the organizational possibilities, the easier it is for them to ferret out mutually beneficial opportunities. It is this enlightened self-interest that drives alignment between corporate and personal visions.

Creative impetus

Environments that encourage and reward creativity produce a greater range of possibilities. The importance of creativity is underlined by studies of new product development. It turns out, for example, to be nine times more productive and much faster to teach creative people about a product area and then give them new product development responsibilities, than to give the same responsibility to technical experts (Stevens *et al*, 1999). The knack here is to encourage and enable people to direct their creative energy where it will produce the greatest momentum. Useful questions here are:

- How much of each individual's creative energy goes into pursuing their own developmental career goals?
- How much goes into pursuing team or business goals?
- How aligned are these, and what can be done to make them more aligned?

Moving horizons

In a dynamic environment, the horizon is constantly shifting. Depending on elevation and what is in the way, we can see further or less far into the future. From an organizational perspective, for example, new competitors constantly appear, so tactics and sometimes strategies have to be under constant review. The same is true for employees. Personal circumstances change almost daily. Employees don't want to know the detail of every minor threat or opportunity the company faces. But they do want enough information to adapt and modify their own plans. Some organizations engage their employees in 'horizon meetings', frequent sessions to share what's happening out there and what it could mean for the business and for them, adapting the content to cover both the big corporate picture and the minutiae that are relevant to them. In return, they find that employees become eyes and ears on the external world, picking up and sharing intelligence from friends, family or visiting the premises of competitors.

Congruent short- and medium-term ambitions

Ambitions can be seen as possibilities, which people have elected to try to make happen. Hence they tend to have a shorter time horizon than visions. The key question here is: 'What do you want to have achieved for yourself and the organization over the next 12 or 24 months?' Understanding the collective ambitions of groups of employees is essential in holding the kind of conversations that will prevent them from having unrealistic expectations, which become energy-sapping when they are unfulfilled. For example, the organization can focus employees' attention away from upward progression and towards sideways opportunities for development, where there are not going to be sufficient promotions to satisfy people's personal ambitions. It can also raise the status of being a member of certain teams, compared with the status of being appointed to lead teams with less status.

Another practical approach to engaging with employees' ambitions is the use of appreciative enquiry in job interviews. The aim is to get the best out of employees by asking them to discuss only their strengths and successes.

This has been particularly successful in identifying talent from minority groups. For example, the UK National Health Service's Breaking Through Programme aims to help black and minority ethnic staff progress into very senior positions. The programme supports participants through targeted education, opportunities to develop track records and mentoring. Selection interviews for the programme are designed to identify people with qualities including high intrinsic motivation, passion for success, self-awareness and resilience. Focusing on their specific positive experiences and attributes and avoiding generic questions – such as where do you see yourself in five years' time – appears to give a much more accurate picture of the individual, especially when coupled with an opportunity for them to discuss how they would like to use their next role to develop in areas where they are less strong (Arkin, 2010).

Following the terrain

Seeing the horizon is one thing. Getting there is another. A lot of energy is wasted in trying to channel talent in directions someone else decides it should go. But a wave tends to wash over the terrain, finding its own path. Instead of seeing strategic planning as a top-down process, it makes a lot more sense to show people the moving horizon and ask them to find their own ways there. It might be less *efficient* (they may go down a lot of blind valleys), but it is arguably more *effective*, because the momentum stays with the employees, who have to make strategy work. When people do go down blind valleys, it's important to help them learn from the experience, rejoining the wave in its next surge forward.

Making the broad conversation happen

If the conversations described here are solely the province of HR, they are unlikely to deliver. This is not a criticism of HR. It's simply that employees want to hear important messages about their careers from leaders, rather than from a staff functionary. So a major challenge for HR is how to persuade top management to accept accountability for leading the career dialogue. Given that the leadership team often pay insufficient attention to managing their own career development, this might seem like a tall order. Part of the solution is to make explicit the relationship between the Talent Wave and delivering the business strategy. If leaders are convinced that the career dialogue will help them resolve their own most significant problems, there's at least a sporting chance that they will engage in the career dialogue with a reasonable level of enthusiasm and authenticity!

CASE STUDY Strengthening dialogue between
the organization and individuals

One interesting idea for enriching the dialogue between the organization and individual employees comes from Rainer von Leoprechting. While developing services for in-house and external recruitments in the European Commission, he has experimented with identifying and categorizing employees' success stories. With an initial sample of 50 employees, he was able to collect a wide range of individual stories relating to a particular time when the individual felt they were successful in managing a project or substantial task.

He collected the different types of success in the form of typical stories that individuals can relate to as either an experience they have lived already or as a project or task they aspire to work on, which they feel plays to their strengths, but perhaps not yet to their experience. The initial sample gave rise to more than 20 frequently occurring stories. Von Leoprechting aims to stimulate dialogue between those people who initiate, facilitate or approve job moves, and employees who have shared their stories. For the former, it should be possible to describe the ideal person for a job role not in terms of a formal job description, but as a combination of relevant stories. For the employee, it should enable them to have conversations with peers and more senior colleagues to understand more fully what kind of roles would be a good match for their particular mix of experience and aspiration, as defined by their stories. It is to be expected that each person's stories will evolve over time, stimulating new conversations and combinations.

Von Leoprechting has brought the concept into the storymatcher initiative (**www.storymatcher.com**) which offers to collect and match people and organizations with a simple information technology (IT) application over the web.

Conversation 4: between social networks

One of the sayings in our country is Ubuntu – the essence of being human. Ubuntu speaks particularly about the fact that you can't exist as a human being in isolation. It speaks about our interconnectedness. You can't be human all by yourself, and when you have this quality – Ubuntu – you are known for your generosity. We think of ourselves far too frequently as just individuals, separated from one another, whereas you are connected and what you do affects the whole world. When you do well, it spreads out; it is for the whole of humanity.

(Archbishop Desmond Tutu, 1999)

The instinct to associate and cooperate with others has been one of the driving forces that has propelled human evolution. Our ability to work in teams, and for teams to work with other teams, has allowed us to build large, complex organizations. Our brain appears to have evolved and to be still evolving to meet the demands of operating in a social environment; for example, each generation appears to be slightly better at social lying and slightly better at detecting social lying than the previous one.

The larger and more complex organizations and societies become, the more important are the skills to create and manage links with other people, who are not part of one's immediate circle of family and friends. There are, in my experience, two critical types of network: those that provide information (how to find out what is or will be happening) and those that provide influence (how to get things done through others). In the context of succession planning, both forms of network are critical for effective job performance and career management. The same individuals, of course, may be members of both networks. Figure 12.1 proposes a rationale for network purpose. Present-based information networks provide the information needed to do current tasks, while present-based influence networks enable people to achieve tasks with the help of others. The more senior people become in an organizational hierarchy, the more reliant they become on these networks. Lack of timely information creates quality problems and

FIGURE 12.1 Why people network

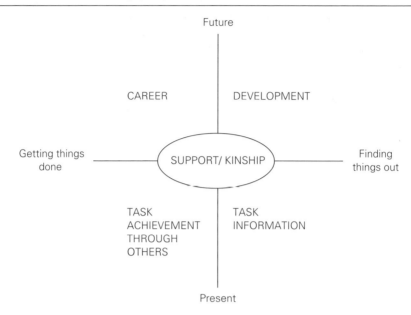

rework, for example, while in a matrix organization, command and control won't work when people don't report to you!

Future-based information networks are the main source for learning about opportunities and for shaping the continuous personal development that helps an employee maintain career momentum. Future-based influence networks are particularly important in securing access to promotion or important learning opportunities, such as joining a strategically critical project group. As I write, there is a political controversy over the fairness of access to internships. Is it right, critics are asking, that these valued learning opportunities should so often be awarded on the basis of influential contacts? Whatever the merits of that debate, it is clear that having a strong and relevant influence network can open doors to career routes that would otherwise be difficult to find, let alone go through.

The figure has one other important element. Right in the middle sits 'kinship'. Defined by the *Oxford English Dictionary* as 'consanguinity' – ie related by blood – the term is more frequently used to describe a broad sense of belongingness, an affinity gained through shared concerns, interests and/or values. This shift in meaning of kinship to a large extent reflects the shift in the nature of networks in the developed Western countries during the past two centuries and more, as the importance of family ties weakens and ties based upon hobbies and occupations have strengthened. The rise of online communities of interest both within organizations and between employees and their external peers is a natural development of this trend.

Traditionally, organizations have talked to their peers at a variety of levels, both hierarchically and in terms of intensity of exchange. The guilds of the Middle Ages originated from the desire of small businesses and their owners to find (and fight for) common cause and to profit from the exchange of information and influence. The Institute of Directors in the UK is a direct descendent of this ancestry; its older brother, the Confederation of British Industry, is a network for the bigger business.

The twentieth century saw the rise of communities of interest representing different specialisms within organizations; for example, accountancy, marketing, public relations and, of course, HR. Most of these set out to provide information exchange and solidarity (securing the reputation and perceived value of their role became a major preoccupation for all of them!), but soon embarked on the maintenance of professional standards and, as a consequence, erecting barriers to practice against non-members. (The coaching 'profession' is going through a very similar evolution.)

Unfortunately, the bigger and more influential these bodies became, the less sense of community they generated. So, for example, HR people have looked elsewhere for the kinship, information and influence exchange they require. They have found it in a variety of ways, including 'unconferences' and, of course, IT-based social networking. LinkedIn alone has hundreds of discussion groups whose members are interested in specific areas of HR, from succession planning to diversity management. Increasingly, these groups are becoming open (ie membership is not confined to a specified type of person or organization), but this risks diluting the strength of the kinship felt by an audience who feel they are true peers in the same boat.

These professional social networks to some extent blur the distinction between individual and organizational networks. The HR person may be a member both on behalf of the organization (eg to import new learning into HR practice within the company) and on their own behalf (eg to enhance their professional reputation and make connections, which may be useful from a career perspective). However, they do not link to the rest of the organization – either other functions or to employees outside of HR – in any significant way.

Organizational social networks may also be either formal (as in the case of professional associations) or informal. The latter are sometimes associated with practices such as price fixing, but can equally be used for much more positive reasons, such as best-practice benchmarking.

For the individual employee, social networks have in many cases become an important part of defining their identity, in both their professional and outside-of-work lives. According to Facebook, this one social network alone has 500 million active users, who each have an average of 130 friends.

Research into social networking suggests that people can on average manage a maximum of 150 strong connections and a much larger number of weak connections (Dunbar, 2010). Strong connections tend to be characterized by a higher quality and frequency of communication, greater trust, greater sense of shared purpose in one or more areas, and more likelihood of putting oneself out for the benefit of the other party. This applies both to individuals and to organizations; studies of company networks show that geographical separation is not a major impediment to the creation and nurturing of informal networks (Casper and Murray, 2005). Weak connections turn out to be more important than might be obvious, especially when it comes to finding new jobs (Granovetter, 1973). Better-connected individuals appear to be more influential, better liked and have high self-esteem (Fisher, 2010) – all characteristics associated with career success. Social networking provides opportunities to engage with a much larger number of weak connections than ever before. And if each of your strong connections is prepared to contact their strong and weak connections on your behalf, the size of your secondary network can potentially be tens of thousands. Research suggests that social networking builds self-esteem (Ellison, 2008) probably because it generates a sense of being supported, even though most of the connections may be weak links.

Networking theory

First, however, let's clarify what we mean by social networks. The pioneer of the concept was John Barnes (1954), who described it simply as 'an association of people drawn together by family, work or hobby'. People can be connected through social familiarities ranging from casual acquaintance to close familial bonds.

Social network theory examines social relationships in terms of nodes (individual actors within the networks) and ties (relationships between the actors). Researchers sometimes create a social network map consisting of all of the relevant ties between the nodes in a network. Even within a small network such as a team, these can become very complicated and techniques such as socio-mapping (**www.sociomap.uk**) make use of sophisticated software to capture this complexity visually.

Social network theory proposes that the attributes of individuals are less important than their relationships and ties with other actors within the network. Hence the studies reported earlier in this book that indicate that high performers are reliant on the quality of their networks.

According to the website Whatis.com, 'Social networking is the practice of expanding the number of one's business and/or social contacts by making connections through individuals.' The intranet has suddenly made this process much easier and, arguably, much less dependent on power or status. The currency of social networking consists of willingness to share information and ideas, to spend time online with other members (albeit asynchronously) and to observe social niceties such as complimenting someone for a particularly useful contribution to a discussion. Social networks, and particularly those with continuing streams of discussion, open opportunities for anyone, at any level in a field, to become introduced to anyone else.

Commentators on social networks frequently refer to the concept of six degrees of separation (Watts, 2003), which claims that any two people on the planet could make contact through a chain of no more than five intermediaries – as long as they are the 'right' connections. Social networking builds internet communities that interconnect with each other to form a theoretical link with anyone else who is also connected to an internet community. As a practical example, I recently wanted to make contact with the civil servant responsible for a specific budget and programme. I contacted my Member of Parliament (MP), who introduced me to a junior minister, who introduced me to a key political adviser, who put me in contact with the person I was aiming at. Had I wanted to contact a similar person in, say, the United States, the chain would have been longer, but still within the bounds of practicality.

Most of the research on social networks focuses on their use for practical purposes, such as doing business or seeking career opportunities. However, it should be borne in mind that the vast majority of social networks do not have this as their primary purpose. Facebook users, for example, tend to seek belongingness over utility. It is an intriguing paradox that people who are otherwise jealous of their privacy will reveal confidences in social space. Employers now routinely use Facebook and other social media as a source of information about the private lives of existing and potential employees. As a result, career-focused people are increasingly learning to use social media for positive reputation management and as a personal advertisement to the jobs market.

Actor-network theory (Latour, 1986) takes networking theory a stage further by equating all actors in a network: individuals, organizations and even IT systems. Because all are important in the efficient functioning of the network, removing an actor damages the network. Networks in this theory are heterogenous – they contain many dissimilar elements, which act and react together.

Social networking by employees is closely associated with creativity. According to Alexander Fliaster (2011): 'HR managers who still hang on to the individualistic view of creative performance should start to rethink... To solve non-trivial, difficult technical problems, knowledge workers cannot just download a ready solution from the corporate intranet. They rely not just on one ad hoc piece of advice but on repeated interactive discussions. Reliable networks, therefore, become vital for problem-solving and work performance.' 'Hire and fire' needs to be replaced by 'hire and wire' (Krebs, 2008). The efficacy of these networks depends considerably on the quality of the relationships between network members – the social element is just as important as the network itself.

Fliaster recommends that companies invest in helping people build networks of friendship and cooperation across the 'structural holes' in the organization – for example, by creating places where they can meet informally (in person or online) to develop a sense of common interest (kinship). Based on our understanding of other close cooperative relationships, such as mentoring, we can surmise that the quality of these relationships (the sense of rapport, shared utility and the perceived value of membership) will be related to characteristics such as trust, a sense of shared values, mutual empowerment, openness and reliability.

A case study by Robert Kelley from Carnegie Mellon University and Janet Caplan at Bell Labs (2009) found that top-performing knowledge workers had stronger and more reliable social ties with colleagues. When they contacted someone for advice, they almost always received a faster response than middle performers. Which is cause and which is effect is not clear. Do high performers do well because of the quality of their networks? Or does quality of network contribute to making a high performer?

The kind of network people create is also a factor. Having a large and diverse network of connections with lots of people is useful in identifying what is happening in an organization and discovering useful clusters of expertise, but less effective in knowledge transfer (Krebs, 2008). However, for influencing purposes, a sparse radial network, in which relatively few people connect you to others who are more distant to you, appears to be more beneficial (Burt, 2000).

In the research for my book *Virtual Coach, Virtual Mentor* (Clutterbuck and Hussain, 2009), I was struck by studies that explored the differences in behaviour of people in face-to-face and online conversations. One particular issue was power dynamics. It seems that people are much less aware and much less influenced by difference in status when communicating by e-mail (Sproull and Kiesler, 1986). So social networks have great potential in promoting honesty in conversations within organizations.

Underpinning social networking is social software, defined as 'software that lets people rendezvous, connect or collaborate by use of a computer network' (Attwell, 2007). Social software can make use of almost any electronic medium, including texting and graphics, web logs, wikis, tools for creating and sharing multimedia and tools for sharing all kinds of different personal knowledge bases including bookmarks and book collections.

From a corporate viewpoint, the only restrictions on social software are often what the IT department will allow through firewalls; and the level of monitoring by companies, to protect against abuse of company computer systems. This latter point can be a significant hindrance to the growth of open, trusting networks. In the case of in-company mentoring, for example, participants are often not unnaturally concerned that comments they make online will not remain private. (Expressing your views of a senior manager in an e-mail might not be the wisest of career moves.) Ways around this issue are conducting exchanges through personal, non-corporate e-mail addresses, or basing communication for the entire mentoring programme on a separate

IT platform. A challenge for the HR and IT departments will be how to reconcile security and the openness required for social networks to flourish; creating protected space for social networks may be an answer.

The opportunity and demand for social networking within organizations is sure to grow, as more and more young people experience personal learning environments (PLEs) in higher education. PLEs use a wide mix of technologies to personalize learning and build informal learning networks amongst students. Inevitably, these networks also include faculty and a variety of outsiders, both individual and organizational. Graham Attwell (2007) explains that: 'If not continuous, learning is now seen as multi-episodic, with individuals spending occasional periods of formal education and training throughout their working life... learning will take place in different contexts and situations and will not be provided by a single learning provider.' At the same time, informal learning will play a much larger role than at present. Attwell continues:

> According to the Institute for Research on Learning, at most, formal training only accounts for 20 percent of how people learn their jobs. Most workers learn their jobs from observing others, asking questions, trial and error, calling the help desk and other unscheduled, largely independent activities (Cross, 2006). Research I undertook into the use of e-Learning in Small and Medium Enterprises found little take up of formal courses. But we found widespread use of the Internet for informal learning, through searching, joining on-line groups and using email and bulletin boards.

Attwell describes a learning environment where there is 'a new ecology of open content, books, learning materials and multi-media, through learners themselves becoming producers of learning materials... Some education institutions are providing blogs for all students and encouraging their use. This is not linked to any course as such, but rather blogging is seen as an important activity for communication and the development of ideas.' For example, Warwick University encourages staff and students to use their websites in any way they wish, to enhance their own or other people's learning.

Companies which take social networks seriously report a range of sometimes unexpected benefits. For example, at US stores Best Buy, about a fifth of the 150,000 employees are signed up to the social network, which was originally designed as a market research tool to share insights from encounters with customers. The network, called Blue Shirt Nation, has evolved into many areas of knowledge sharing and colleague support. Particularly impressive, however, is that staff turnover amongst members of the network is a sixth of the company average.

Social networking and succession planning

In the context of succession planning, individual employees, HR and senior management all belong to a number of social networks. However, the interconnectedness between those networks does not appear to be very efficient. I propose that two key factors, which would promote this connectedness, are currently at too low a level to be sufficiently impactful. One is *interest*. How much do the actors in the different networks care about each other's exchanges of information and influence? One of the perennial complaints of HR, for example, is that senior managers are not really interested in people issues. Solving technical problems is much more psychologically rewarding. Line managers typically don't read HR journals; and (from quasi-experiments I have conducted over the years with HR people) HR rarely read journals on business strategy, corporate governance and the like. Similarly, the trivia of employees' daily lives has little interest for HR, while the dull bureaucracy of HR management has little to excite employees.

The second factor influencing connectedness is *perceived utility*. Or to put it another way, what's the point? What value can be added to the purpose of one network by engaging with another? Employers already increasingly use social networks as general recruitment resources, identifying potential employees from the networks they belong to and the way they participate in them. Research by the University of Mainz in Germany and the University of Texas finds that Facebook profiles are generally reliable as reflections of the person's personality on four out of the 'big five' personality traits (the exception being neuroticism, which is particularly hard to assess from general information). This suggests that general impressions of potential job candidates from their Facebook profile are a useful element in filtering applications. Other research finds that it is possible to identify personality traits from analysing the language used in blogs (Yarkoni, 2010).

To a large extent, perceived utility generates interest. Then a third factor kicks in: *accessibility*, that is: how easy is it for a meaningful information exchange to happen between networks? A simple example of this in practice occurred for me years ago with the HR department of a large utility. The HR professionals were frustrated that they could not engage the business leaders (the top 200) with people issues. Interviews with the leaders revealed that the problem wasn't that they didn't want to know, more that they had other priorities and had little time to focus on anything not immediately relevant to their roles. The solution was for HR to select every two weeks or so the articles or books which would have greatest relevance to people issues in that business, and to précis these in a two-page bulletin. Combined with senior management's guilt about not having taken people issues sufficiently seriously, this produced a general change of behaviour, with topics raised in the bulletin being raised at management meetings. In this case, a critical 'actor' was how the connection between the two communities of interest was made.

The potential for meaningful conversations, especially about career issues, as a result of connecting the separate employer and employee networks is still emerging. But speculating under the three headings of interest, utility and accessibility, we can surmise that:

- HR should be interested in capturing the ambitions and evolving identities of existing and potential employees, recognizing that the formal systems of data capture are constantly out of date and prone to misinformation, on the basis that people fear to be fully open. HR should also be tracking the careers of former employees, who the organization might wish to re-recruit. After all, who better to slot into a role than someone who already knows and has learned to work within the corporate culture, and who has gained new skills, knowledge and experience? (One of the most powerful networks which could be created is between mentors and mentees, some of whom will have left the organization. One financial services company told me that it saves millions of dollars annually in re-recruitment fees, when former employees contact their old mentor for advice on their next career move.)

- Talented employees should be interested in understanding how the HR and senior management group thinks about succession and talent development. Much of this information is intangible and often only accessible in the informal chat rooms frequented by HR professionals.

- HR should explore the world of social networking more fully to identify better ways to influence the career development and career decisions of talented employees; and in turn to be influenced by evolving trends in the aspirations of employees generally. One of the big issues, for example, is how to identify hidden talents – skills and interests used by employees in areas outside of their work, but not in their job. If you want to make full use of talent available, you have to view employees holistically.

- Talented employees can develop their networking skills (perhaps with help from the company) to gain greater access to potential job opportunities.

- HR might benefit from giving employees greater access to career and talent management data by rethinking how people find out about jobs. In a large transport organization, HR worked out that only one person in five looked internally first for their next job. The problem was partly fear of negative reaction from their current boss or team, but more importantly a lack of information to identify where interesting vacancies might arise. We designed a theoretical system that involved a 'blog' about each department and the roles within it. So, for example, the role of marketing assistant was defined not in terms of a job description, but in vignettes by current job holders of their working day, the joys and the frustrations of the job and how the role contributed to team and organizational goals. Other information important for job searchers included the background and qualifications of people who were currently and previously in the role, how long on average people stayed, what roles they moved on to, and so on.

- Talented employees might consider how to make their own profiles more accessible to HR and to managers who influence succession planning decisions. Some organizations give all employees the option to maintain their own blog and personal website on the intranet. Effective career management may in these circumstances have similarities with website optimization on the general internet – how do you ensure that your internal blog gets noticed? Author Neil Schaffer, who has studied in depth how headhunters and HR mine social networks to find suitable job candidates advises talented managers and professionals to 'differentiate themselves in every aspect of their profile... populate their profile with keywords that will resonate with employers they want to attract'. He also advises joining multiple LinkedIn groups relevant to their sector or profession. While Schaffer's focus is on reputation management external to the person's employer, the same messages appear to apply to the internal career market.

Integrating organizational and employee social networks

Integration between social networks is already happening, according to Henry Holtzman, chief knowledge officer of MIT's Media Lab. Increased visibility inevitably leads to some merging between social spheres, such as family, friends and work (Fisher, 2010). The step to integrating organizational and employee social networks is therefore not as large as it might initially seem.

In general, most social networking is unfocused, in terms of both what people give to their networks and the rewards they look to from them. If proactive network management has wider job and career benefits, however, there is a case for employers to support employees by providing skills training in network management, access to wider people resources, and technology platforms that support networking. So, for example, they might:

- Promote communities of interest around specific job roles, technical specialisms or other areas of perceived commonality, such as gender, nationality or disability. These communities need not be limited to the organization – the key question is: 'Who do we collectively and individually know, who could add value to this network?'
- Assign members of the Talent Wave the task of developing networks that will provide access to potential recruits, to market or technological information, or some other valuable resource.

- Help employees add value to existing social networks by, for example, facilitating the wider dissemination of responses to individual requests for information, or by creating topic bulletins that network members will want to circulate to other networks, of which they are a part.

Employers can develop closer cooperation with non-competitive strong connections, to enlarge and enhance the collective talent pool. Large Japanese companies facing difficult times have sometimes loaned employees to companies in their supply chain. The benefits of this include retaining talent, maintaining relationships with key business partners, and two-way importing of know-how, particularly in the context of quality management and cost saving. Pixar and Google both encourage employees to create networks that allow them to pursue their own special interests. Indeed, inevitably, these networks cross the internal and external boundaries of the organization, but that helps to ensure a healthy flow of ideas and technical knowledge into the business, and opens up the potential pool of employees. What distinguishes both of these companies is that they are comfortable with a certain amount of chaos. They don't attempt to control these networks – that would make them much less effective.

Making this informal process more transparent could have major advantages for all the collaborating organizations. Yes, there is some danger of losing key people, but this is at least balanced by having a wider pool of talent to draw on. Moreover, the arguments about holding on to talent have in many cases already been made, in great depth, in the context of moving talent between divisions and departments within the same organization.

The critical questions here include:

- Where is the best developmental opportunity for a member of the Talent Wave, regardless of which organization they currently work in?
- What leadership qualities and characteristics, skills and experiences will be common needs for the organizational partners?
- What kind of collaborative developmental programmes (such as action learning sets) can we create that will develop Talent Waves that stretch across organizational boundaries?
- How can we use employees' personal social networks to reinforce this corporate collaboration and vice versa?
- How can we ensure that talented employees look first for new career roles within the consortium?
- How can we support and sustain social networks across all the organizations, so opportunities become known to those employees who might benefit most from them?

This 'free trade area' in talent may seem radical, but we already see practical examples of similar collaboration in people development. Companies such as Lloyds TSB and An Post, the Irish post office, have gone outside corporate boundaries and into their network of strong connections to find mentors for talented employees. Public sector organizations in some local areas of the UK have combined resources to create mutually accessible pools of coaches and/or mentors. The National Health Service, police, local government and higher education have been particularly active in this regard.

One organization which has taken the idea of boundaryless succession seriously is Cancer Research, UK. It has established an active, internet-driven network that links existing, former and potential employees. When existing employees travel to other countries, they are encouraged to meet with alumni and potential employees, building relationships that will create opportunities to align future needs by the organization with the interests and capabilities of a much wider range of talented people. This is particularly important for the younger generations of researchers. Says Christine Lloyd, former director of HR: 'Gen X were all about career ladders and having a clear career pathway. GenY have been brought up in a connectivity world – that's how their minds are wired differently.'

The concept of the Hakathon, originated by Facebook to conscript software engineers inside and outside the company into informal product development groups, has potential as a boundary-breaking tool for talent development as well. Creating social network space where people throughout the company (or at a minimum, everyone in the Talent Wave) can bring their ideas about how development could be made more effective, can energize humdrum HR practices.

Online jobs marts allow people to bid for jobs and link their social networks with others to recruit people from outside. Companies often pay a recruitment bonus to employees who introduce a friend to the organization, but it's rare for employees to make full use of their social networks. Yet potentially an employee who uses social networks really well could equal or surpass their salary through recruitment bonuses earned by tapping into numerous weak nodes in their social networks.

Benefits of integrating organizational and individual social networks

Integrating these networks benefits both the organization and its Talent Wave in numerous ways:

- Talent will gravitate to attractive situations and opportunities (more open networks will make these more visible) that utilize and allow them to develop their strengths.

- Private conversations will emerge between people at different points on similar career ladders (informal and formal mentoring and coaching).

- New career ladders and directions will emerge as a result of dialogue between employees, HR and senior line managers.

- Talent clusters will form more readily – groups of talented people who collaborate on projects and use their own social networks (internal and external) as resources.

- Talent identification will become a more dynamic, constantly adjusting process as continuous feedback between managers and their peers and direct reports and other stakeholders provides a more rounded picture of who is actually making things happen and how they are putting core values into practice. Widening the pool of people who recommend others in LinkedIn style references will overcome many of the problems of boss nomination. However, it is probably too much to hope that the determined sociopath will not learn how to manipulate this system as well, so safeguards will need to be built in to ensure an appropriate counterbalance of comment from others.

- Assessment and development centres will emerge not as centrally organized activities to identify talent but as talent-driven (demand-led) ways of satisfying calls for development support by the Talent Wave.

- 'Open' continuous professional development (CPD) – where talented employees can gather continuous feedback on areas of development need, making behavioural learning and personal evolution a more collaborative effort.

This is far from being an exhaustive list. The practice, if not the concept, of integrated employee and employer social dialogue is sufficiently new that we are still discovering its possibilities.

Supporting employee-focused social networking

In my correspondence with social networking experts on these issues, I was particularly struck by the coherence of comments by Gareth Jones, a UK consultant who has explored social networks in the workplace extensively. He concludes that innate conservatism within HR has meant that the profession has not kept pace with employees in its use of social networks. He observes that: 'HR networks are notable for their formality, which by definition means that they are not that "social"!' Such social networks as there are for HR professionals – such as Toolbox for HR, ConnectingHR (**www.connectinghr.org**) and HRevolution (**www.thehrevolution.org**) – are relatively recent and have relatively small membership. He suggests four reasons for HR's failure to exploit social networks, and explains them as follows:

- *It's new* – 'Social networks' have emerged from the personal side of our lives, not the professional. As such, the adoption and recognition of the value they can bring is currently low. HR is not unique in this – it is the same for pretty much all professions apart from the digitally and technically focused ones.

- *It's social* – by definition, its roots are in the social, personal arena and this feels uncomfortable for HR and organizations in general where the personal and professional sides of our lives are encouraged to be kept separate or only allowed to overlap under controlled circumstances. Social networks are largely informal and bring with them a level of personal involvement and sharing that can make HR professionals feel uncomfortable.

- *Lack of control* – social networks tend to be supported and enabled by technologies that are relatively new and, more importantly, not controlled by the organization. These technologies are very open and tend to push the boundaries in terms of what is professional versus personal, with no control beyond the individual user.

- *Fear* – connected to lack of control. Right now, most HR professionals are aware of social networks, but they are more preoccupied with how their employees are using them and what they may be saying about the company/leaders/each other than they are about using them themselves for either personal or professional benefit. The fear of an employee saying something 'inappropriate' dominates most discussions amongst HR professionals on the subject.

Becoming more comfortable with social networks would allow HR access to all sorts of conversations from which it is currently largely excluded. Jones declares that:

> the days of the employee survey are numbered, chiefly because of its staged manner and lack of frequency. Using internal social networks of which all professional managers and leaders are part – regardless of status – gives an organization access to real-time feedback and information. I call this 'real-time engagement' and the benefits are enormous.

> HR professionals need to shift their mind-set from one of supervisor to participant. They need to join in the conversation, rather than try and control it from the outside, using policies or sanctions. This is a wider issue for the organization, but given the people focus of the HR profession, they should really be totally engaged in the dialogue themselves, as a peer (regardless of seniority).

> Ultimately, it's not about the tools. What organizations need to do is embrace a more social, peer to peer, two-way and conversation-led communications strategy. Becoming comfortable with having an open dialogue, online or in a place that is visible to people inside *and* outside the organization is the key. Once you get past this cultural hurdle, the tools become secondary.

> Social networks are blurring the lines between employees, customers and potential employees – distinctions between groups of individuals that organizations have been keen to keep in place historically. The truth is we are all one and the same, just at different points in our consumer lifecycle.

HR should step away from the controlling approach. There is a distinct and positive feature of social networks that can work to an organization's benefit – the power of the crowd. If someone speaks out within a social framework, and their accusations are unfounded, then the rest of the network tends to take care of the issue and will address the balance/inaccuracy without the organization or brand having to do so themselves. If, however, the issue is a real one, an organization can no longer ignore it and the crowd will amplify the issue. The best way to address this risk, is to a) be part of the conversation and b) be authentic in how you position your brand and interest.

I could not have said it better!

If we follow this logic, then HR can take a number of steps to provide practical support for career and developmental social networks. For example, it can:

- Engage with employees and with IT to design social network support systems that meet employees' ideas of what is helpful.

- Encourage employees to set up their own groups and discussion streams – providing the tools but not the direction.

- Create databases of career and development relevant information driven by employee requests for knowledge, rather than by what HR thinks people ought to know. If this is facilitated like a wiki, employees can share information and reports which they think will be useful to others. Some HR resources might also be diverted towards finding answers to employees' questions, where the network doesn't have sufficient information.

- Build trust between HR and users of social networks by being role models for supportive networking behaviour.

- Educate employees (and everyone in HR) in how to use social networks more effectively.

- Examine all HR systems and repositories of information from the perspective of what genuinely needs to be confidential. The fewer secrets employees perceive HR to hold, the higher the level of trust that can be developed. Workforce analytics and people strategy documents belong in the open space of the career and development networks, not in locked cabinets!

- Encourage HR practitioners who attend conferences to report their learning not just to HR peers, but to anyone who is interested in the topic in question. (It's relatively easy for social networkers to request notification of relevant new filings.)

- Invite outsiders, such as subject specialists in careers and development, to contribute to HR's own social networks; and make these conversations more widely available to the employee-run social networks.

- Most important of all, resist the temptation to grab back control. Live with the uncertainty and enjoy the thrill of surfing the Talent Wave!

Summary

The creation of dialogue between the networks of employees and those of employers raises many questions. The greater the level of connectivity between them and the wider the boundaries of these communities are stretched, the less practical it becomes to control the content and nature of conversations. A critical challenge for HR therefore, is: 'Can we summon the courage and skill to let go?'

CASE STUDY Connect Us

Global electronics company Philips has what it calls a social-powered community, titled Connect Us. Like a LinkedIn group, employees can ask questions of the community, share their thoughts and challenges and connect directly to the leaders. They exchange information in real time and on average receive 3.4 answers, with more than 25 per cent of the answers coming from a different sector of the business and 38 per cent from a different job function. Within 12 months of launch, there were over 23,000 members of the network. Initially, it took up to three weeks for people to become comfortable with using the network, particularly at top management levels, but the learning curve has shortened considerably with more users. Senior managers were particularly encouraged to participate, to provide perspective and share their insights with others.

When initially launched, people placed all sorts of personal and other information on their blogs, including pictures of their family dogs, but social norms soon established themselves and the network settled down as a professional exchange. Asking people the question, 'What are you working on?' when they log on helps to reinforce the work orientation of the network.

Accessible from anywhere, including the company intranet and mobile applications such as Blackberry and iPhone, the network provides ideas for Philips's weekly employee television programme, *Philips News Network* (PNN), which is also on YouTube. The aim of the network was primarily achieving greater business performance, 'to stream information to people's groups so employees can collaborate and become faster at completing tasks and finding solutions'. But it has immediate practical implications for personal and career development.

Succession planning for a dynamic world

> If you want to reach a state of bliss, then go beyond your ego and the internal dialogue. Make a decision to relinquish the need to control, the need to be approved, and the need to judge.
>
> (Deepak Chopra)

The central message of this book has been that, if organizations really want to have the right people in the right jobs at the right time, they need to stop trying to impose artificial and simplistic processes aimed at exerting control and based on linear assumptions about the systems involved, and shift instead to a strategy of enabling and supporting the Talent Wave to advance, based on the recognition that talent development and succession are complex, adaptive systems.

Working within a complex, adaptive system

The lessons I've gathered from dozens of reflective HR practitioners in the research for the book are many and varied. It's clear there is no single blueprint for working within a complex adaptive system of talent development and succession. However, some common themes do emerge from the hundreds of conversations I have had with HR practitioners and observers. These are:

- the need for courage;
- harnessing the energy of the Talent Wave;
- ensuring that talent development and succession systems enable rather than control;
- making sure that the four conversations or dialogues happen, and supporting them in quantity and quality.

The need for courage

'We're from HR – we don't do courageous', said a seasoned HR director from a Fortune 500 company in jest when presented with some of the ideas reproduced in this book. In the ensuing discussion, it became clear that courage was not a descriptor that HR instinctively applied to itself, or expected others to associate with HR. Yet 'Gutsy HR', all 20 senior practitioners agreed, was essential if organizations are to achieve a dynamic talent management and succession culture. So what would courageous HR look like, in this respect? Some of the ideas from my conversations with HR professionals are:

- Change the role and the language. Make it clear to all stakeholders that they are there to enable, not to control – for example, by allowing a greater voice from employees in how the talent management and succession planning processes are run. Stop talking about talent management and refer instead to talent support and development. Similarly, replace succession planning with succession facilitation. Do less to employees and more with them.

- Decrease reliance on simplistic models and frameworks, such as the nine-box grid and leadership competencies. That's not to say that they need to abandon these completely, merely that they should use them as a (small) part of the data that inform talent identification and succession decisions.

- Stand up to organizational psychopaths and, where necessary, block their progress, even if they have powerful allies. This can be the toughest call of all, especially when the employee has a record of delivering results by being ruthless. If the HR director's objections are over-ruled, then it's time to resign and to be public about why.

- Challenge the culture that values conformity and box-ticking over originality and personal maturity. Be prepared to sponsor and protect talented people who don't conform to leaders' biases about what a good leader looks like.

- Challenge the notion of the single leader wherever it influences talent identification and succession – including at the top table.

- Challenge top management to change their assumptions and behaviours. Be sure of your ground, then stand it. 'All the measures and criteria in the world will not withstand the interference of the "human" element; those senior people in an organization who over-ride HR's analysis for succession planning and make their own decisions regarding who is ready to step up to the next level' (comment from LinkedIn group, 2011).

It's not just HR that needs to be courageous, however. Leaders and employees both need to develop courageous habits. For leaders, courage includes:

- being honest with themselves about how their own biases and stereotypes distort their views of talent;
- taking risks on appointments, to allow people to show what they can do;
- taking responsibility for and learning from the appointments they make; attempting to be as dispassionate as possible in assessing how well a favourite has really performed.

For talented employees, courage involves:

- taking responsibility for managing your own career and self-development;
- being honest with yourself, to develop authenticity;
- taking on roles for the learning opportunities they offer, rather than for increased status and income;
- having honest conversations about your career ambitions with your boss and other stakeholders.

Harnessing the energy of the Talent Wave

When sound engineers want to reduce the impact of, say, traffic noise, they can either block it or superimpose a counter-wave that has the same effect. What happens now in so many organizations is that HR and leaders un-intentionally counter and dilute the energy of their Talent Waves. Every time someone leaves disappointed at not being able to apply their talents, the Talent Wave is diminished. In contrast, when one wave superimposes itself on another travelling in the same direction, their momentum is combined. The big question is: how do you make it more likely that this will happen?

In Chapters 9 to 12, we have explored some of the practical ways in which organizations can reinforce and sustain the energy of the Talent Wave through more effective dialogue. In Chapter 9, we looked at the inner dialogue. It's clear that people who know themselves and know what they want from their careers are likely to have more focused energy than those who don't. In Chapter 10, we looked at the dialogue between talented employees and their immediate stakeholders in the workplace. The energy here comes from constantly adjusting roles and responsibilities so that talented employees are in continuous learning mode. In Chapter 11, we identified ways to align collective employee and employer aspirations, so that the energy of the Talent Wave flows as much as possible in the same direction. And in Chapter 12, we saw how social networks can reinforce the power of the Talent Wave, by making it easier for them to build on each other's creativity and energy.

Taken together, the four conversations provide the most comprehensive approach yet to helping HR and the organizations it serves overcome their addiction to linear thinking and stop trying to play Canute. HR's future role might be compared to surfing on top of the wave – the best vantage point to keep top management informed about where the wave is going and what it is capable of achieving.

Ensuring that talent development and succession planning systems enable rather than control

So what on earth can HR do in relation to succession planning? If the answer is to enable rather than control the process, there are lots of ways in which they can exert a positive influence. These include:

- *Creating conditions that encourage self-organization.* For example, the more data people have on jobs, the more they can direct themselves towards or away from them. The time to have that information is not when a vacancy occurs, but well before that. It is interesting that in choosing a holiday hotel or resort, we can go online and gather masses of data including the experiences, good and bad, of people who have been there before, yet it's relatively hard to find out what a job in the next department is really like. Useful information for talented people might include:
  - What are the excitements, challenges and downsides of the role?
  - Where have previous incumbents gone on to?
  - How long do people typically stay in that role?
  - What are the natural stepping stones from the role?
  - What personal strengths does it demand?
  - How much of a learning environment does it provide?

  Other ways of supporting self-organization might be to:
  - Build networks and communities of interest devoted to the creation of new roles and transformation of old ones.
  - Follow Google's example and encourage employees to take a proportion of their time to work on their own projects. On the one hand this creates new job opportunities; on the other, it helps to develop the core skills and strengths of talented employees.
  - Create a 'succession supermarket', where people can shop around for roles they would like to grow into and engage with HR in creating development plans that might take them there.
  - Have annual sessions with all leaders about what they can do to ensure their successor is different to and better than they are. Encourage and support them in having conversations with people

widely outside their own department, to widen the potential succession pool.

- *Invest in creating attractors.* An attractor in chaos theory is something that creates a state of equilibrium. An example of an attractor might be a lake in a mountain range. While the water flow in mountain streams may be chaotic in depth, direction and velocity, it will seek out the same low point in which to congregate. In companies, certain job roles may be attractors (for example, you have to have spent some time in sales, or overseas, to make it into top management) and these attractors may be artificially or chaotically created. Other attractors might be senior managers who have a reputation for developing others; or high flyers willing to take on more junior people as crew on their personal ship. Talented employees will gravitate towards them.

    The value of having attractors is that you don't have to have elaborate plans of how to move people into roles – they will find their own way there and remain until they are ready to move on. If they do not move on swiftly enough for the organization's needs, then new attractors may be required.

- *Accept suboptimal efficiency.* Instead of trying not to make mistakes in selecting talent and making appointments, focus on frequent experiments. Take measured risks and try to change the culture from one that rewards not making mistakes to one that rewards learning from mistakes.

- *Stimulate requisite variety.* Widen the definition of talent and monitor how diverse the Talent Wave is. The critical question is not whether we have enough talent, but whether we have enough variety of talent. In a recent book on Diversity Mentoring (Clutterbuck *et al*, 2012), my colleagues and I explore the evolution of corporate approaches to diversity. From an initial focus on achieving *equal opportunities* (problem-based, tactical, numerical and legislation-driven), companies moved their attention to *diversity management* (opportunity-based, strategic, changing thinking and behaviours, driven by organizational need). Now, many organizations are making a further shift to *leveraging difference* (individual-focused, both tactical and strategic, with a wider definition of talent, valuing difference in all its forms, and driven by alignment between individual and organizational needs). Leveraging talent is also characterized by the quality of conversation between employees and the organization.

- *Promote connectivity.* As a small piece of utterly unscientific research, I have been asking people about how they found their best job (or how it found them) and how they found their best direct report. I've been struck by how often the answer relates to a chance conversation or unexpected connection. It seems that the formal systems sometimes simply provide a backup to the informal. Without wanting to take this observation to an extreme, it suggests that, given sufficient connectivity, people will gravitate to the roles that they contribute most to. The core of connectivity in the workplace is conversation. A critical challenge for HR is: 'How do we support people in making and using the kind of connections which will benefit both themselves and the organization?' Those connections may be both internal and external to the company.

● *Be attentive to iteration.* Feedback loops can be positive or negative. Where the system is not producing the quality and quantity of leaders required, or where the energy of the Talent Wave appears to be blocked, the probability is high that negative feedback loops are occurring. By trying to understand the system, HR can identify positive loops and provide additional support (and hence momentum). In some cases, it may also be possible to counter negative feedback loops, by making people aware of them and engaging them in changing them.

My argument here is not that HR should adopt a laissez-faire approach to talent development and succession, but that it should influence by supporting the natural tendencies of the system, avoiding the temptation to try to exert control and obstruct the natural forces of the Talent Wave. And the primary vehicle for supporting the system is the quality and scope of the conversations that happen within it.

Making sure the four conversations happen

The good news here is that HR doesn't have to stop measuring and monitoring. It simply has to focus on measuring and monitoring the right things. Some of the key measures are:

● *Are the conversations happening?*
  - Are they happening continuously or only at long intervals (for example, every 6 or 12 months)?
  - Does everyone have a personal development plan? If they do, is it a live document that forms part of their career and developmental dialogues?
  - What proportion of people are taking part in the social networks? Do the people identified as having greatest potential play a greater or lesser role than average in contributing to these networks?
● *What's the quality of conversation?*
  - Is it primarily developmental or remedial? Focused on strengths or weaknesses?

- Do people feel that their boss, HR and their colleagues are all supportive of their development and career aspirations?
- What is the depth of the conversations?
- Do people feel they are being listened to about their developmental needs and career aspirations?
- Do people feel able to be open and honest with themselves and with others about developmental and career issues?

● *Are the conversations having the desired effect?*
- Do people feel more confident, better informed and purposeful in their career planning?
- Do line managers feel confident that there is a large and diverse enough wave of talent coming through at each level?
- Do people feel they can take the risks of unconventional moves?
- What is the proportion of conventional to unconventional job moves?
- Do people have a sense of being in charge of and responsible for their own careers?
- How clear are employees about how their aspirations align with those of the organization? Is that sense of alignment increasing or decreasing?
- What is the level of maturity of people in contention for senior roles?

Other metrics might cover a deeper analysis of job moves, energy levels and overall perception of the talent development and succession processes. Job move analysis includes ratios of:

● horizontal to vertical moves;
● continuity to transformational roles (ie established to newly created);
● internal to external hires;
● developmental to consolidative (ie appointments aimed at giving someone learning opportunities versus those that recognize and reward previous learning and existing abilities).

At an even deeper level, it is useful to examine a longitudinal cross-sample of appointments to assess issues such as:

● What was needed in this role – a caretaker or a transformer? And what kind of person was actually appointed?
● Tenure – when was the right time for the incumbent to move on and what happened?
● Legacy – how much was left to the next incumbent to clear up afterwards? What problems were created or parked as too difficult? To what extent did direct reports develop over the period?

- What were the performance results for the team in the short term, medium term and long term?
- What is the stakeholder assessment of this appointment (boss, direct reports, other teams)? How well did they think it worked out?

Measuring energy levels is more difficult. The aim here is to assess how dynamic the Talent Wave is. Suggested areas for measurement include:

- How much effort (talented) employees put into their own and other people's career management and personal development.
- Setting and achievement of stretch goals at individual, team and organizational levels.
- Learning intensity (how quickly people achieve learning objectives).
- Ratio of learn–exploit–coast for individuals, teams and the organization as a whole, compared to the levels aspired to.
- Proportion of designated key roles that changes annually. (This is analogous to employee turnover statistics – too high or too low is equally a warning sign.)

As we saw in Chapter 1, succession planning doesn't currently have much of a positive reputation, at any level in organizations. Practical areas of measurement might be:

- How fair and transparent do employees see the selection process for succession to be?
- How confident is top management in the quality and breadth of the talent available for succession at each level in the organization?
- Is HR perceived as a help or a hindrance in ensuring that talent rises to where it can contribute most?

To ensure that HR doesn't fall into the old traps of confusing measurement with being in control, it's helpful to be clear about the purpose of these and other measures. It is not to control, except in the sense of identifying obstructions. It is to ensure that its own creative energy is focused on facilitating the immense energy of the Talent Wave.

So can we prevent the wrong people getting to the top?

This book wouldn't be complete if it didn't come full circle to the question in the introduction. Throughout the chapters, I have referred to the problem that any system designed to identify and reward talent is open to manipulation by those skilled enough and motivated enough to fake it. What's more, it is extremely difficult to distinguish between the creative genius who will inspire others to great things, and the fatally flawed individual who will bring about corporate tragedy. However, organizations can do a lot to create the climate in which it is easier to detect and contain psychopathic managers, while allowing both their own and other people's talents and creativity to flourish. The key, of course, is taking a much more systemic perspective of the organization and the talent available to it.

Among the practical steps organizations can take, under the guidance of insightful HR, are the following:

- Seek to control less and enable more.
- Genuinely value difference and, in particular, leadership diversity.
- Take a view of performance that is much wider than normal, and from several perspectives: what makes a positive contribution, tangibles and intangibles, short term and medium term, how the person's performance is viewed by multiple stakeholders, and so on.
- Take legacy into account when assessing performance in a previous role.
- Give people opportunities, encouragement and support – then see what they can do with them. Help them learn from mistakes and setbacks.
- Look at every HR procedure, and competencies in particular, from the perspective of how you can distinguish between someone who sets out to tick the boxes, and someone who genuinely lives the values.
- Assess the maturity of candidates for significant roles – if they operate mainly at a level of maturity below that, which would be ideal for the role, what support will enable them to contribute; or what would help them become more mature?
- Never allow anyone with a potential fatal flaw to achieve unfettered control; place much more emphasis on collegiate leadership than on individual leadership. The best place to start with this is at the top (where the psychopath can do most harm), to provide a role model for balanced leadership.

One practical way of ameliorating the effects of putting the wrong person into a role is to take a more systemic approach to annual reviews. Instead of just reviewing individual performance, review team performance and review the role itself. What has changed in the context, purpose and challenges of this role? What conclusions can we draw about a 'best-fit' leader for this role as it now stands, or can be predicted to evolve in the next 12 months? What opportunities are there to reshape the role, delegate key tasks to potential future leaders? Use the review to explore with the incumbent whether the new challenges motivate them sufficiently and play to their strengths. If they do, what development needs do they have and what support do they need? If they don't, what new roles can be created to play to their strengths and interests? It's about seeing each role not as a fixed-term tenancy, but as a learning opportunity of indeterminate length, defined by the evolving requirements of both the role and the role holder.

Conclusion

I usually start out on the journey of writing a book with a difficult question. In this case, it was the question: *'If succession planning works, how do the wrong people so often get to the top?'* Seeking an answer carries with it something of an obligation to search also for potential solutions. I hope I've shown that standard approaches to talent and succession are deeply flawed and also that there are practical ways in which those flaws can be overcome. It does require deep reflection and a shift in perspective on the part of HR, away from its dependence on simple, linear models. But this is still an evolving profession, and where the courageous lead, in time others will no doubt follow.

REFERENCES

Chapter 1

Ahrens, T (2005) *High-Growth Companies: Driving the Tiger*, 2nd edn, Gower, Aldershot

Alimo-Metcalfe, B (1998) 360 degree feedback and leadership development, *International Journal of Selection and Assessment*, **6** (1), pp 35–44

Anon (2008) *The Glass Cliff*, report from the Canadian Institute for Advanced Research, Toronto

Anon (2009) The crisis: mobilizing boards for change, *McKinsey Quarterly*, March

Babiak, P, Newman, CS and Hare, R (2010) Corporate psychopathy: talking the walk, *Behavioral Sciences and the Law Special Issue: International Perspectives on Psychopathy, An Update*, **28** (2), pp 121–302

Barsh, J and Yee, L (2011) *McKinsey Quarterly*, Sept [online] https://www.mckinseyquarterly.com/Organization/Talent/Changing_companies_minds_about_women_2858

Bennett, JT, Moss, SE and Duffy, MK (2011) Predictors of abusive supervision: supervisor perceptions of deep-level dissimilarity, relationship conflict, and subordinate performance, *Academy of Management Journal*, **54** (2), pp 279–94

Cannella, AA and Harris, IC (2002) Women and racial minorities in the boardroom: how do directors differ? *Journal of Management*, **28**, pp 747–63

Casserley, T and Megginson, D (2009) *Learning from Burnout*, Butterworth Heinemann, Oxford

Charan, R (2006) Conquering a culture of indecision, *Harvard Business Review* (Jan), pp 108–17

Charan, R, Drotter, S and Noel, J (2001) *The Leadership Pipeline: How to build the leadership powered company*, Jossey-Bass, San Francisco

Clutterbuck, D (1975) Einar Thorsrud: apostle of employee democracy, *International Management*, Oct, pp 28–34

Clutterbuck, D (2000) *The Learning Teams Project*, Herts Business Link (now Exemplas) on behalf of European Social Fund

Clutterbuck, D, de Haan, E, Lucas, B and Winter, J (2010) *Development at the Top*, White paper from Clutterbuck Associates, Ashridge Management College, The Talent Foundation and Career Innovation

Deci, EL, Koestner, R and Ryan, RM (1999) A meta-analytic review of experiments examining the effects of extrinsic rewards on intrinsic motivation, *Psychological Bulletin*, **125** (6), pp 627–68

Garman, AN and Glawe, J (2004) Succession planning, *Consulting Psychology Journal: Practice and Research*, **56** (2), pp 119–28

Gladwell, M (2008) *Outliers*, Allen Lane, London

Goldsmith, W and Clutterbuck, D (1997) *The Winning Streak Mark II*, Orion, London

Greenhaus, J and Callaman, G (2006) *Encyclopedia of Career Development*, SAGE Publications, London

Hammond, J and Keeney, RL (2006) The hidden traps in decision making, *Harvard Business Review*, Jan, pp 118–26

Hirsh, W (2000) *Succession Planning Demystified*, IES Report 372

Laske, O (2009) *Measuring Hidden Dimensions of Human Systems*, Interdevelopmental Institute Press, Melford, MA

Lombardi, M (2010) *Succession Planning: Sustainable leadership for the future*, Aberdeen Group report, Boston

Mankins, M and Steele, R (2006) Stop making plans; start making decisions, *Harvard Business Review*, Jan, pp 76–84

Martinko, MJ and Gardner, WL (1987) The leader/member attribution process, *Academy of Management Review*, **12**, pp 23–249

Ordonez, LD, Schweitzer, ME, Galinsky, AE and Bazerman, MH (2009) Goals gone wild: the systemic side effects of overprescribing goal setting, *Academy of Management Perspectives*, **23** (1), pp 6–16

Peter, L and Hull, R (1969) *The Peter Principle: Why Things Always Go Wrong*, William Morrow & Company, New York

Rogelberg, S (ed) (2007) *Encyclopedia of Industrial and Organizational Psychology*, SAGE Publications, London

Rothwell, W (2000 [2005]) *Effective Succession Planning: Ensuring leadership continuity and building talent from within*, 2nd edn, AMACOM, New York (3rd edn 2005)

Thomas, DA (2001) The truth about mentoring minorities: race matters, *Harvard Business Review*, **79** (4), pp 98–107, 168

Westphal, J and Stern, I (2007) Flattery will get you everywhere (especially if you are a male Caucasian): how ingratiation, boardroom behaviour and demographic minority status affect additional board appointments at US companies, *Academy of Management Journal*, **50** (2), pp 267–88

Chapter 2

Clutterbuck, D and Dearlove, D (1995) *Routes to the Top*, Kinsley Lord, London

Earley, PC and Mosakowski, E (2000) Creating hybrid team cultures: an empirical test of transnational team functioning, *Academy of Management Journal*, **43** (1), pp 26–49

Edmondson, A (1999) Psychological safety and learning behaviour in teams, *Administrative Science Quarterly*, **44**, pp 350–83

Gall, J (1975) *Systemantics: how systems work and especially how they fail*, Pocket Books, New York

De Geus, A (1997) *The Living Company*, Harvard Business School Publishing, Boston

Hamel, G (2009) *The Facebook Generation vs the Fortune 500*, Blog, http://hr.wtgalumni.com.media_detail,php?id=304

Chapter 3

Casserley, T and Critchley, W (2010) Perennial philosophy, *People Management*, 12 August, pp 20–24

Casserley, T and Megginson, D (2009) *Learning from Burnout*, Butterworth Heinemann, Oxford

Cohen, W (1998) *The Stuff of Heroes: The Eight Universal Laws of Leadership*, Longstreet Press, Atlanta

Coyle, D (2009) *The Talent Code*, Random House, New York

Gladwell, M (2008) *Outliers*, Allen Lane, London

Goldsmith, W and Clutterbuck, D (1984) *The Winning Streak*, Weidenfeld, London

Goldsmith, W and Clutterbuck, D (1997) *The Winning Streak Mark II*, Orion, London

Greenleaf, RK (1977) *Servant Leadership: A Journey into the Nature of Legitimate Power and Greatness*, Paulist Press, New Jersey

Kouzes, JM and Posner, BZ (1987) *The Leadership Challenge*, Jossey-Bass, Oxford

Kouzes, JM and Posner, BZ (2011) *Credibility: How leaders gain and lose it, why people demand it*, revised edn, Jossey-Bass, San Francisco

Vanderbroeck, P (2010) Odysseus and the seduction of leadership, *Provocations: A Journal from The Trinity Forum*, www.ttf.org/index/journal/print-2/odysseus-as-leader

Wageman, R, Nunes, DA, Buruss, JA and Hackman, JR (2008) *Senior Leadership Teams: What It Takes to Make Them Great*, Harvard Business Press, Boston

Zenger, J and Folkman, J (2009) Ten fatal flaws that derail leaders, *Harvard Business Review*, June

Chapter 4

Ahrens, T (1999) *High Growth Companies: Driving the Tiger*, 2nd edn, Gower, Aldershot

Alimo-Metcalfe, B (1998) 360 degree feedback and leadership development, *International Journal of Selection and Assessment*, 6 (1), pp 35–44

Alimo-Metcalfe, B and Alban-Metcalfe, J (2009) *Engaging leadership: Creating Organisations that Maximise the Potential of Their People*, CIPD Research Insight, Wimbledon

Anon (2004) The seed of Apple's innovation, *Business Week*, 12 April

Anon (2010) *Personnel Today*, 20 April, p 24

Antonakis, J and Dalgas, O (2009) Predicting elections: child's play, *Science*, 323, p 1183

Atwater, L, Waldman, D and Cartier, P (2000) An upward feedback field experiment: supervisor's cynicism, follow-up and commitment to subordinates, *Personnel Psychology*, 53, pp 275–97

Bennis, W (2010) *Learning to Lead*, 4th edn, Basic Books, New York

Bennis, Warren and Thomas, Robert J (2002) *Geeks and Geezers*, Harvard Business School Press, Boston

Bertlett, J (2010) *An Employeeship Model and its Relation to Psychological Climate: A study of congruence in the behavior of leaders and followers*, Doctoral thesis

Bishop, CH (2009) *The Seven Deadly Sins of Talent Management*, occasional paper

Bolden, R and Gosling, J (2006) Leadership competencies: time to change the tune? *Leadership*, 2 (2), pp 147–63

Boyatzis, R (1982) *The effective Manager: A model for effective performance*, John Wiley, Chichester

Bruckmüller, S and Branscombe, N (2010) The glass cliff: when and why women are selected as leaders in crisis contexts, *British Journal of Social Psychology*, 49 (3), pp 433–51

Buckingham, M (2001) Don't waste time and money, *Gallup Management Journal*, 3 Dec

Casserley, T and Megginson, D (2009) *Learning from Burnout*, Butterworth Heinemann, Oxford

Charan, R, Drotter, S and Noel, J (2001) *The Leadership Pipeline: How to build the leadership powered company*, Jossey-Bass, San Francisco

Claxton, G and Lucas, W (2010) *New Kinds of Smart: How the science of learnable intelligence is changing education*, McGraw-Hill, Maidenhead

Cosack, S, Guthridge, M and Lawson, E (2010) *Retaining Key Employees in Times of Change*, Occasional Paper McKinsey Organization Practice, August

Drucker, P (1990) *Managing the Nonprofit Organization: Principles and Practices*, Collins, Glasgow

Dweck, CS (1986) Motivational processes affecting learning, *American Psychologist*, **41** (10), pp 1040–48

Dweck, CS (2000) *Self-theories: Their role in motivation, personality, and development*, Psychology Press, Abingdon

Fliaster, A (2011) Organisational learning: the social network, *CIPD newsletter*, April

Gladwell, M (2008) *Outliers*, Little, Brown & Company, London

Goldsmith, M (2003) All of us are stuck on suck-ups, *Fast Company Magazine*, 1 December

Goldsmith, W and Clutterbuck, D (1997) *The Winning Streak Mark II*, Orion, London

Gravells, J and Wallace, S (2011) *Dial M for Mentor: Reflections on mentoring in film, television and literature*, Informations Age publishing, Charlotte, NC

Grimley, BN (1998) *The Accuracy and Utility of Upward Appraisal*, MSc dissertation, (Occupational and Organisational Psychology), University of East London

Groysberg, B (2010) *Chasing Stars: The Myth of Talent and the Portability of Performance*, Princeton University Press, Princeton

Haragon, A (2000) Building an innovation factory, *Harvard Business Review*, **78** (3), pp 157–66

Harris, M and Schaubroeck, J (1988) A meta-analysis of self-supervisor, self-peer and peer-supervisor ratings, *Personnel Psychology*, **41**, pp 43–62

Hawkins, P (2011) *Leadership Team Coaching*, Kogan Page, London

Hollenbeck, GP, McCall, MW and Silzer, RF (2006) Leadership competency models, *Leadership Quarterly*, **17** (4), pp 191–202

Menkes, J (2011) *Better Under Success*, Harvard Business Review Press, Boston

Michaels, E, Handfield-Jones, H and Axelrod, B (2001) *The War for Talent*, Harvard Business School Press, Boston

Kayes, DC (2006) *Destructive Goal Pursuit: The Mount Everest Disaster*, Palgrave Macmillan, Basingstoke

Kleisner, K, Kocnar, T, Rubesiova, A and Flegr, J (2010) Eye color predicts but does not directly influence perceived dominance in men, *Personality and Individual Differences*, **49** (1), pp 59–64

Kluger, A and DeNisi, A (1996) The effects of feedback interventions on performance: a historical review, meta-analysis and preliminary feedback theory, *Psychological Bulletin*, **119**, 254–85

Ordonez, LD, Schweitzer, ME, Galinsky, AE and Bazerman, MH (2009) Goals gone wild: the systemic side effects of overprescribing goal setting, *Academy of Management Perspectives*, **23** (1), pp 6–16

Pfau, B and Kay, I (2002) Does 360 degree feedback negatively affect company performance? *HR Magazine*, **47** (6)

Pfeffer, J and Sutton, R (2006) Evidence-based management, *Harvard Business Review*, Jan, pp 63–72

Ready, DA and Conger, JA (2007) Make your company a talent factory, *Harvard Business Review*, **85** (6), pp 68–77

Sinatra, A (2010) Notes for those whose huge responsibility it is to identify and develop talent, in *Growing Talent*, ed H Borensztejn, pp 287–306, Marshall Cavendish, London

Sorcher, M and Brant, J (2002) Are you picking the right leaders? *Harvard Business Review*, Feb, pp 122–29

Tate, W (2009) *The Search for Leadership: An Organisational Perspective*, Triarchy Press, Axminster

The Times (2008) Too cautious: how army rated woman who went on to lead 3000 against the Nazis

Vanderbroeck, P (2010) The traps that keep women from reaching the top and how to avoid them, *Journal of Management Development*, **29** (9), pp 764–70

Wageman, R, Nunes, DA, Buruss, JA and Hackman, JR (2008) *Senior Leadership Teams: What It Takes to Make Them Great*, Harvard Business Press, Boston

Warren, AK (2009) *Cascading Gender Biases, Compounding Effects: An Assessment of Talent Management Systems*, Catalyst, New York, www.catalyst.org/publication/292/cascading-gender-biases-compounding-effects-an-assessment-of-talent-management-systems%22

Woodward, D (2011) How to create an entrepreneurial culture, *Director*, www.director.co.uk/MAGAZINE/ 2011/6_June/innovation_64_10.html

Chapter 5

Allen, DG, Bryant, PC and Vardman, JM (2010) Retaining talent: replacing misconceptions with evidence-based strategies, *Academy of Management Perspectives*, **24**, pp 48–64

Arthur, MB and Rousseau, DM (1996) The boundaryless career as a new employment principle, in *The Boundaryless Career*, ed MB Arthur and DM Rousseau, pp 3–20, Oxford University Press, New York

Baumgarten, P, Desvaux, G and Devillard, S (2007) *What Shapes Careers? A McKinsey Global Survey*, https://www.mckinseyquarterly.com/What_shapes_careers_A_McKinsey_Global_Survey_2078

Briscoe, JP and Hall, DT (2006) The interplay of boundaryless and protean careers: combinations and implications, *Journal of Vocational behavior*, **69**, 4–18

Cascio, WF (2006) The economic impact of employee behaviors on organizational performance, *California Management Review*, **48** (4), pp 41–60

Crush, P (2009) *HR Magazine*, Interviews with Scott Northcutt, www.hrmagazine.co.uk/hr/interviews/1014972/interview-scott-northcutt-human-resources-director-dhl, Accessed 12 April 2012

Griffeth, RW, Hom, PW and Gaertner, S (2000) A meta-analysis of antecedents and correlates of employee turnover: update, moderator tests, and research implications for the next millennium, *Journal of Management*, **26**, 463–88

Ibarra, H and Lineback, K (2005) What's your story? *Harvard Business Review*, **83** (1), 64–71

Inkson, K and King, Z (2011) Contested terrain in careers: a psychological contract model, *Human Relations*, 36, 37–57

James, A, Bibb, S and Walker, S (2008) *A Summary Report of the 'Tell It How It Is' Research Talentsmoothie*, Newbury, www.talentsmoothie.com

Latack, JC (1984) Career transitions within organizations: an exploratory study of work, nonwork, and coping strategies, *Organizational Behavior and Human Performance*, 34 (3), 296–322

Lee, TW, Mitchell, TR, Holtom, BC, McDaniel, LS and Hill, JW (1999) The unfolding model of voluntary turnover: a replication and extension, *Academy of Management Journal*, 42, pp 450–62

Louis, MR (1982) Managing career transition: a missing link in career development, *Organizational Dynamics*, 10 (4), pp 68–77

Mainero, LA and Sullivan, SE (2006) *The Opt-Out Revolt: Why people are leaving companies to create kaleidoscope careers*, Davies-Black, Mountain View, CA

Mitchell, TR, Holtom, BC, Lee, TW, Sablynski, CJ and Erez, M (2001) Why people stay: using job embeddedness to predict voluntary turnover, *Academy of Management Journal*, 44, pp 1102–21

Peiperl, MA and Baruch, Y (1997) Back to square zero: the post-corporate career, *Organizational Dynamics*, 25 (4), pp 7–22

Segers, J, Inceoglu, I, Vloeberghs, D, Bartram, D and Hendricks, E (2008) Protean and boundaryless careers: a study on powerful motivators, *Journal of Vocational Behavior*, 73 (2), pp 212–30

Shaw, J, Delery, J, Jenkins, G and Gupta, N (1998) An organization-level analysis of voluntary and involuntary turnover, *Academy of Management Journal*, 41, 511–25

Shaw, JD, Gupta, N and Delery, JE (2005) Alternative conceptualizations of the relationship between voluntary turnover and organizational performance, *Academy of Management Journal*, 48, pp 50–68

Sitkin, BS, See, KE, Miller, CC, Lawless, MW and Carton, AM (2011) The paradox of stretch goals: organizations in pursuit of the seemingly impossible, *Academy of Management Review*, 36 (3), pp 544–66

Smith, S and Paquette, S (2010) Creativity, chaos and knowledge management, *Business Information Review*, 27 (2), pp 118–23

Sullivan, SE and Baruch, Y (2010) Advances in career theory and research: a critical review and agenda for future exploration, *Journal of Management*, 35 (6), pp 1542–71

Thomas, DA and Gabarro, JJ (1999) *Breaking Through: The making of minority executives in corporate America*, Harvard Business School Press, Boston, MA

Chapter 6

Charan, R, Drotter, S and Noel, J (2001) *The Leadership Pipeline: How to build the leadership powered company*, Jossey-Bass, San Francisco

Davies, MR (2009) Unlocking the value of exceptional personalities, in *The Perils of Accentuating the Positive*, ed RB Kaiser, pp 135–58, Hogan Press, Tulsa, OK

Gauthier, A (nd), *Stages of leadership Development*, www.alaingauthier.org/Stages_of_Leadership_Development.pdf

Kegan, R (1982) *The Evolving Self*, Harvard University Press, Cambridge, MA

Kegan, R (1994) *In Over Our Heads: The mental demands of modern life*, Harvard University Press, Boston, MA

Kram, K (1980) *Mentoring Processes at Work: Developmental Relationships in Managerial Careers*, Doctoral dissertation, Yale University

Kram, K (1988) *Mentoring at Work*, University Press of America, Lanham, MD

Laske, O (2006) *Measuring Hidden Dimensions: The art and science of fully engaging adults*, Vol 1, IDM Press, Medford, MA

Laske, O (2009) *Measuring Hidden Dimensions Of Human Systems*, Vol 2, IDM Press, Medford, MA

Levinson, D (1978) *The Seasons of a Man's Life*, Alfred Knopf, New York

Piaget, J (1985) *The Equilibration of Cognitive Structures: The central problem of intellectual development*, University of Chicago Press, Chicago, IL

Rooke, D and Torbert, W (2005) Seven transformations of leadership, *Harvard Business Review*, Apr

Schein, E (1999) *Process Consultation Revisited*, Addison-Wesley, Reading, MA

Chapter 7

Charan, R, Drotter, S and Noel, J (2001) *The Leadership Pipeline: How to build the leadership powered company*, Jossey-Bass, San Francisco, CA

De Meuse, KP, Dai, G and Wu, J (2011) Leadership skills across organizational levels: a closer examination, *Psychologist-Manager Journal*, **14**, pp 120–39

Freedman, A (1998) Pathways and crossroads to institutional leadership, *Consulting Psychology Journal*, **50**, pp 131–51

Galef, J (2011) The perils of metaphorical thinking, *Measure of Doubt* blog site, 2 April, http://measureofdoubt.com/ 2011/04/06/the-perils-of-metaphorical-thinking/

Goldsmith, M and Reiter, M (2007) *What Got You Here Won't Get You There*, Hyperion, New York

Jacques, E (1964) *Time-Span Handbook: The use of time-span of discretion to measure the level of work in employment roles and to arrange an equitable payment structure*, Heinemann, London

Jacques, E (1978) *A General Theory of Bureaucracy*, Halstead Press, New York

Jacques, E (1989) *Requisite Organization*, Cason Hall, Alington, VA

Kaiser, RB (2011) The leadership pipeline: fad, fashion, or empirical fact? *Psychologist-Manager Journal*, **14**, pp 71–75

Kaiser, RB and Craig, SB (2011) Do behaviors related to managerial effectiveness really change with organizational level? An empirical test, *Psychologist-Manager Journal*, **14**, 92–119

Kaiser, RB, Craig, SB, Overfield, DV and Preston, Y (2011) Differences in managerial jobs at the bottom, middle, and top: a review of empirical research, **14**, pp 76–91

Katz, D and Kahn, RL (1978) *The Social Psychology of Organizations*, 2nd edn, Wiley, New York

Mann, FC (1965) Toward an understanding of the leadership role in formal organizations, in *Leadership and Productivity*, ed R Dubin, GC Homans, FC Mann and DC Miller, pp 68–103, Chandler, San Francisco, CA

McCartney, C (2010) Floating asscts, *People Management*, 1 July, pp 26–27

Chapter 8

Winter, J and Jackson, C (2009) *The Conversation Gap: Using dialogue to build trust and inspire performance*, Career Innovations, Oxford

Chapter 9

Amundson, N (2009) *Active Engagement: Enhancing the career counseling process*, 3rd edn, Ergon Communications, Richmond, BC

Bramston (2008) *Investigating the Issue of Stress in the Workplace in the 21st Century*, Thesis submitted to the University of Bristol as a part requirement for the Doctor of Education programme

Campbell, J (1949) *The Hero with a Thousand Faces*, Pantheon Press, New York

Clutterbuck, D (2003) *Managing Work–Life Balance*, CIPD, Wimbledon

Ermann, D (1987) *Corporate and Governmental Deviance: Problems of organizational behavior in contemporary society*, Oxford University Press, Oxford

Forret, ML and Dougherty, TW (2004) Networking behaviours and career outcomes: differences for men and women, *Journal of Organizational Behavior*, 25 (3), pp 419–37

George, B (2011) Why leaders lose their way, *HBR Blog Network*, June 8

Goldsmith, M (2007) *What Got You Here Won't Get You There*, Hyperion, New York

Ibarra, H (1999) Provisional selves: experimenting with image and identity in professional app lication, *Administrative Science Quarterly*, 22, pp 764–91

Ibarra, H and Lineback, K (2005) What's your story? *Harvard Business Review*, 83 (1), pp 64–73

Rothwell, W (2003) Competency-based succession planning: do I fit in? The individual's role in succession planning, *Career Planning and Adult Development Journal*, 18 (4), 120–35.

Schwartz, B (2004) *The Paradox of Choice – Why More Is Less*, Harper Perennial, New York

Simon, H (1993) Satisficing, in *The McGraw-Hill Encyclopaedia of Economics*, 2nd edn, ed D Greenwald, pp 881–86, McGraw-Hill, New York

Steele, CC and Francis-Smythe, J (2007) Career anchors – an empirical investigation, *Proceedings of the British Psychological Society's 2007 Occupational Psychology Conference, Bristol, England*

Chapter 10

de Bono, Edward (1985) *Six Thinking Hats: an Essential Approach to Business Management*, Little, Brown & Company, London

Bramston (2008) *Investigating the Issue of Stress in the Workplace in the 21st Century*, Thesis submitted to the University of Bristol as a part requirement for the Doctor of Education programme

Clutterbuck, D (2007) *Coaching the Team at Work*, Nicholas Brealy, London

Clutterbuck, DA (2010) *Development at the Top: Who really cares?* Consortium paper/report of survey, Ashridge, Career Innovation, Clutterbuck Associates, The Talent Foundation

Dragoni, L, Tesluk, PE, Russell, JEA and In-Sue, OH (2010) Understanding managerial development: integrating developmental assignments, learning orientation, and access to developmental opportunities in predicting managerial competencies, *Academy of Management Journal*, **24** (2), pp 731–43

Dweck, CS (1986) Motivational processes affecting learning, *American Psychologist*, **41**, pp 1040–48

Dweck, CS and Leggett, EL (1988) A social-cognitive approach to motivation and personality, *Psychological Review*, **95**, pp 256–73

Ferrar, P (2006) *The Paradox of Manager as Coach: Does being a manager inhibit effective coaching?* thesis submitted to Oxford Brookes University

Gratton, L and Ghoshal, S (2002) Improving the quality of conversations, *Organizational Dynamics*, **31** (3), pp 209–23

McCauley, CD, Ruderman, MN, Ohlott, PJ and Morrow, JE (1994) Assessing the development components of managerial jobs, *Journal of Applied Psychology*, **79**, pp 544–60

Souerwine, A (1985) What to do with the plateaued manager, *Issues*, **3**, pp 32–33 (PA Management Consultants journal)

Winter, J and Jackson, C (2009) *The Conversation Gap: Using dialogue to build trust and inspire performance*, Career Innovations, Oxford

Chapter 11

Arkin, A (2010) In the mix, *PM Guide to Assessment*, 1 October

Collins, J and Porras, J (1994) *Built To Last*, HarperBusiness, New York

Collins, J and Porras, J (1996) Building your company's vision, *Harvard Business Review*, **74** (5), pp 65–77

Stevens, G, Burley, J and Divine, R (1999) Creativity + Business discipline = Higher profits faster from new product development, *Journal of Product Innovation Management*, **16** (5), pp 455–68

Chapter 12

Attwell, G (2007) Personal learning environments – the future of eLearning? *eLearning Papers*, www.elearningpapers.eu., **2** (1), January

Barnes, J (1954) Class and committees in a Norwegian island parish, *Human Relations*, **7**, pp 39–58

Burt, RS (2000) The network structure of social capital, in *Research in Organizational Behavior*, ed BM Shaw and RI Sutton, pp 345–423, Elsevier Science, Oxford

Casper, S and Murray, F (2005) Careers and clusters: analyzing the career network dynamic of biotechnology clusters, *Journal of Engineering and Technology Management*, **22** (1–2), pp 51–74

Clutterbuck, D and Hussain, Z (2009) *Virtual Coach, Virtual Mentor*, Nicholas Brealy, London

Cross, J (2006) The low-hanging fruit is tasty, *Internet Time Blog*, retrieved 12 October 2006 from http://internettime.com/?p=105

Dunbar, Robin (2010) *How Many Friends Does One Person Need?* Faber & Faber, London

Fisher, R (2010) Generation F, *New Scientist*, 10 July, pp 39–41

Fliaster, A (2011) Organisational learning: the social network, *CIPD newsletter*, April

Granovetter, MS (1973) The strength of weak ties, *American Journal of Sociology*, 78 (6), pp 1360–80

Kelley, RE and Caplan, J (2009) How Bell Labs creates star performers, *Harvard Business Review*

Krebs, V (2008) *Managing the Connected Organization*, Orgnet.com

Latour, B (1986) 'The Powers of Association': Power, Action and Belief. A new sociology of knowledge? Sociological Review* monograph 32, ed J Law, pp 264–80, Routledge & Kegan Paul, London

Sproull, L and Kiesler, S (1986) Reducing social context clues: electronic mail in organizational communication, *Management Science*, 32 (11), pp 1492–1512

Tutu, D (1999) *No Future Without Forgiveness*, Image, Cape Town

Watts, D (2003) *Six Degrees: The Science of A Connected Age*, Norton, New York

Yarkoni, T (2010) Personality in 100,000 words: a large-scale analysis of personality and word use among bloggers, *Journal of Research in Personality*, 44 (3), pp 363–73

Chapter 13

Clutterbuck, D, Kochan, F and Poulson, K (2012) *The Diversity Mentoring Casebook*, McGraw-Hill, Maidenhead

INDEX

NB page numbers in *italics* indicate a figure in the text